what did you eat yesterday? 5
fumi yoshinaga

#33. 3

#34. 23

#35. 41

#36. 59

#37. 79

#38. 99

#39. 117

#40. 135

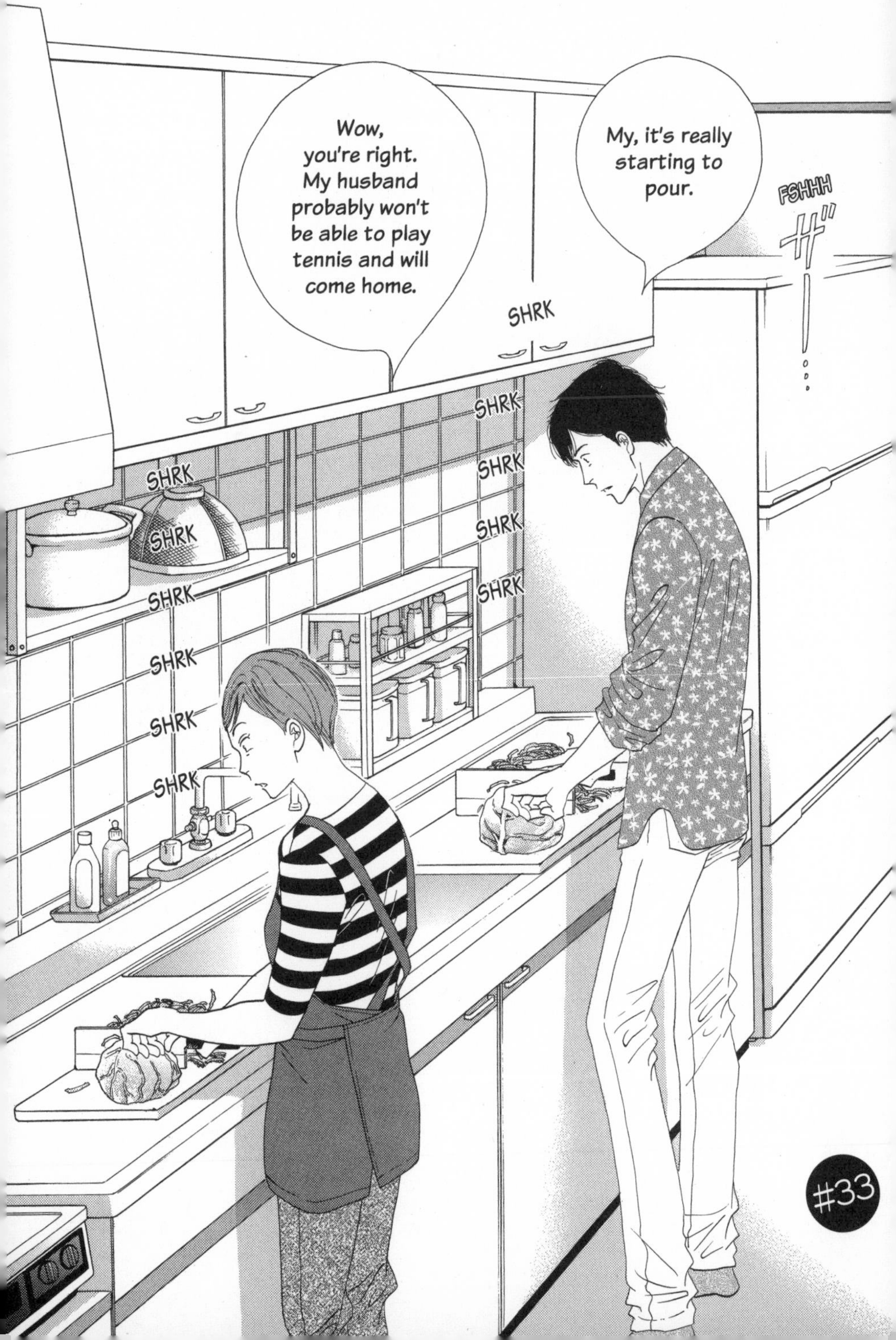
FSHHH
ザ"
My, it's really starting to pour.
Wow, you're right. My husband probably won't be able to play tennis and will come home.
SHRK
SHRK
SHRK
SHRK
SHRK
SHRK
SHRK
SHRK
SHRK
SHRK
SHRK
SHRK
#33

That store sometimes sells things in a crazy way.

New Takaraya was absurd today. Two cabbages for 200 yen, and three for 200 yen too. That's just not fair.

But Mr. Kakei.

SHRK SHRK SHRK SHRK SHRK SHRK

If you weren't around I couldn't have carried them home.

SHRUK SHRUK SHRUK SHRUK

SO, THE TWO ARE MAKING COLESLAW WITH THE ONE EXTRA CABBAGE TODAY.

WRRR

Yes. Our family recipe is to use dressing vinegar and mayo and sugar, and to stir it up roughly...

Phew, my oh my.

Okay, one cabbage, one carrot, all julienned!

Flavor with mayo?

It impresses me that you have such a big pot. You really are a homemaker.

I see.

I heard you can avoid making it too salty by doing the salt last.

In about thirty minutes, once the cabbage is flattened out, add some salt and pepper and it's done.

I can't even imagine having two cutting boards at our place.

Using a big pot instead of a bowl

GCHAK

Mom!

Oh please. We have two only because I cook with my daughter when we're making New Year's dinner or have guests. My husband loves bringing guests over...

Excuse us! Please don't mind.

I brought everyone from the tennis club because it was raining...

See.

No, Mr. Tominaga, I'll pay for myself. Or actually, I was going to leave soon.

I'll pay for Mr. Kakei and you, honey. Oh, we got drinks too.

Excuse me!

Oh honey, I ordered a bunch of pizzas from my cell earlier for lunch.

They said it'll take about fifty minutes because of the rain. Please have some too, Mr. Kakei.

Guess the coleslaw is coming out now.

Huh? Um, hello.

Hello.

Here, this is Mr. Kohinata.

And he's the Mr. Kakei we were talking about!

Please don't go home! I brought Mr. Kohinata because I thought you'd be here.

What are you talking about!

Mr. Kohinata! Come, come!

I thought you guys might get along being both gay!

THAT'S ALL !!

You see, Mr. Kohinata is gay!

I mean, you're gay too, no?

So!

CHEERS!!

Okay then, cheers!!

STUNNED...

8

Would you listen to my sad story from just the other day?

Well, we might as well chat.

Want me to get it, Mr. Yabe? Which one? Oh excuse me, then um, the teriyaki chicken please.

Really, Mr. Tominaga? Get along just 'cause we're both gay?

Hah.

...

That's rough.

I know.

Yes...

ド JOLT
キ!!

He quit his job and was kicked out of his company dorm, and stumbled into my house.

Oh, you have a boyfriend.

So I'm living with my boyfriend.

9

Oh, Wataru is my boyfriend. Imagine a beautiful boy like Gilbert.

But Wataru puts the chain on the door and locks me out when I'm just a little late to come home...

I'm supposed to be in a superior position.

Uh huh...

Here, coleslaw. I'll pass it around so take some.

KNOCK KNOCK
KNOCK KNOCK
KNOCK KNOCK
KNOCK KNOCK
KNOCK KNOCK
KNOCK
KNOCK

Wataru... Wataruuu...

So even though it's my own home, I have to knock and plead in a soft voice so I don't look bad to the neighbors.

Oh please, you must be up. Please let me in!

Of course I'll try calling but he won't pick up.

Daisaku.

Kakei's image

Why are you so late?

KCHAK

!

Please open up...

KNOCK

KNOCK KNOCK

KNOCK

KNOCK

KNOCK KNOCK

KNOCK

KNOCK

KNOCK KNOCK KNOCK KNOCK KNOCK

Wata-ruuu

I'm sorry, Wata-ruuu

KNOCK KNOCK

SQUEAK

BTAM

CREAK

I'm sure you could have sent an email.

I'm sorry.

I'm sorry, Wataru. There was an unexpected business dinner with a client...

Again, just Kakei's imagination

...

I'm sorry...

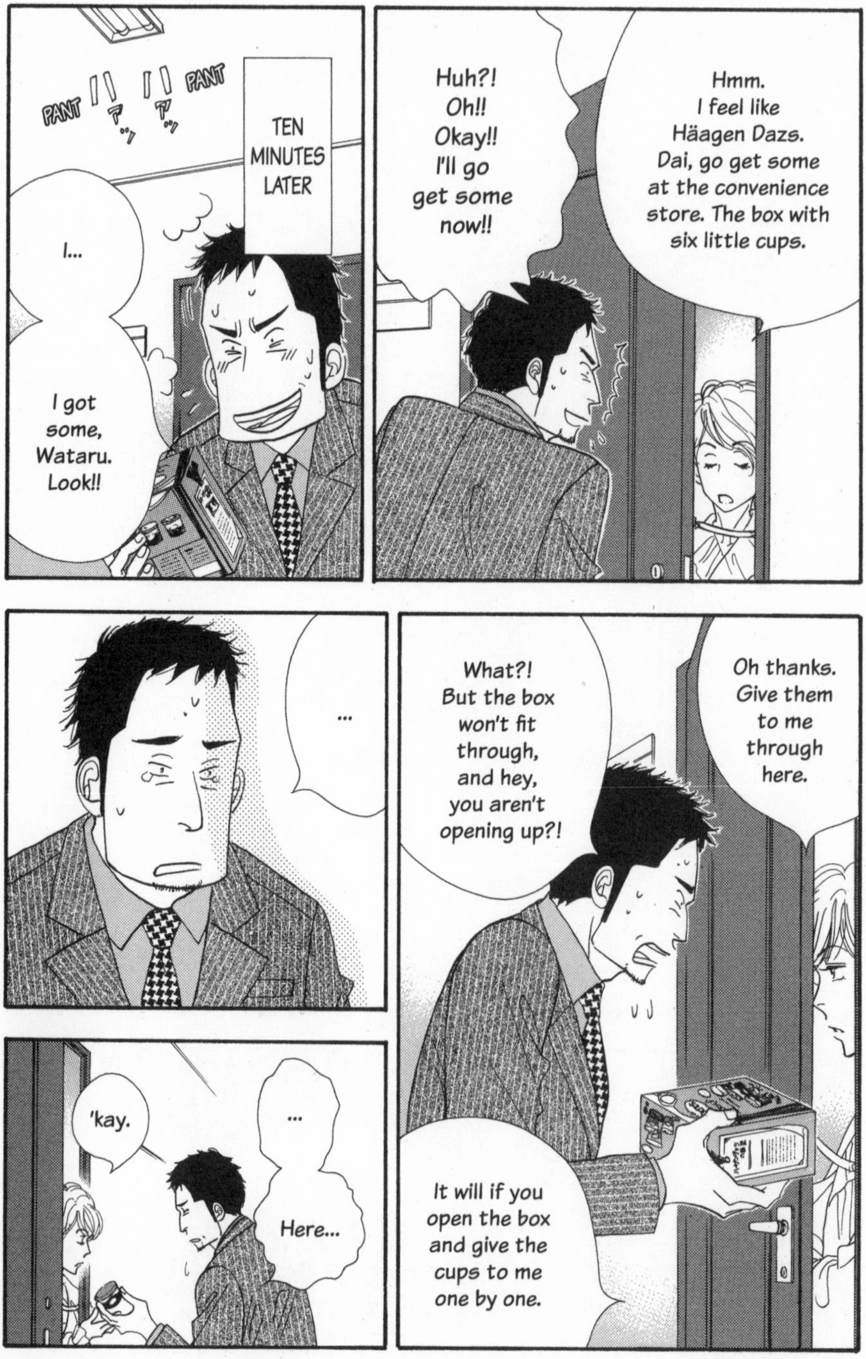
Hmm. I feel like Häagen Dazs. Dai, go get some at the convenience store. The box with six little cups.
Huh?! Oh!! Okay!! I'll go get some now!!
TEN MINUTES LATER
PANT PANT
I...
I got some, Wataru. Look!!
Oh thanks. Give them to me through here.
What?! But the box won't fit through, and hey, you aren't opening up?!
It will if you open the box and give the cups to me one by one.
...
...
Here...
'kay.

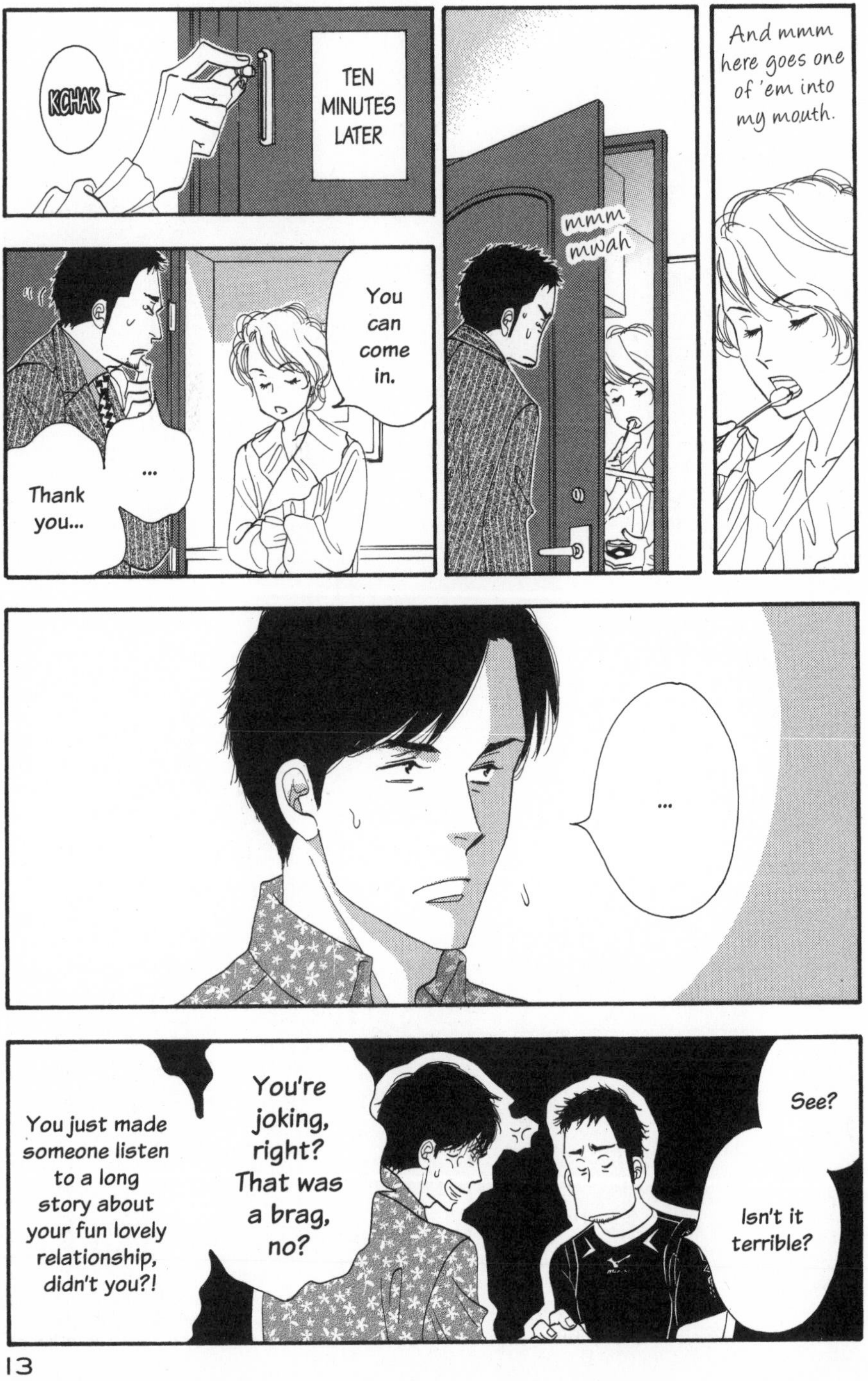
And mmm here goes one of 'em into my mouth.
mmm mwah
TEN MINUTES LATER
KCHAK
You can come in.
...
Thank you...
...
See?
Isn't it terrible?
You're joking, right? That was a brag, no?
You just made someone listen to a long story about your fun lovely relationship, didn't you?!

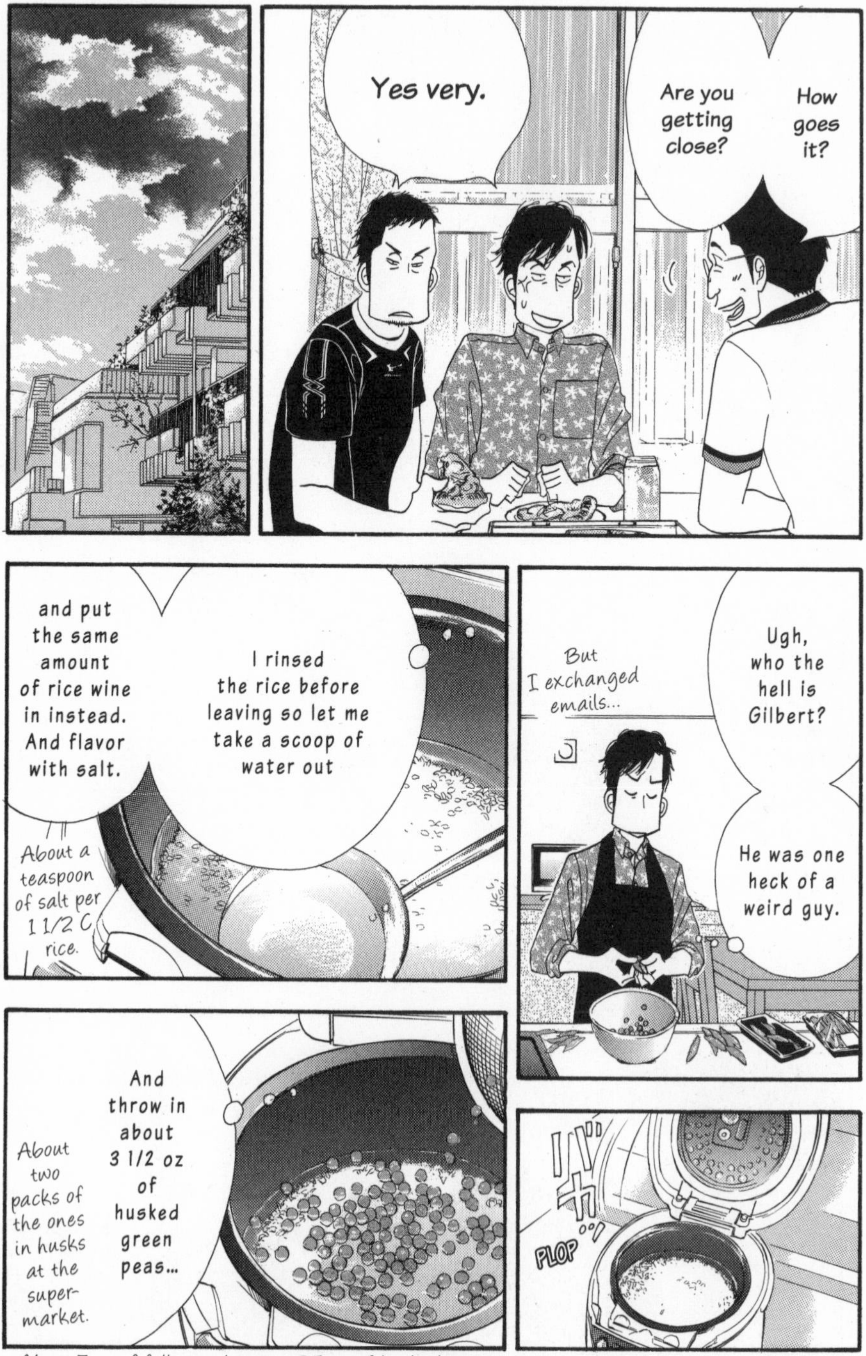
How goes it?
Are you getting close?
Yes very.
Ugh, who the hell is Gilbert?
He was one heck of a weird guy.
But I exchanged emails...
I rinsed the rice before leaving so let me take a scoop of water out
and put the same amount of rice wine in instead. And flavor with salt.
About a teaspoon of salt per 1 1/2 C rice.
And throw in about 3 1/2 oz of husked green peas...
About two packs of the ones in husks at the super-market.
PLOP

About 7 oz of full peas become 3.5 oz of husked peas.

Cook the rice.
PIP
CO
TIMER
I don't have much time today, so I'll just do some quick sides.
TOK
TOK
TOK
Roughly chop 1/2 nub garlic, and cut one onion into thin arches.
Next, cut a slice of chicken thigh into eighths and lightly salt-and-pepper.
FZZZZZZZ
Once both sides of the thighs are cooked to a crisp take it out and put aside.
SHHH
JZT

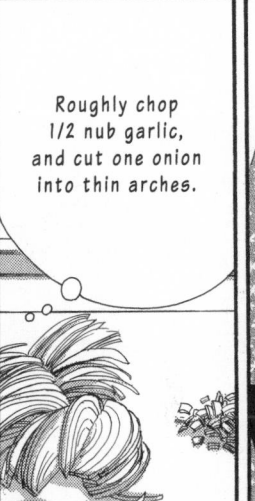

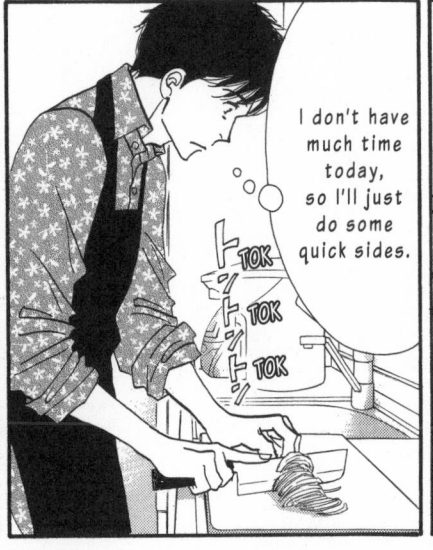

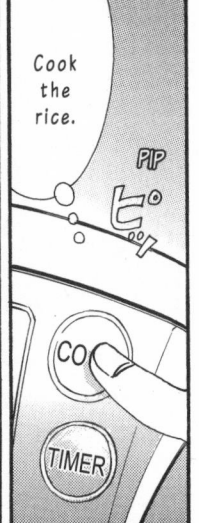

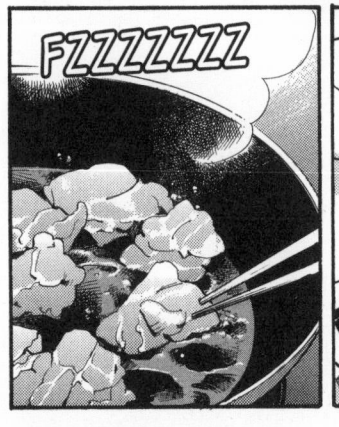

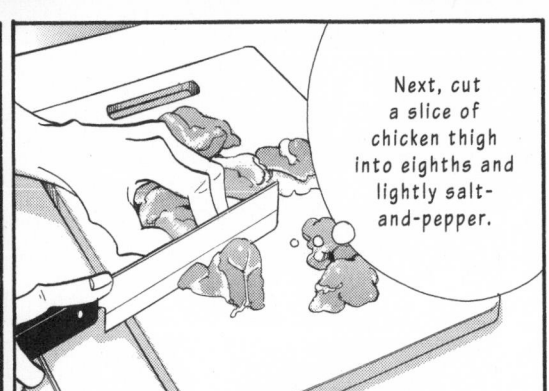

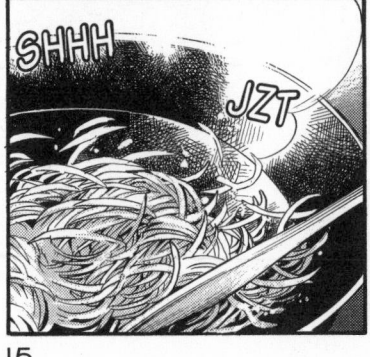

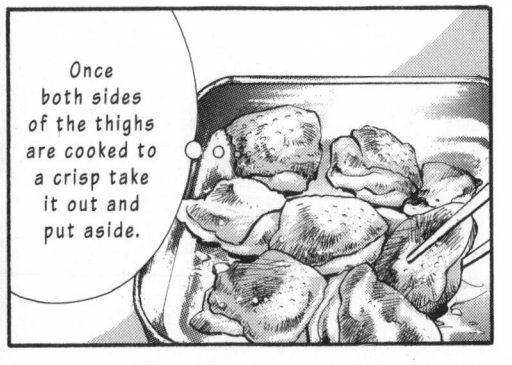

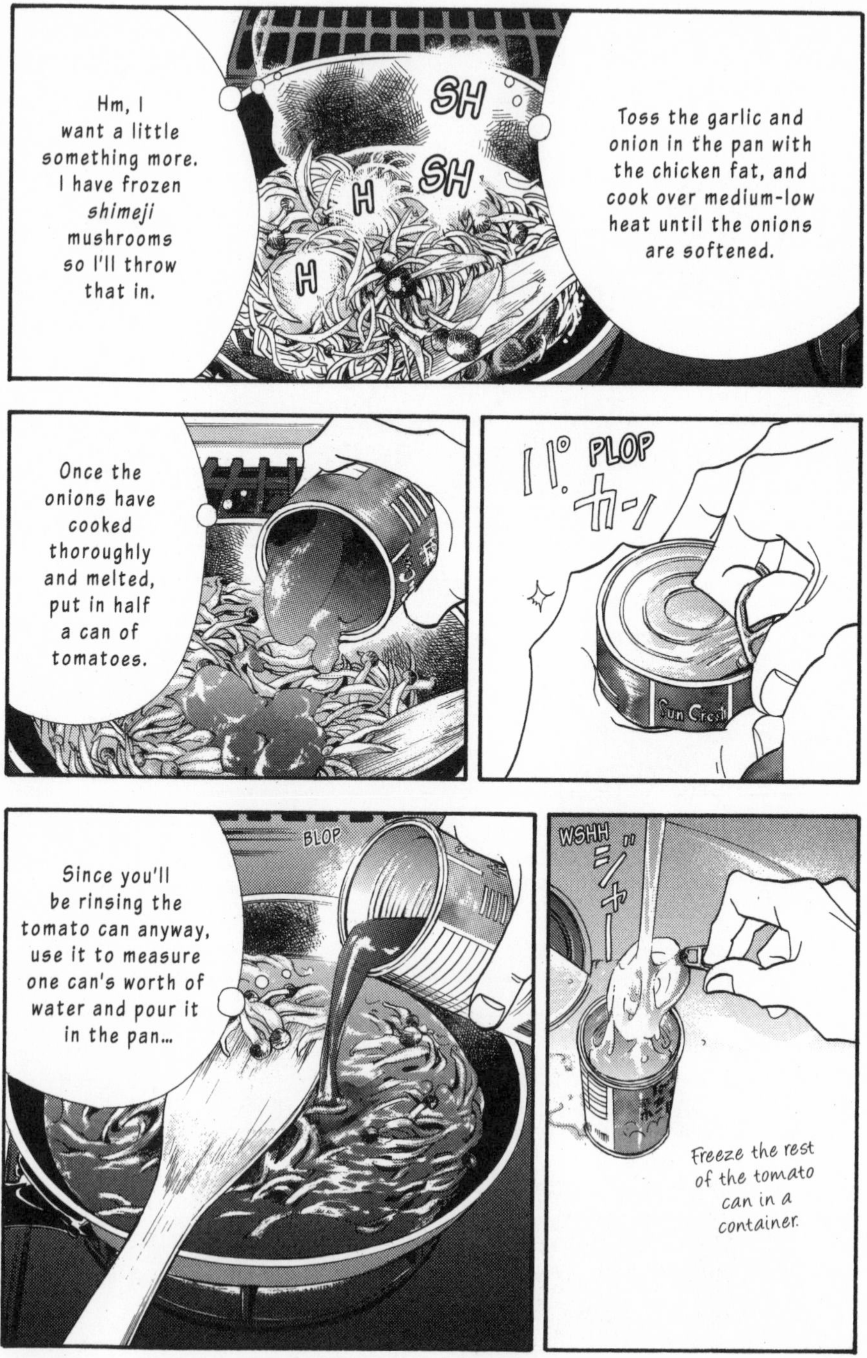
SH
SH
H
H
Toss the garlic and onion in the pan with the chicken fat, and cook over medium-low heat until the onions are softened.
Hm, I want a little something more. I have frozen *shimeji* mushrooms so I'll throw that in.
PLOP
Sun Cresi
Once the onions have cooked thoroughly and melted, put in half a can of tomatoes.
WSHH
Freeze the rest of the tomato can in a container.
BLOP
Since you'll be rinsing the tomato can anyway, use it to measure one can's worth of water and pour it in the pan...

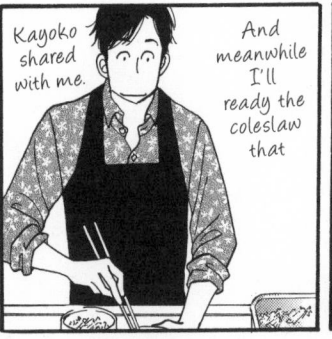

and throw in a cube of consommé and boil for a while on low.
If water runs low I can just add.
And meanwhile I'll ready the coleslaw that
Kayoko shared with me.
And yesterday's leftover, stewed string beans and potatoes.
TUMP
I'm home!
Wah! This smell!
It's bean rice, isn't i~t? Thank you, Shiro, I love bean ri~ce ♡
Oh, you're back.
I don't know why but I always want to have bean rice at least once before spring's over.

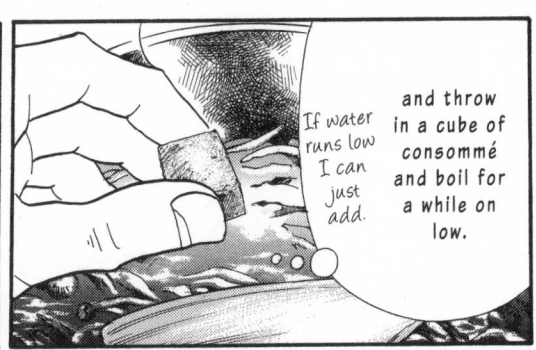

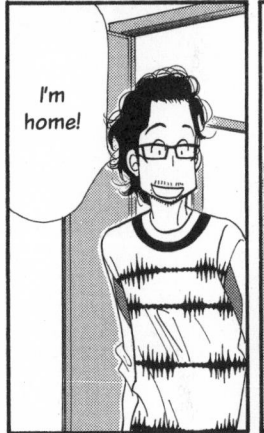

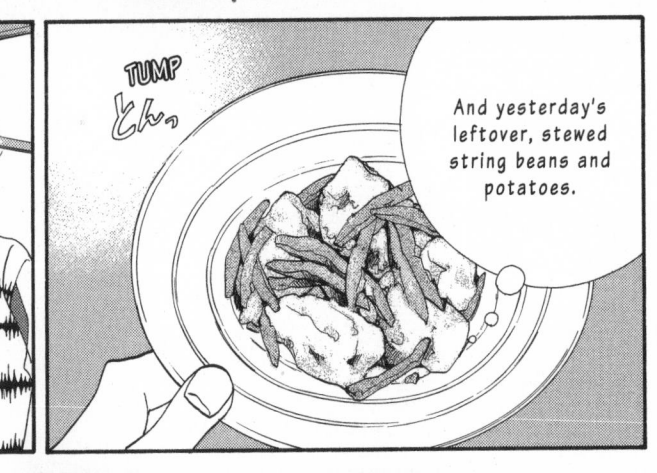

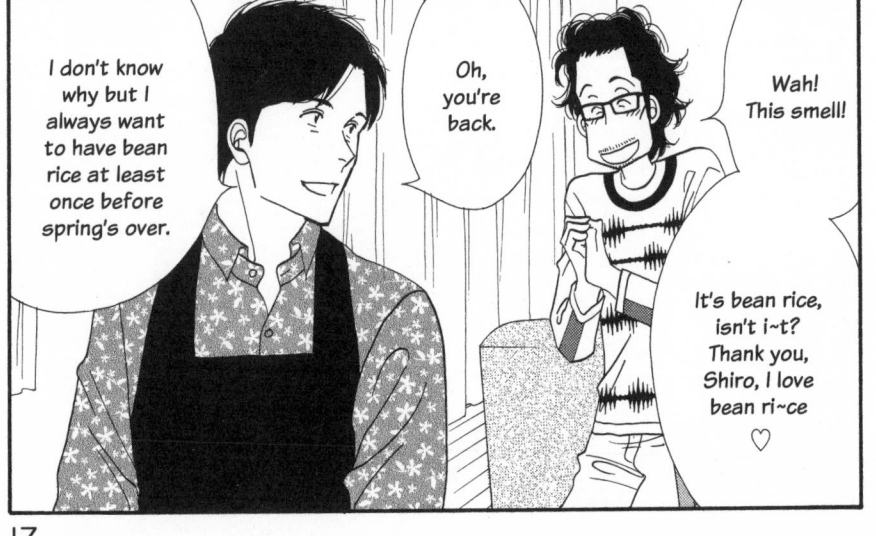

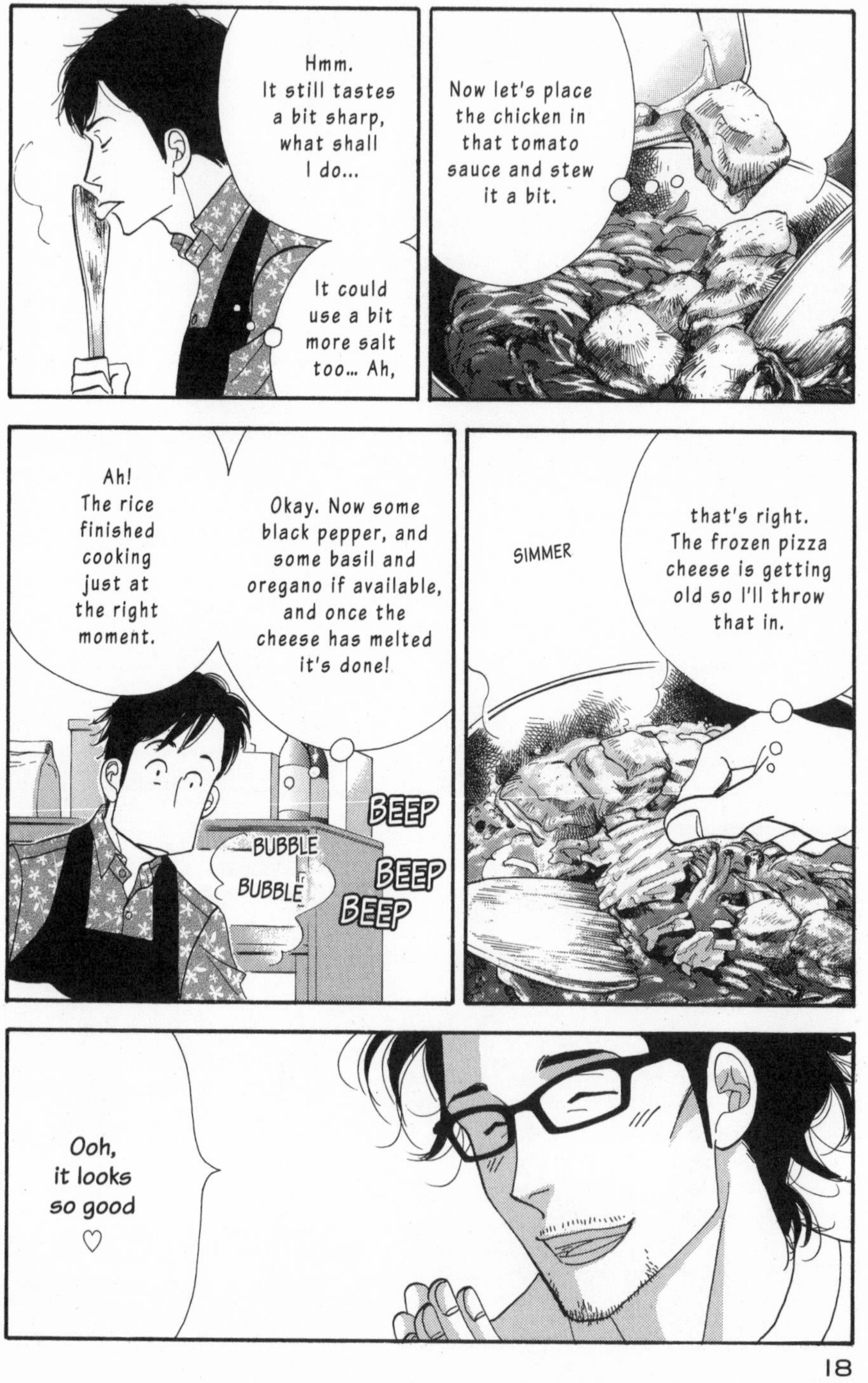
Now let's place the chicken in that tomato sauce and stew it a bit.
Hmm. It still tastes a bit sharp, what shall I do...
It could use a bit more salt too... Ah,
that's right. The frozen pizza cheese is getting old so I'll throw that in.
SIMMER
Ah! The rice finished cooking just at the right moment.
Okay. Now some black pepper, and some basil and oregano if available, and once the cheese has melted it's done!
BUBBLE
BUBBLE
BEEP
BEEP
BEEP
Ooh, it looks so good ♡

- Bean rice
- Tomato stewed chicken
- Coleslaw
- Stewed string beans and potatoes

The light saltiness of the bean rice, so good ♡

Mmmmm.

GASP

Hm?

But sorry, I did it quick today, the chicken might be too big and hard to eat...

Oh yeah, Kenji, today, at Kayoko's place...

Oh, there's cheese in it.

And this tomato chicken, whatta deep flavor. Delicious.

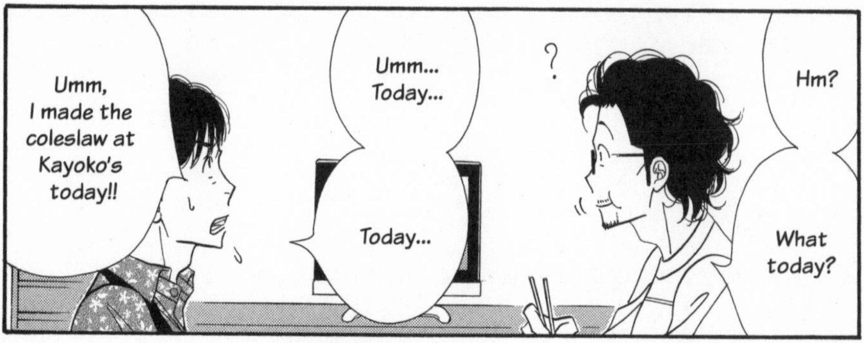
Hm?
What today?
?
Umm... Today...
Today...
Umm, I made the coleslaw at Kayoko's today!!

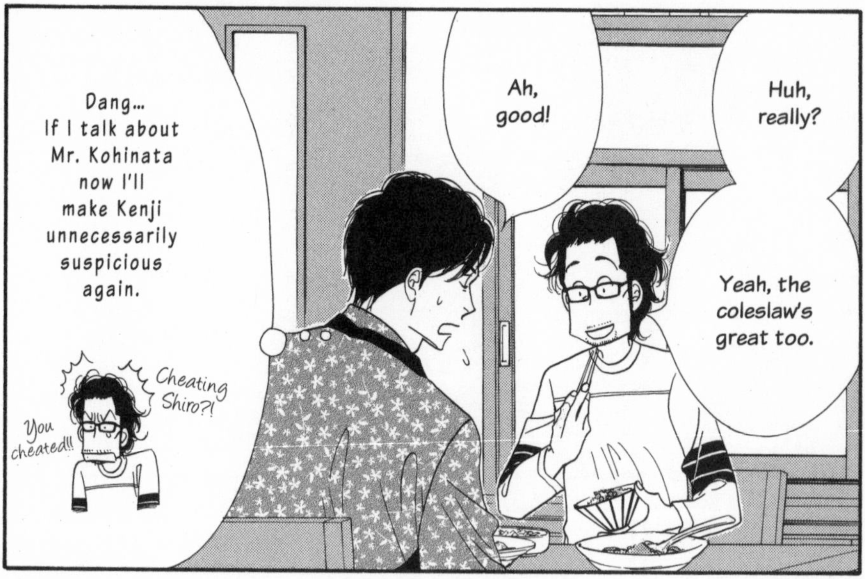
Huh, really?
Yeah, the coleslaw's great too.
Ah, good!
Dang... If I talk about Mr. Kohinata now I'll make Kenji unnecessarily suspicious again.
Cheating Shiro?!
You cheated!!

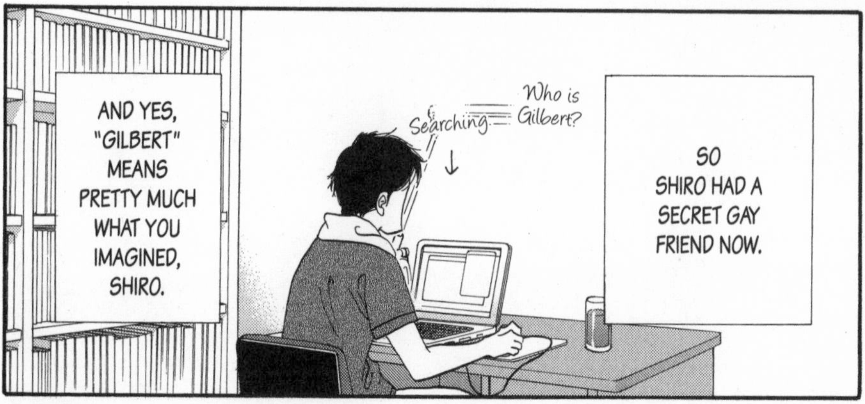
SO SHIRO HAD A SECRET GAY FRIEND NOW.
Who is Gilbert?
Searching
AND YES, "GILBERT" MEANS PRETTY MUCH WHAT YOU IMAGINED, SHIRO.

#33 END

Stewed string beans and potatoes (serves four)

1. Cut four medium-sized potatoes into fourths or fifths, and cover in water and boil.

2. Once the water starts to boil, throw in a bag of string beans cut in half. Then pour in some noodle sauce to about where it's drinkable but rather salty.

3. Boil over medium heat until the liquid is gone.

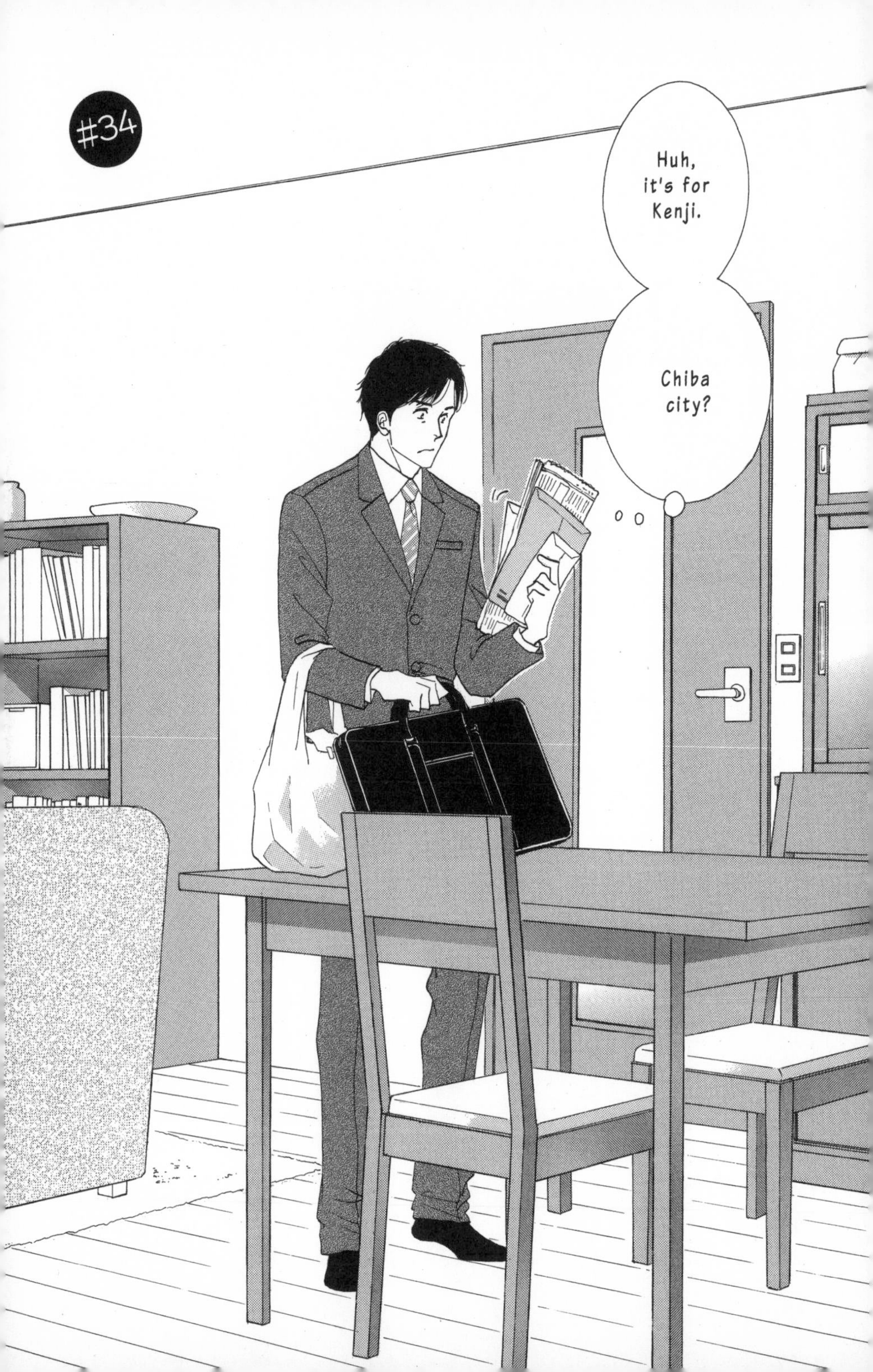
#34
Huh, it's for Kenji.
Chiba city?

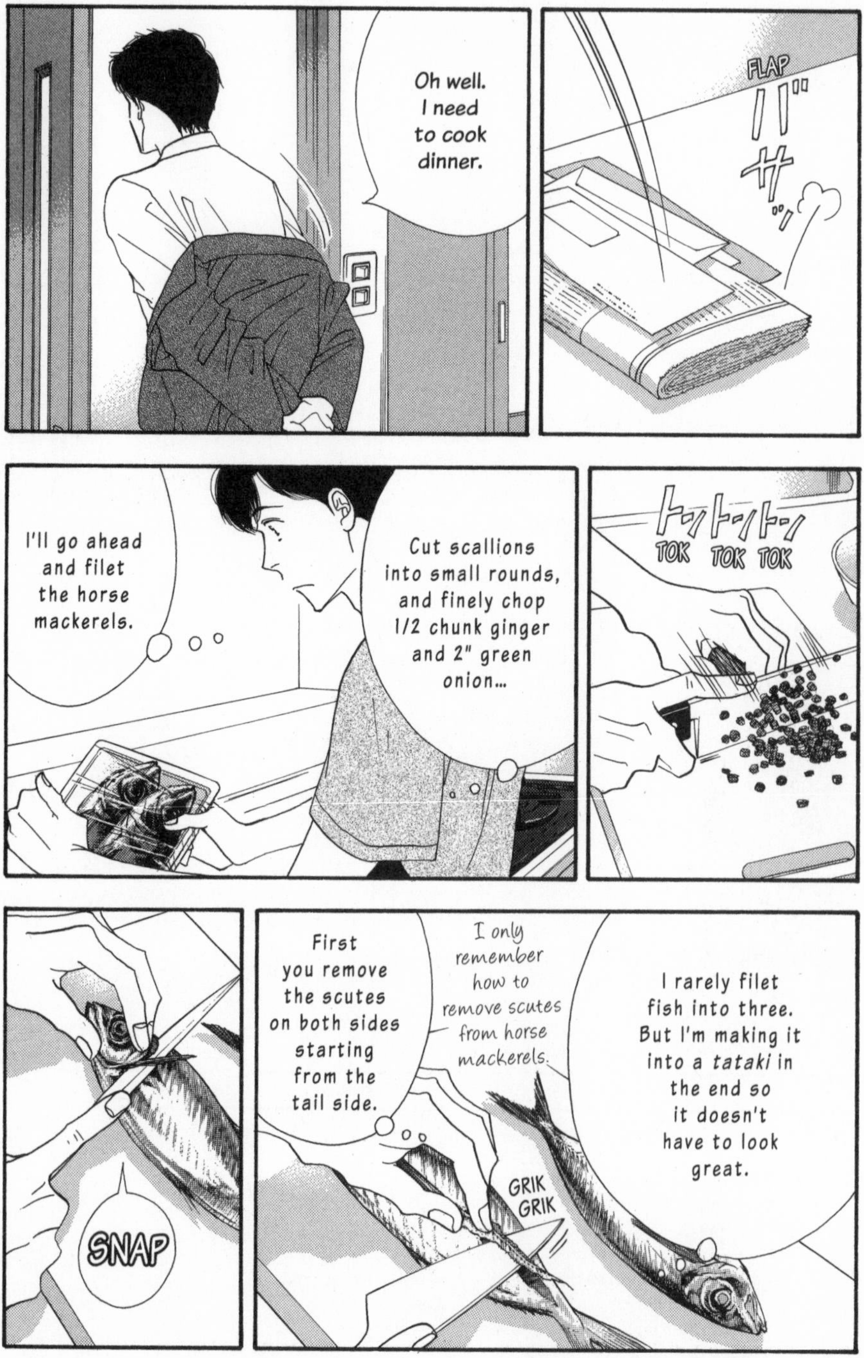
FLAP
バサッ
Oh well. I need to cook dinner.
トッ トッ トッ
TOK TOK TOK
Cut scallions into small rounds, and finely chop 1/2 chunk ginger and 2" green onion...
I'll go ahead and filet the horse mackerels.
I rarely filet fish into three. But I'm making it into a *tataki* in the end so it doesn't have to look great.
I only remember how to remove scutes from horse mackerels.
First you remove the scutes on both sides starting from the tail side.
GRIK GRIK
SNAP

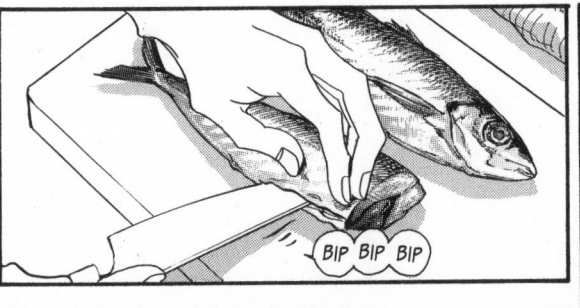

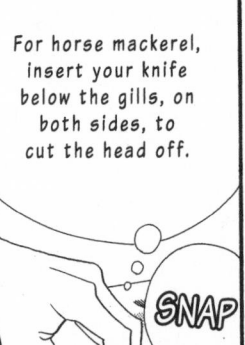

For horse mackerel, insert your knife below the gills, on both sides, to cut the head off.
SNAP
BIP BIP BIP
Cut the stomach open about an inch and a half from the head and dig out the intestines.
Do it on a newspaper so you can wrap it up and throw it away.
KTT KTT
FSHHH
Wash off the remaining blood and intestines and use a towel or paper towels to remove moisture.
Same thing with the other one.
FSHHH
Wash off knife and cutting board often and keep dry.

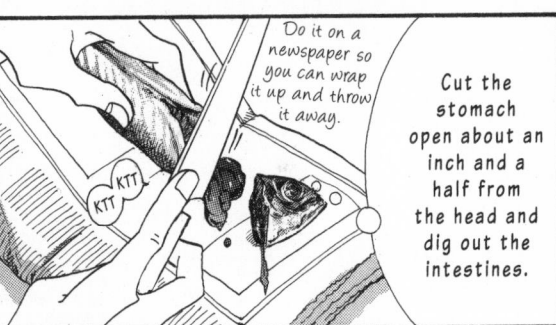

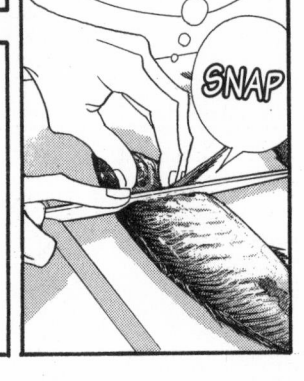

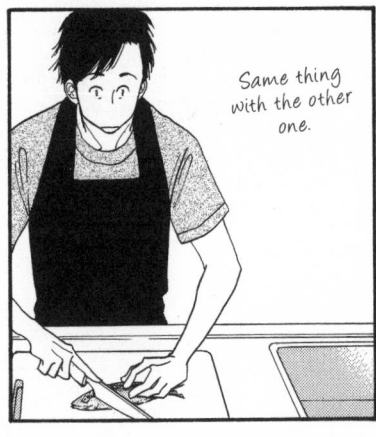

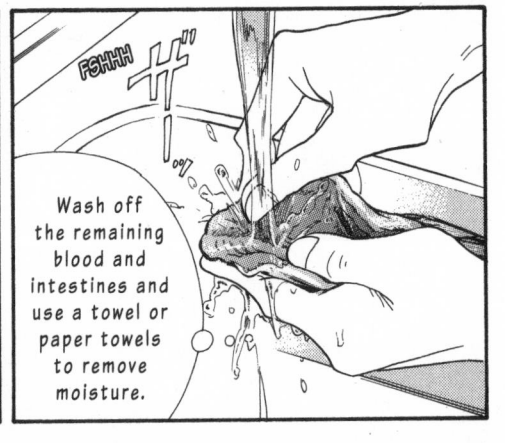

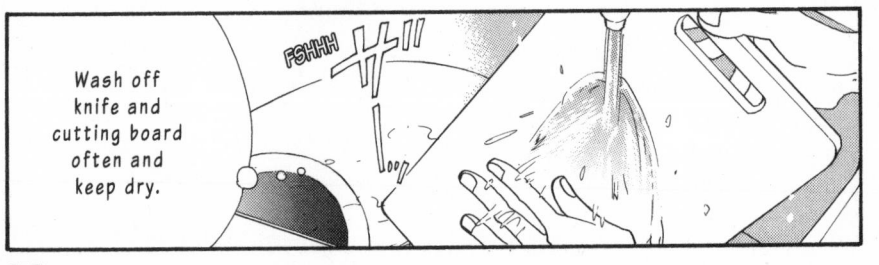

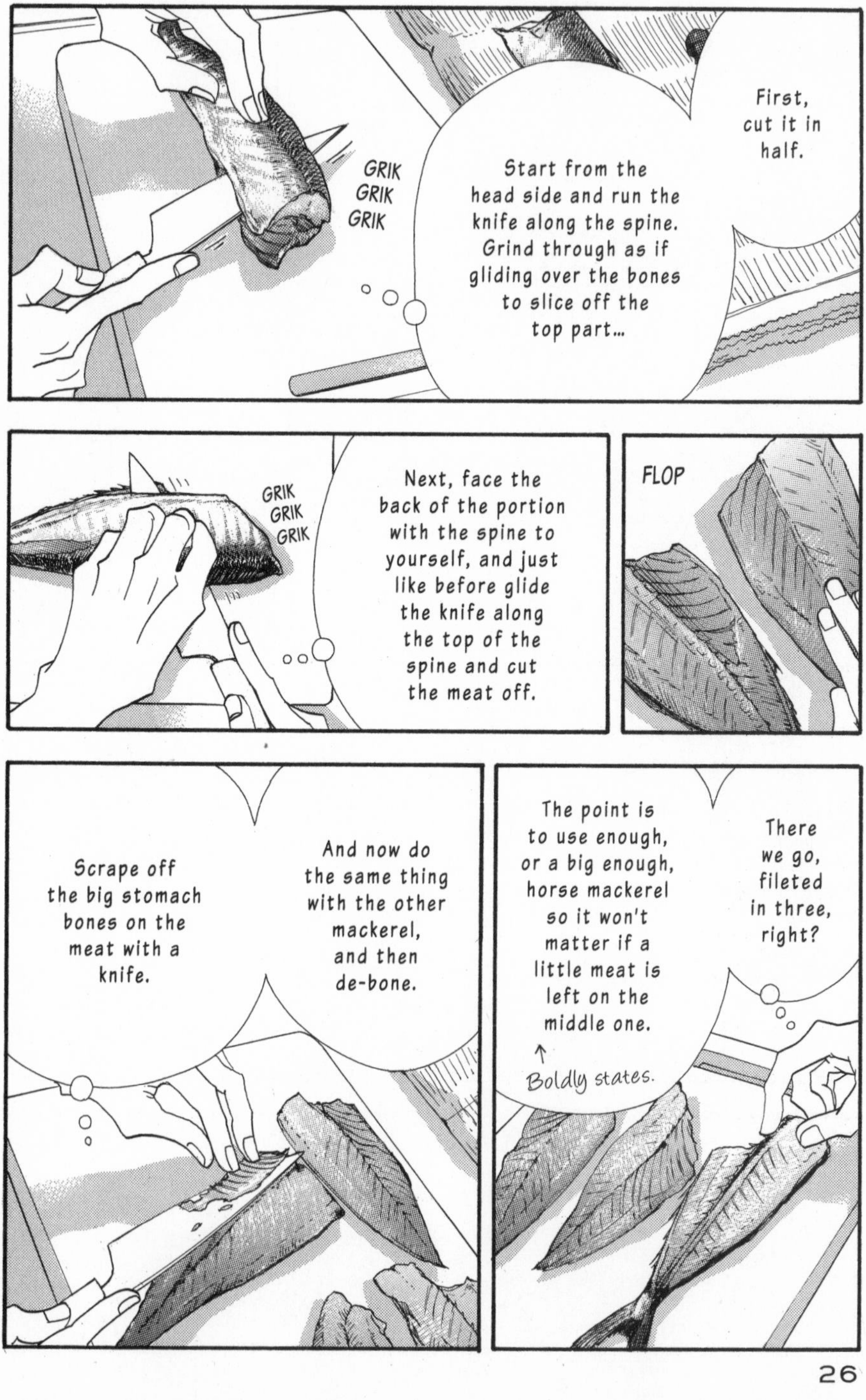
First, cut it in half.
Start from the head side and run the knife along the spine. Grind through as if gliding over the bones to slice off the top part...
GRIK GRIK GRIK
FLOP
Next, face the back of the portion with the spine to yourself, and just like before glide the knife along the top of the spine and cut the meat off.
GRIK GRIK GRIK
There we go, fileted in three, right?
The point is to use enough, or a big enough, horse mackerel so it won't matter if a little meat is left on the middle one.
Boldly states.
And now do the same thing with the other mackerel, and then de-bone.
Scrape off the big stomach bones on the meat with a knife.

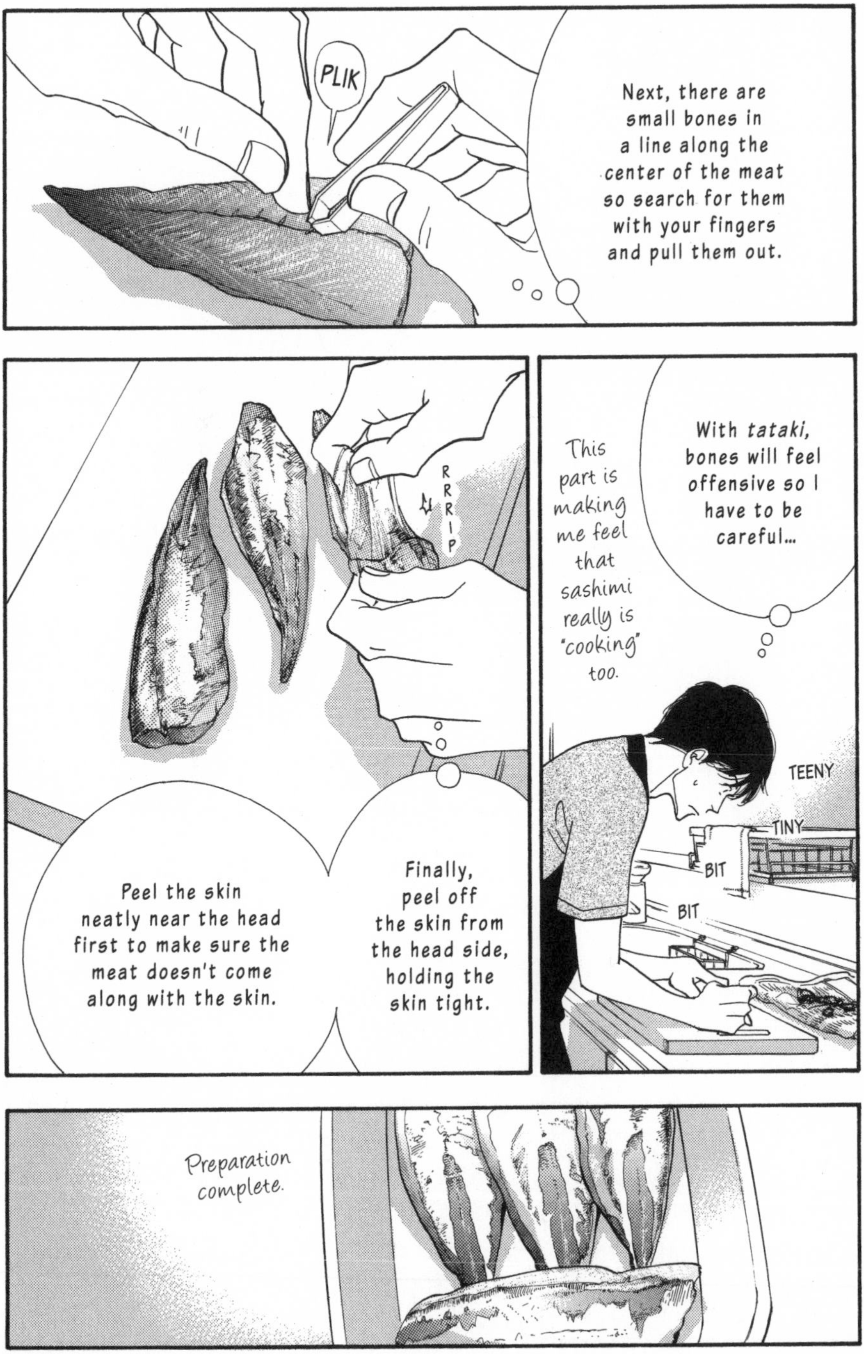

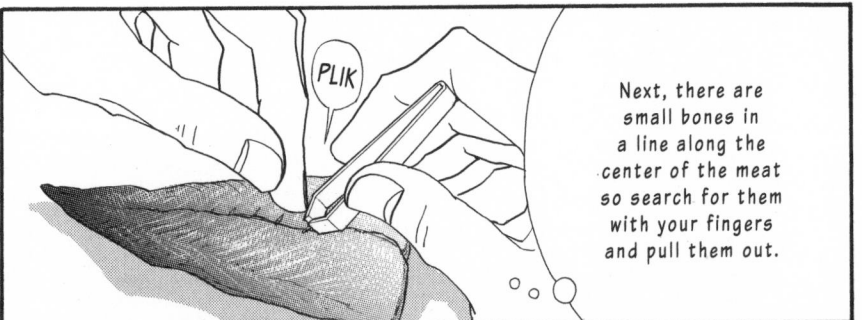

PLIK

Next, there are small bones in a line along the center of the meat so search for them with your fingers and pull them out.

RRRIP

This part is making me feel that sashimi really is "cooking" too.

With *tataki*, bones will feel offensive so I have to be careful...

TEENY

TINY

BIT

BIT

Peel the skin neatly near the head first to make sure the meat doesn't come along with the skin.

Finally, peel off the skin from the head side, holding the skin tight.

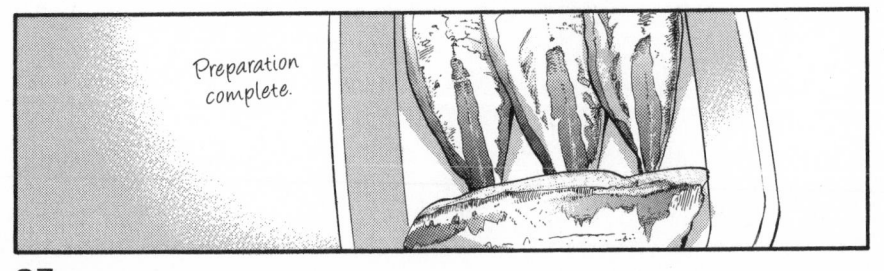

Preparation complete.

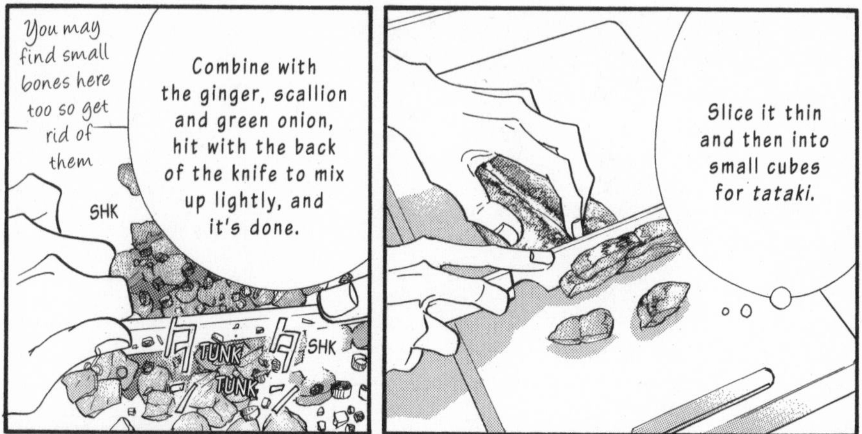
Slice it thin and then into small cubes for *tataki.*
Combine with the ginger, scallion and green onion, hit with the back of the knife to mix up lightly, and it's done.
You may find small bones here too so get rid of them
SHK
SHK
TUNK
TUNK

Note: "tataku" = to hit

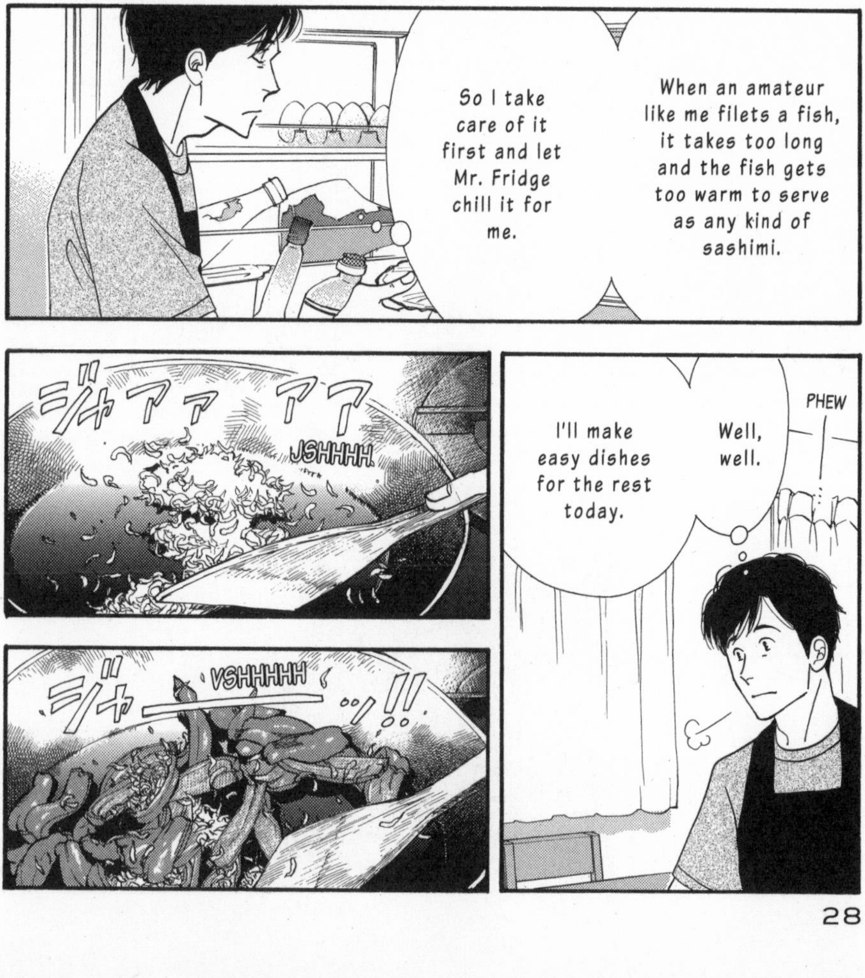
When an amateur like me filets a fish, it takes too long and the fish gets too warm to serve as any kind of sashimi.
So I take care of it first and let Mr. Fridge chill it for me.
PHEW
Well, well.
I'll make easy dishes for the rest today.
JSHHHH
VSHHHHH

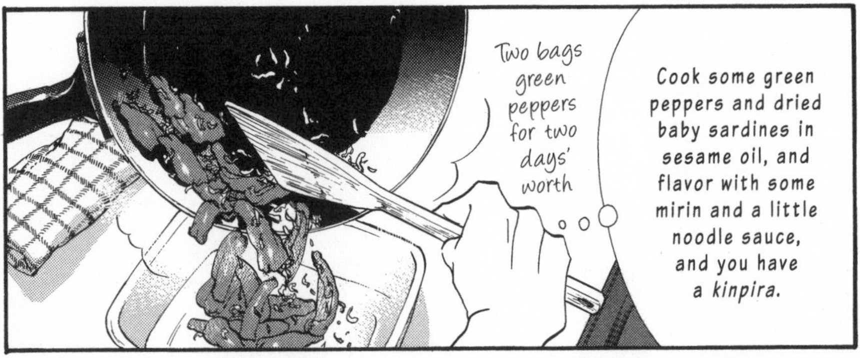
Cook some green peppers and dried baby sardines in sesame oil, and flavor with some mirin and a little noodle sauce, and you have a kinpira.
Two bags green peppers for two days' worth

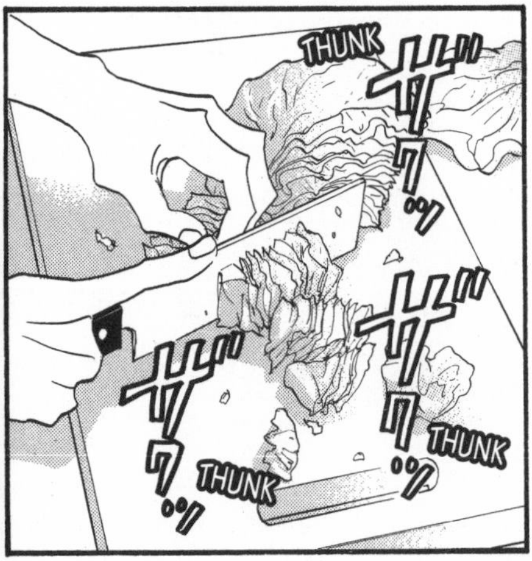
THUNK
THUNK
THUNK

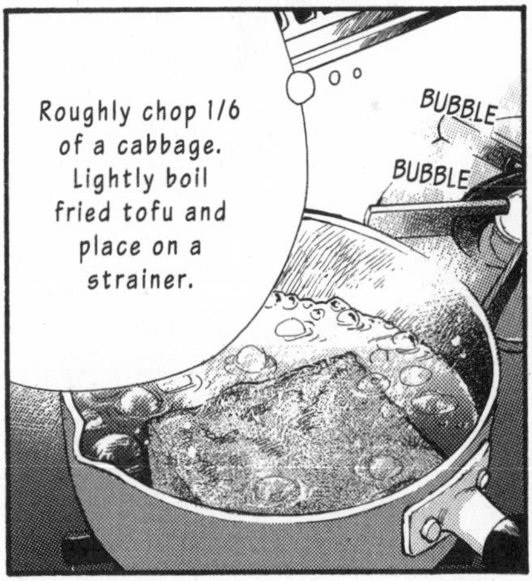
Roughly chop 1/6 of a cabbage. Lightly boil fried tofu and place on a strainer.
BUBBLE
BUBBLE

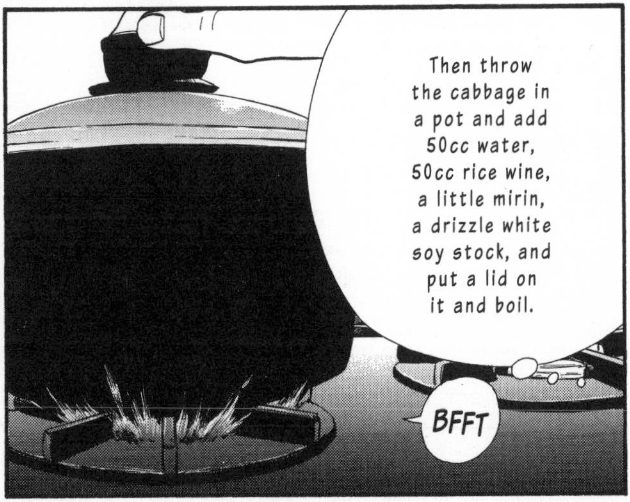
Then throw the cabbage in a pot and add 50cc water, 50cc rice wine, a little mirin, a drizzle white soy stock, and put a lid on it and boil.
BFFT

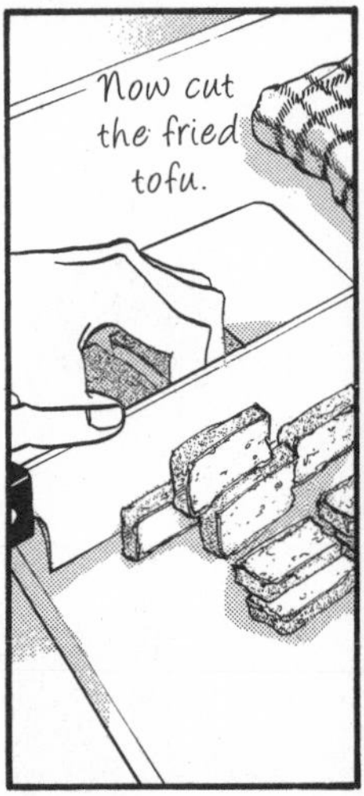
Now cut the fried tofu.

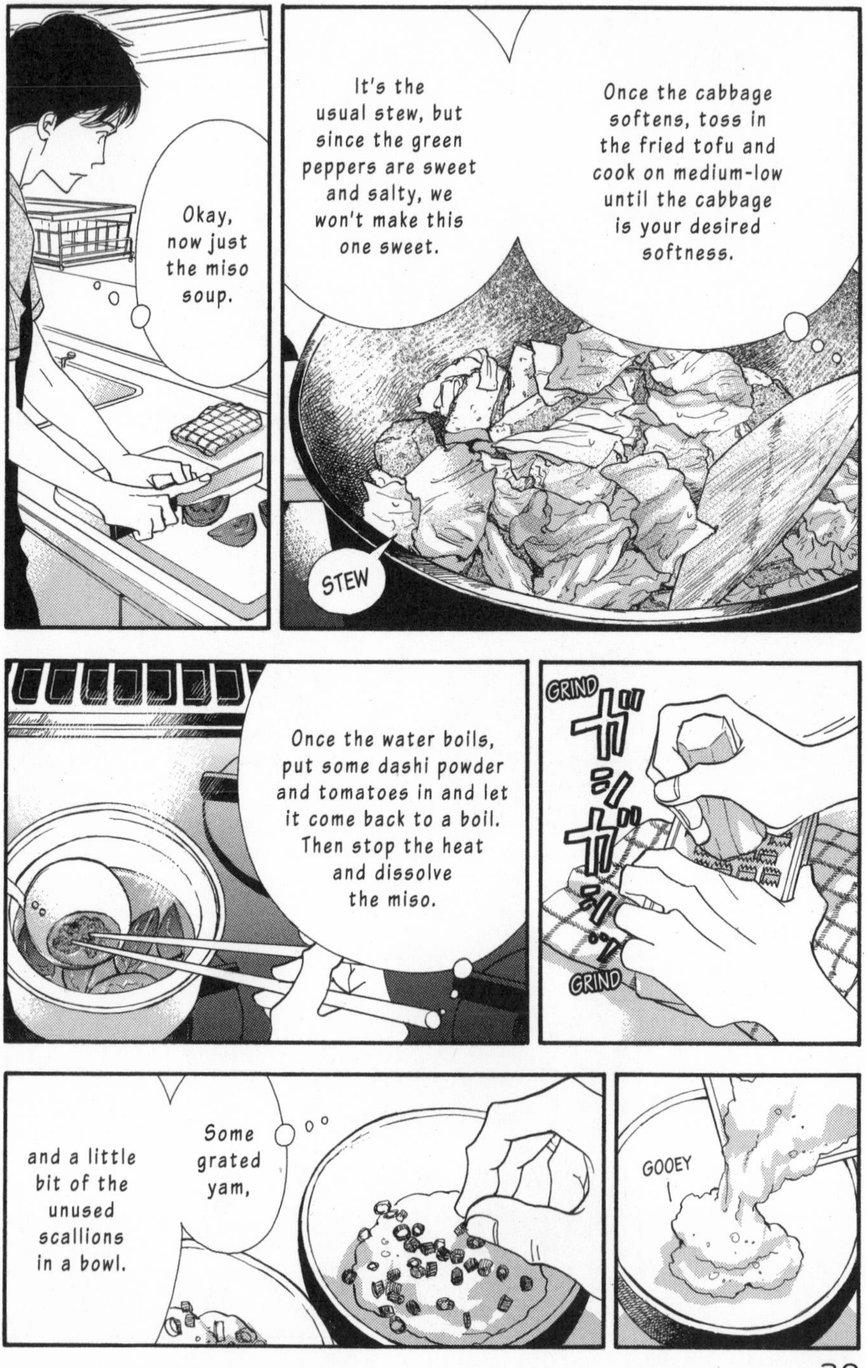

Okay, now just the miso soup.

It's the usual stew, but since the green peppers are sweet and salty, we won't make this one sweet.

Once the cabbage softens, toss in the fried tofu and cook on medium-low until the cabbage is your desired softness.

STEW

Once the water boils, put some dashi powder and tomatoes in and let it come back to a boil. Then stop the heat and dissolve the miso.

GRIND

GRIND

and a little bit of the unused scallions in a bowl.

Some grated yam,

GOOEY

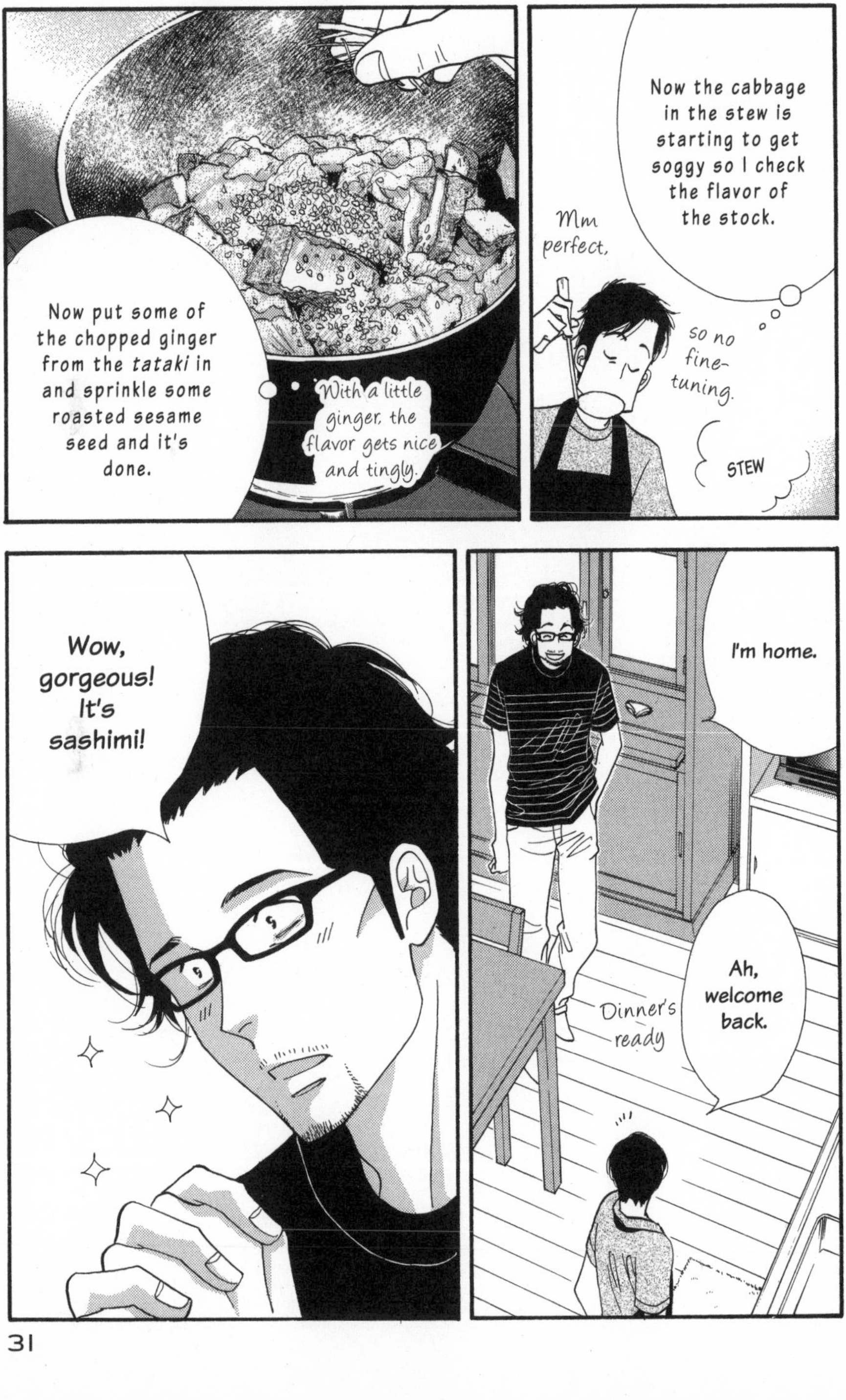
Now the cabbage in the stew is starting to get soggy so I check the flavor of the stock.
Mm perfect,
so no fine-tuning.
STEW
Now put some of the chopped ginger from the *tataki* in and sprinkle some roasted sesame seed and it's done.
With a little ginger, the flavor gets nice and tingly.
I'm home.
Ah, welcome back.
Dinner's ready
Wow, gorgeous! It's sashimi!

- Horse mackerel tataki
- Stewed cabbage and fried tofu
- Kinpira of green peppers and dried baby sardines
- Miso soup with tomatoes and Chinese yam

Mm! It's good!

And this stewed cabbage is the one I said I liked before. Happy ♡

Now let's see how it is.

Well, they had pretty big sashimi-grade horse mackerels for 100 yen each. I couldn't pass that up.

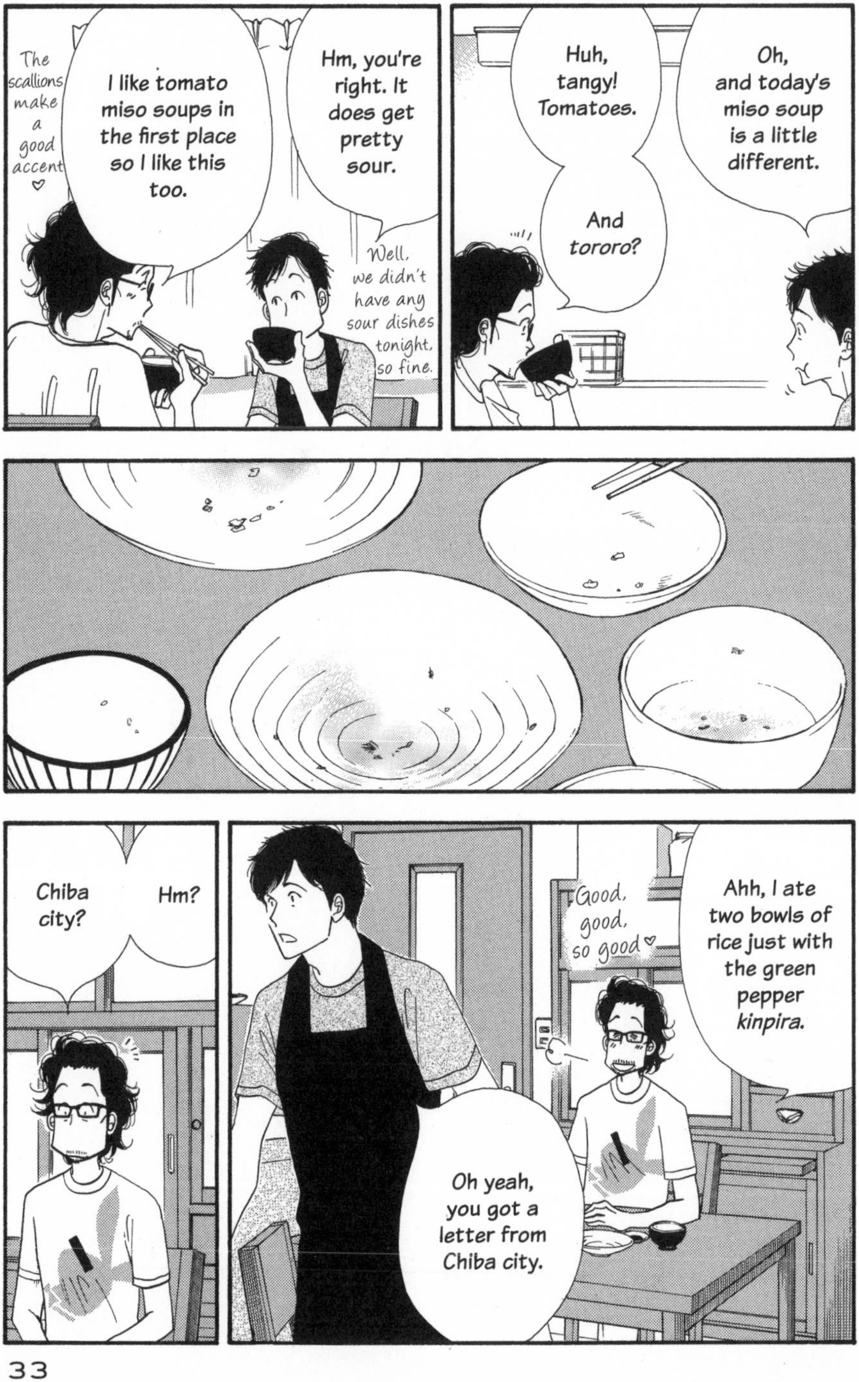
Oh, and today's miso soup is a little different.
Huh, tangy! Tomatoes.
And tororo?
Hm, you're right. It does get pretty sour.
Well, we didn't have any sour dishes tonight, so fine.
I like tomato miso soups in the first place so I like this too.
The scallions make a good accent ♡
Ahh, I ate two bowls of rice just with the green pepper kinpira.
Good, good, so good ♡
Oh yeah, you got a letter from Chiba city.
Hm?
Chiba city?

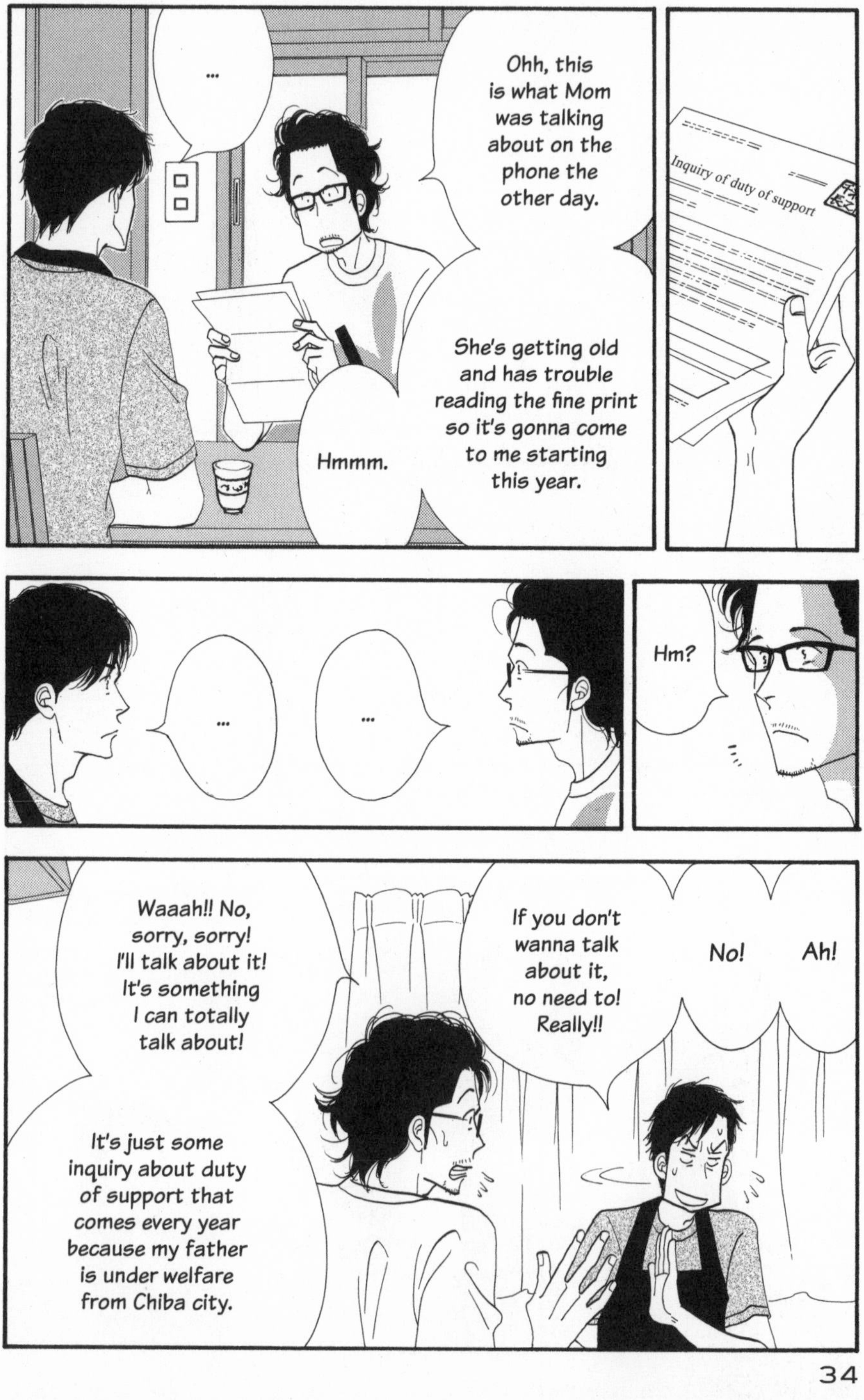
Inquiry of duty of support
Ohh, this is what Mom was talking about on the phone the other day.
...
She's getting old and has trouble reading the fine print so it's gonna come to me starting this year.
Hmmm.
Hm?
...
...
Ah!
No!
If you don't wanna talk about it, no need to! Really!!
Waaah!! No, sorry, sorry! I'll talk about it! It's something I can totally talk about!
It's just some inquiry about duty of support that comes every year because my father is under welfare from Chiba city.

To me he was just some man who came once every few years to steal money and abuse our family only to vanish again.

Masae! Get the bankbook 'n wallet and run!!

Shut up, you old hag, just gimme the money!!

EEK
EEK
EEK

WAAH
WAAH
WAAH
Okay!

Kenji

When I was big enough to think, my dad had already run away with a woman and almost never came home.

BAM
BAM
BAM
BAM
BAM

Mineko!!   Mineko,

Open up, I know you're there 'cause you're closed on Tuesdays!!

And the last time my dad came was when I was a high school freshman.

But we got by since my mom had a beauty salon in the area, and since he only came back once in a while and she didn't know how to get a divorce, she never got divorced.

SIP

Ke-
Kenji?!

Who are
you?

Wha...

SHRUKK

LOOM

He just went
home that day.
He was always
faint-hearted.
He had to get
drunk to come
home.

It was just my height
that had grown,
and my heart was
a fluffy princess's,
but my dad had no
idea his son would
look like that.

What is this?
"Inquiry"?
"Duty of
support"?

And then about
twenty years ago,
a notice from
Chiba city came
to my mom.

We would like you to support within your income. Please reply using the enclosed sheet."

The Welfare Act requires that we contact close relatives as defined by civil law for support first.

"Your husband Kenichi Yabuki has applied for welfare benefits.

YUP

I'll reply: "No extra income, cannot support."

It's not like it leaves me cold, but...

Ugh, to think such a socially inept man could actually ask for help from someone and apply for welfare...

So since then, that kinda offered proof that my dad is still alive.

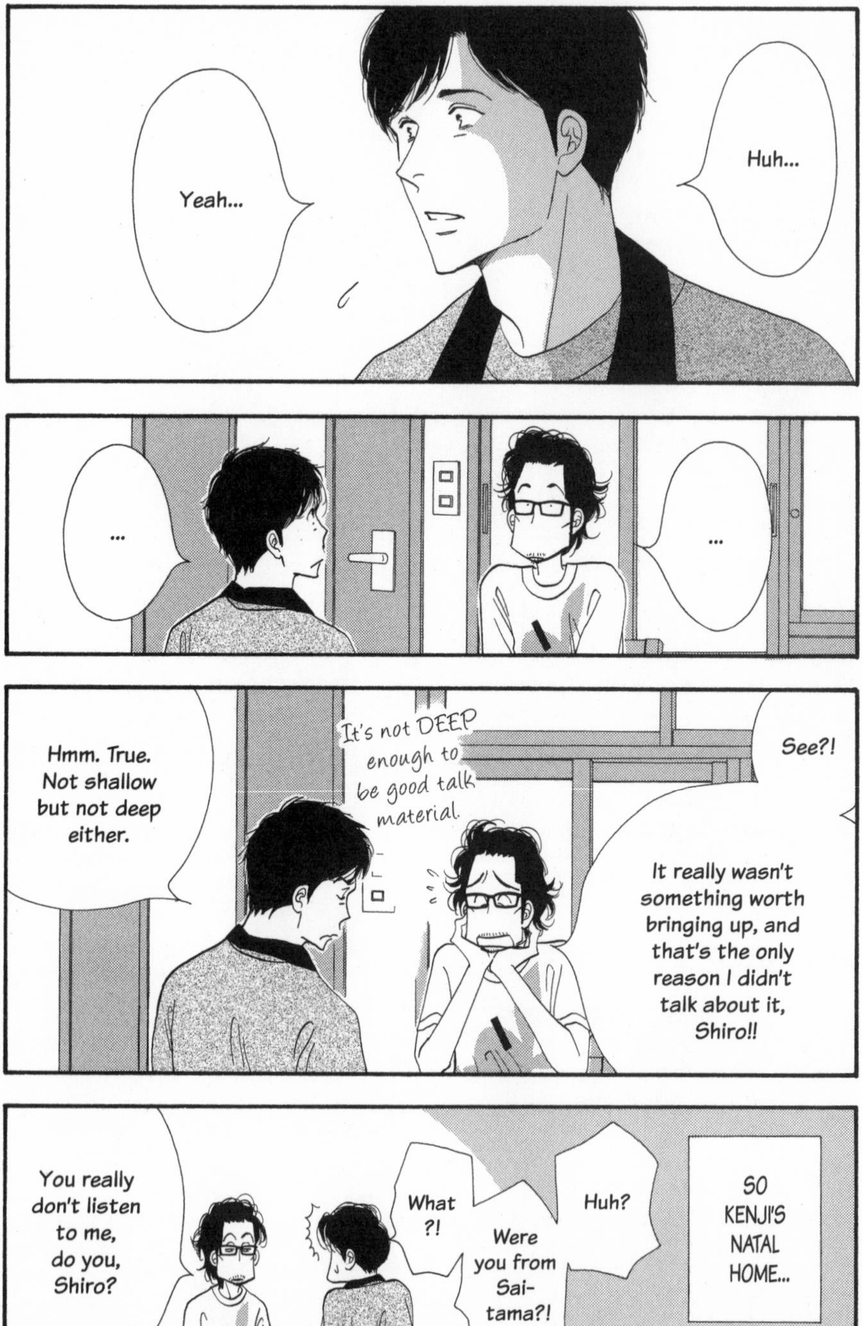
Huh...
Yeah...
...
...
See?!
It really wasn't something worth bringing up, and that's the only reason I didn't talk about it, Shiro!!
It's not DEEP enough to be good talk material.
Hmm. True. Not shallow but not deep either.
SO KENJI'S NATAL HOME...
Huh?
Were you from Sai-tama?!
What?!
You really don't listen to me, do you, Shiro?

#34 END

Miso soup with tomatoes and chinese yam

It's still good if you take out the yam
and just make a tomato miso soup.
Only heat the tomato for a brief while.

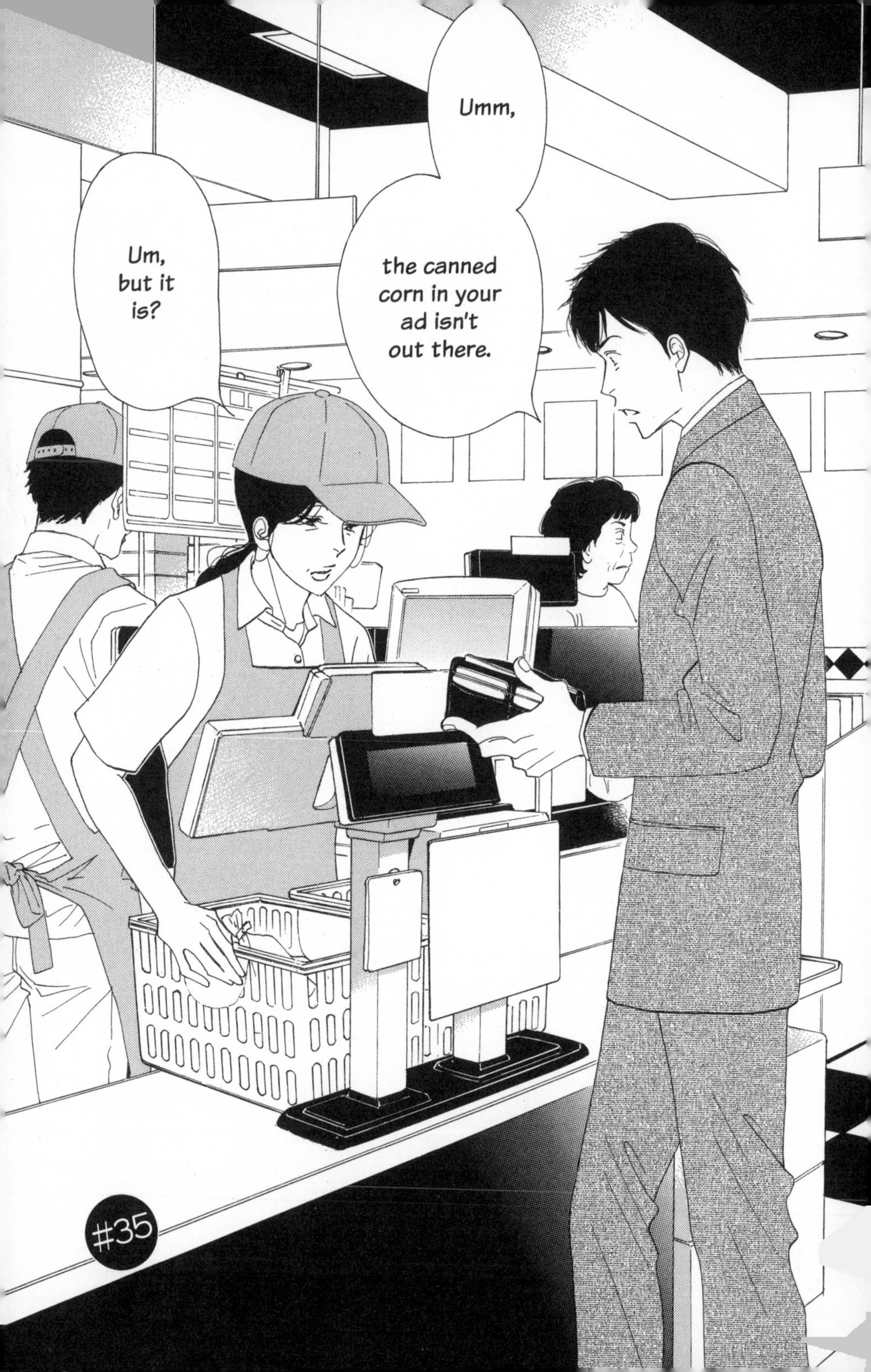
Umm,
the canned corn in your ad isn't out there.
Um, but it is?
#35

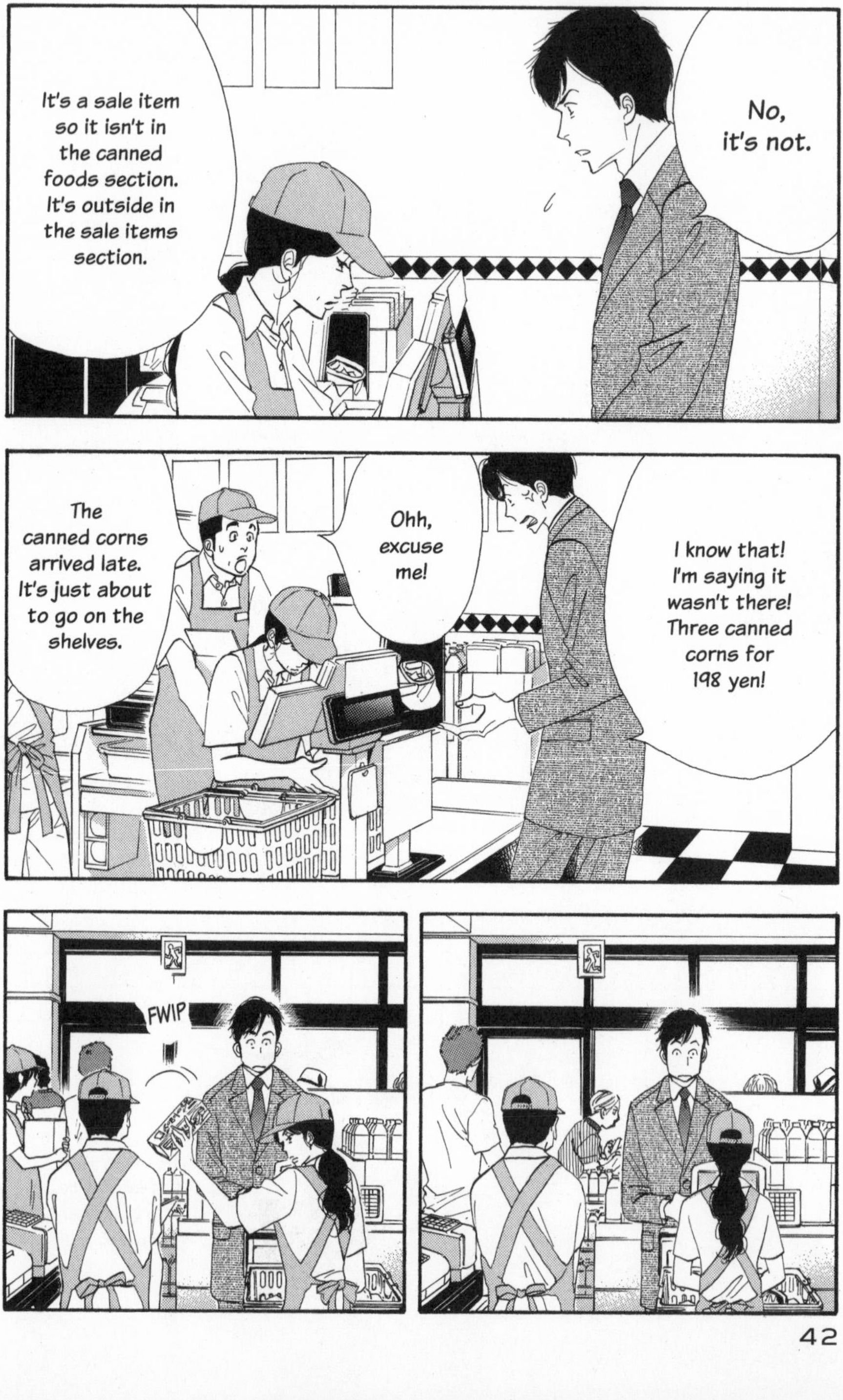
No, it's not.
It's a sale item so it isn't in the canned foods section. It's outside in the sale items section.
I know that! I'm saying it wasn't there! Three canned corns for 198 yen!
Ohh, excuse me!
The canned corns arrived late. It's just about to go on the shelves.
FWIP

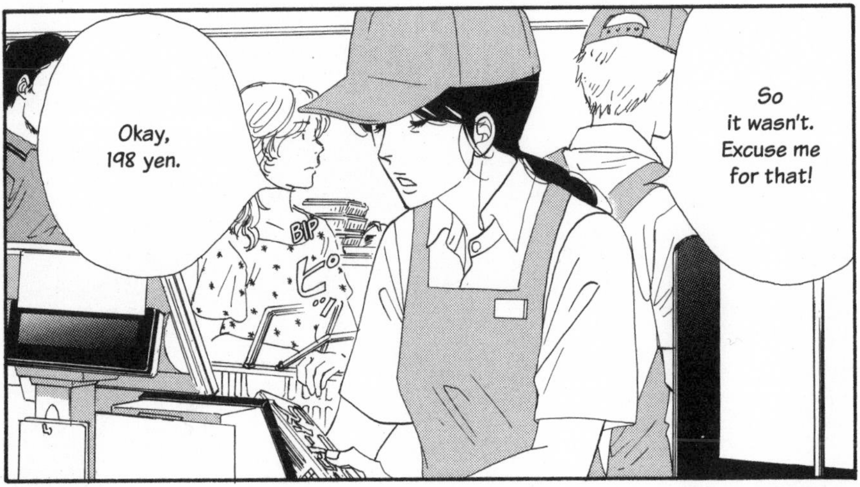
So it wasn't. Excuse me for that!
Okay, 198 yen.
BIP

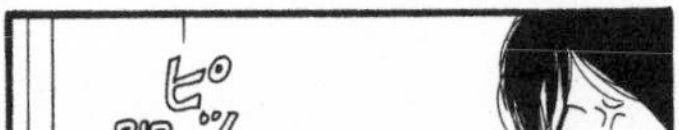
BIP
BIP
BIP
BIP
...
...

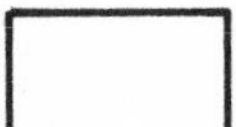
AND ANOTHER DAY

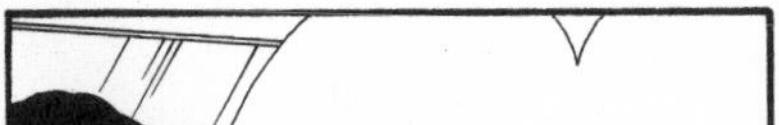
Huh?
It's Thursday but the 105-yen skim milk isn't here!

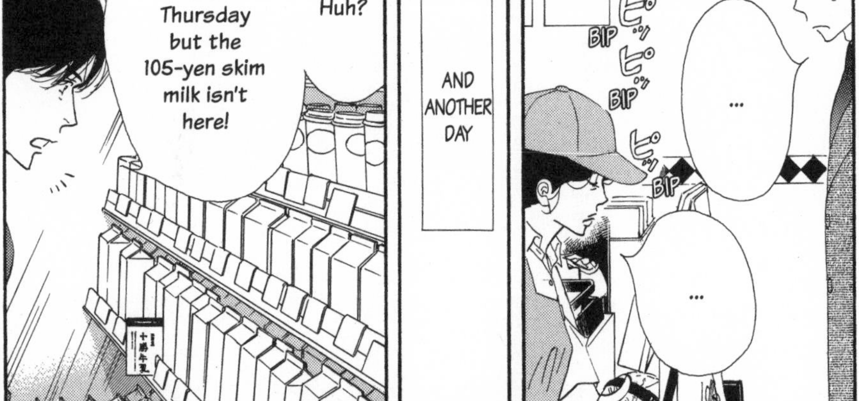
Oh, that's not a mistake. We quit doing the Thursday sale for skim milk starting this week.
Here, take a closer look at our ad!

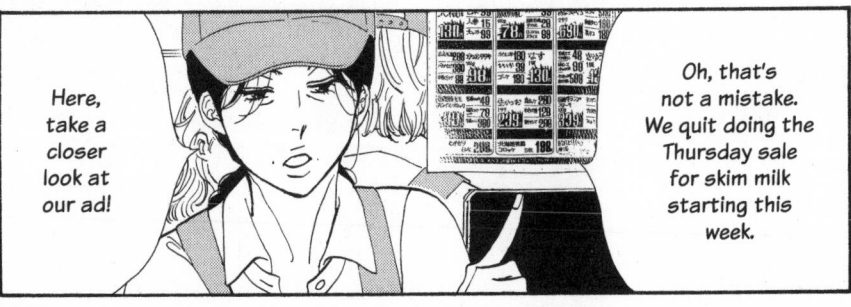

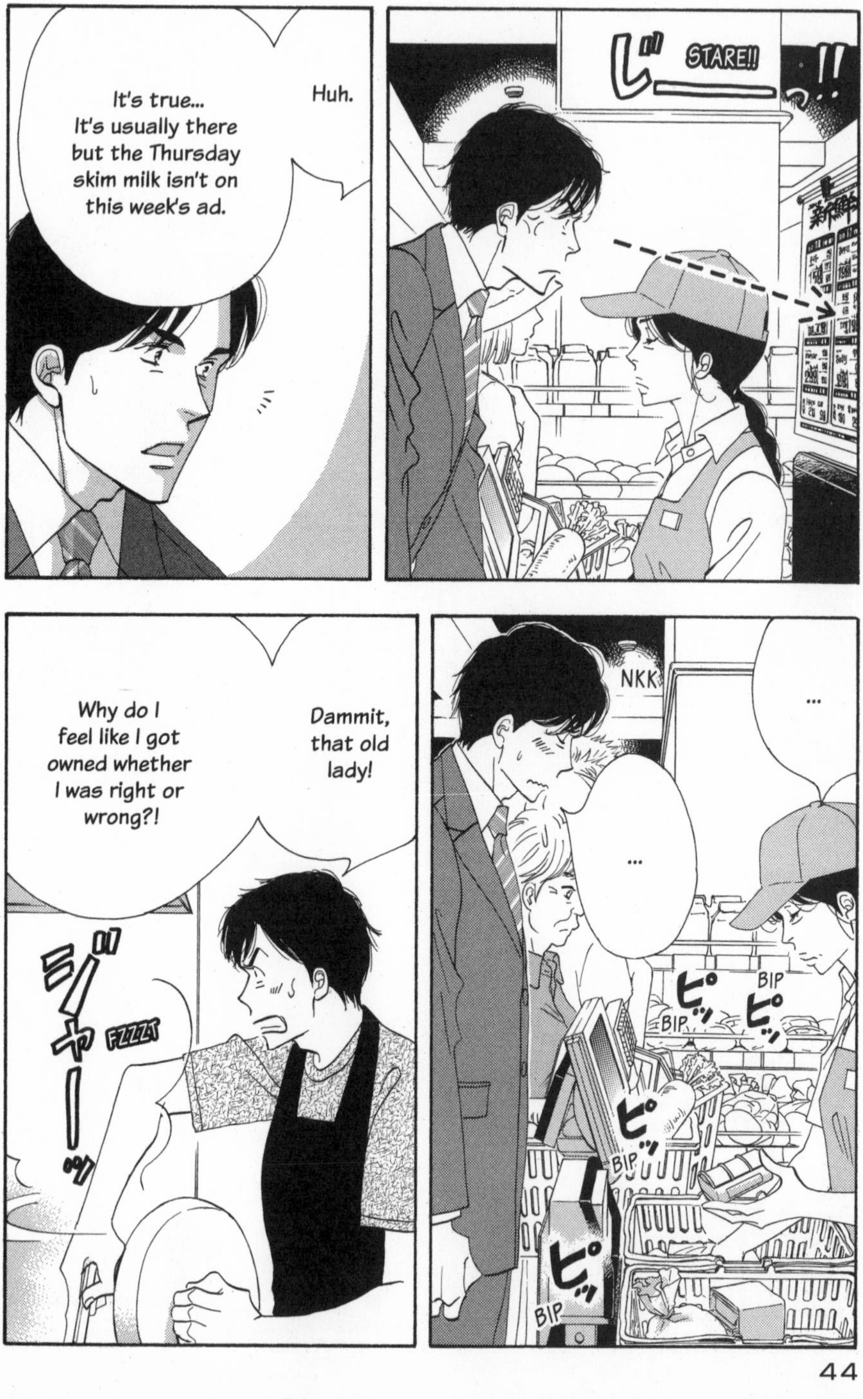

STARE!!
Huh.
It's true... It's usually there but the Thursday skim milk isn't on this week's ad.
...
NKK
...
BIP
BIP
BIP
BIP
Dammit, that old lady!
Why do I feel like I got owned whether I was right or wrong?!
FZZZT

When the three onions cooked in vegetable oil become soft,

lower the heat to medium low, and keep cooking until they are caramelized.

ジュ
ウ
ウ

SZZ

Huh.

I did it on pretty strong flames, but the onions do cook quicker this way.

FZZZT

This way I can cut up other veggies in the meantime.

The knack for cooking onions: don't stir too much, and not on too low.

Lesson learned.

I remember cooking onions super-slow on super-low heat before and going through hell.

Leave it for a spell, pretend you're stirring the bums up with the onions, and repeat.

Two hours already.

It's not turning brown...

SHH

45

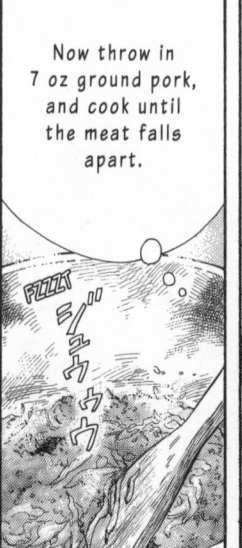

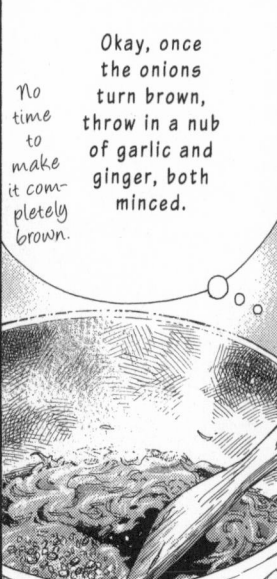

Still, you mustn't burn them completely.
Oops
FZZZ
And don't forget cooking the rice either.
Oops
Okay, once the onions turn brown, throw in a nub of garlic and ginger, both minced.
No time to make it completely brown.
Now throw in 7 oz ground pork, and cook until the meat falls apart.
FZZZT
ジュウウウ
And once enough fat comes out of the meat, throw in a bunch of sliced rounds of eggplants and halved string beans.
Five or six medium-sized eggplants, about two bags of string beans.
PLOP
Next in, one red and one yellow paprika sliced vertically.
FZZZ

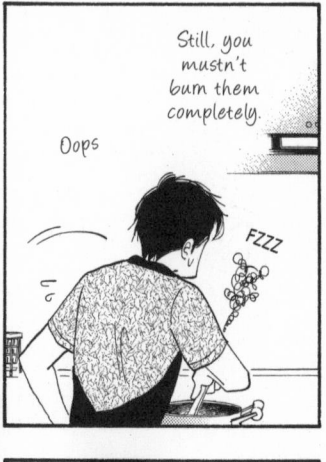

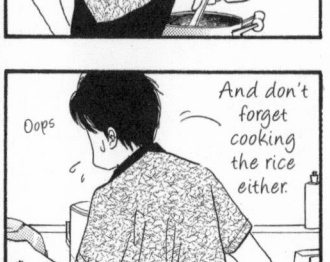

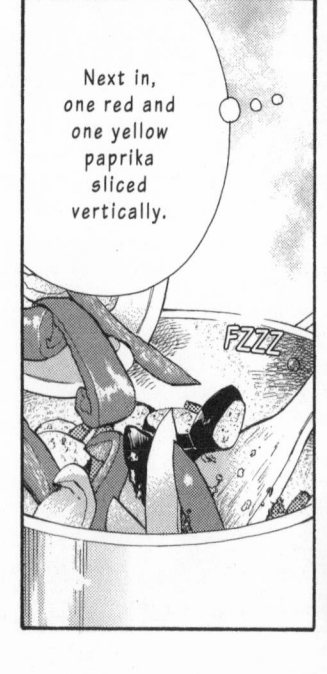

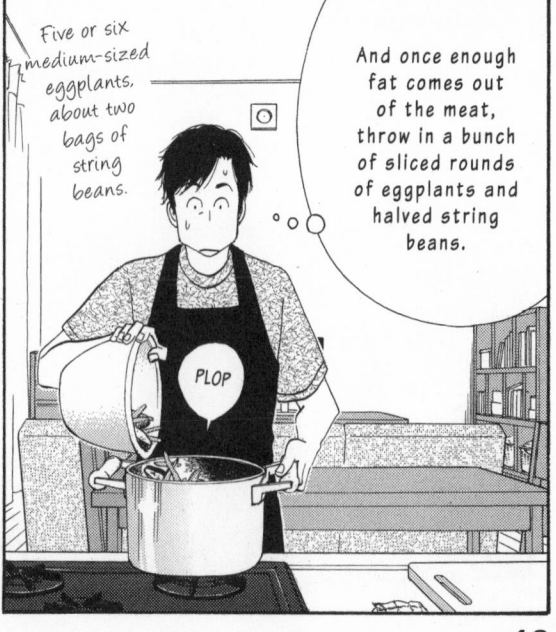

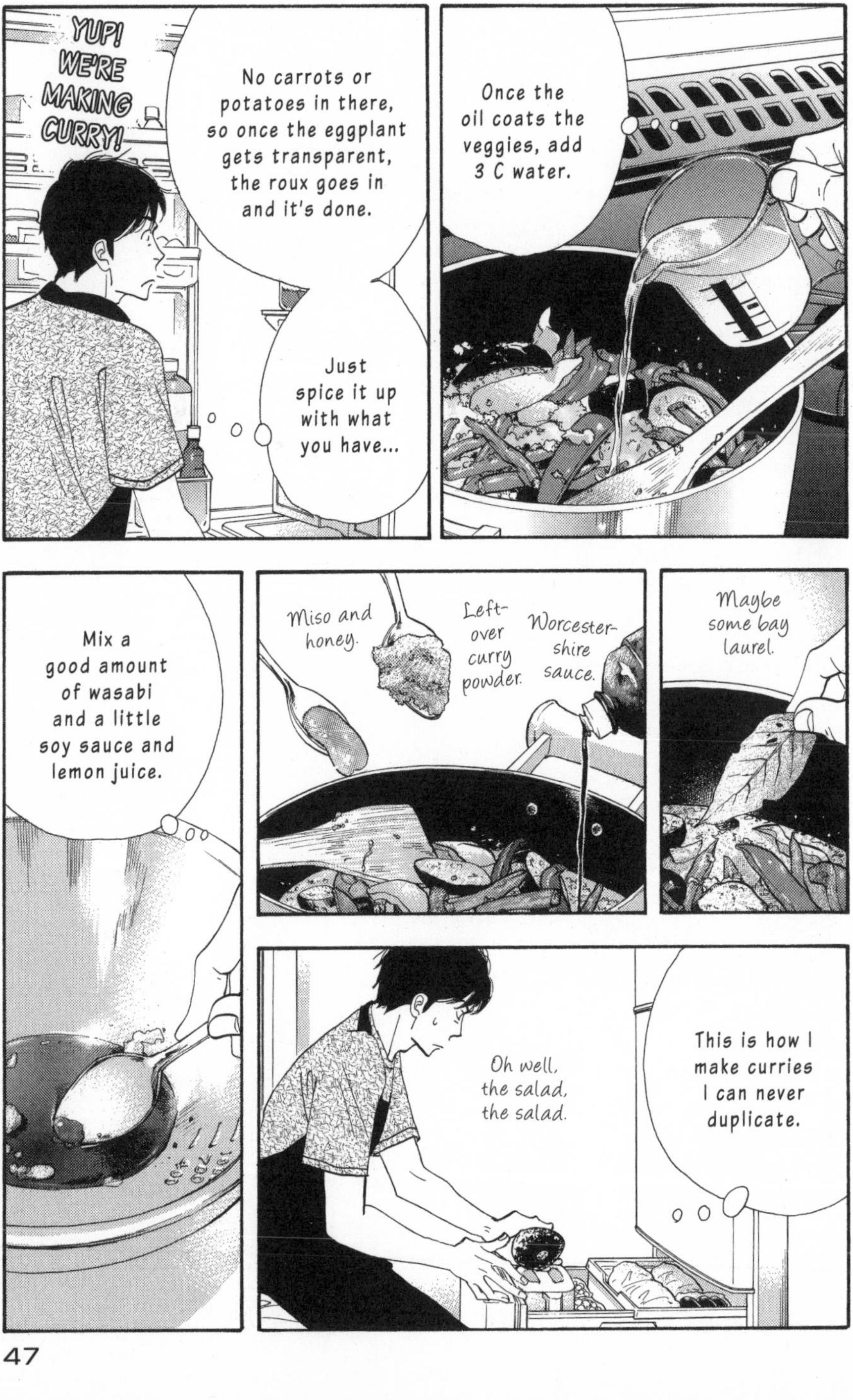
Once the oil coats the veggies, add 3 C water.
YUP! WE'RE MAKING CURRY!
No carrots or potatoes in there, so once the eggplant gets transparent, the roux goes in and it's done.
Just spice it up with what you have...
Maybe some bay laurel.
Worcester-shire sauce.
Left-over curry powder.
Miso and honey.
This is how I make curries I can never duplicate.
Oh well, the salad, the salad.
Mix a good amount of wasabi and a little soy sauce and lemon juice.

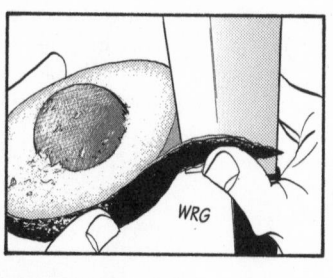

SSST
PLOP
WRG
TOK
TOK
Cut one avocado and one tomato into bite-sized pieces.
Mix it up with the wasabi soy sauce from earlier, and sprinkle some shaved bonito, and that's it.
Okay, add five servings roux and okras sliced on the bias, and boil a bit.
About two packs of okras too.
SIMMER
SIMMER
SIMMER
Eggplants, okras, tomatoes, and string beans.
It's summer...

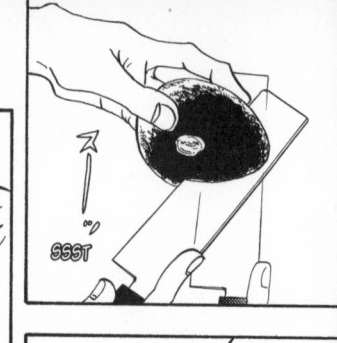

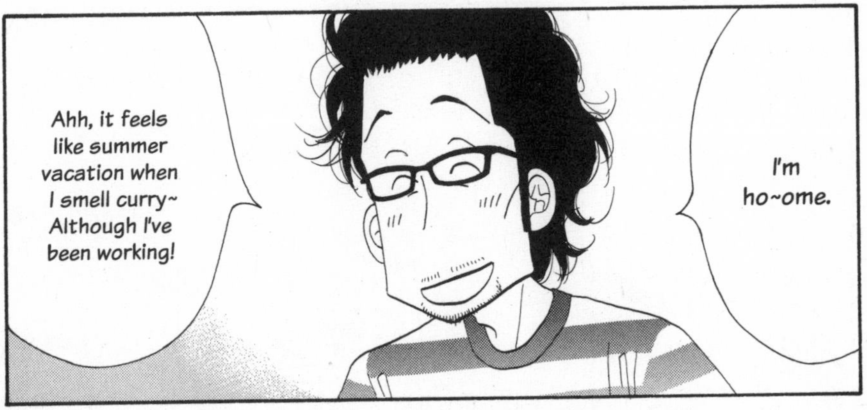
I'm ho~ome.
Ahh, it feels like summer vacation when I smell curry~ Although I've been working!
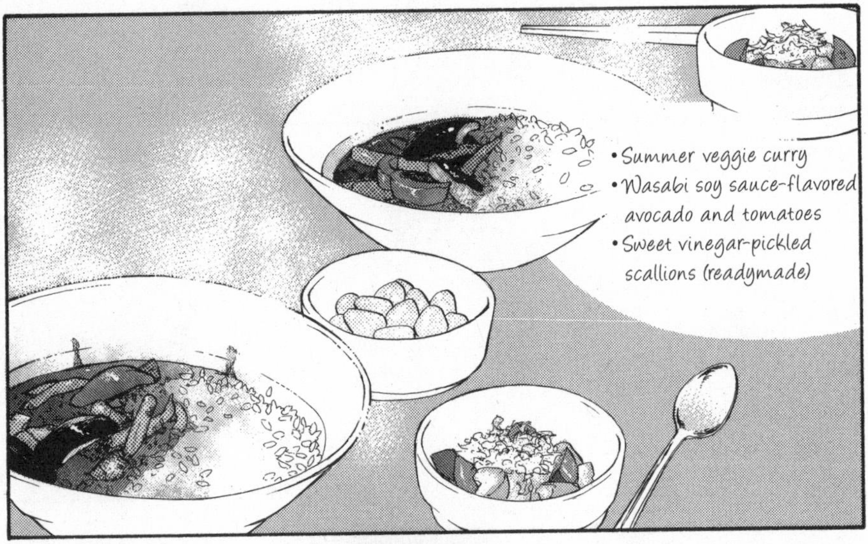
•Summer veggie curry
•Wasabi soy sauce-flavored avocado and tomatoes
•Sweet vinegar-pickled scallions (readymade)
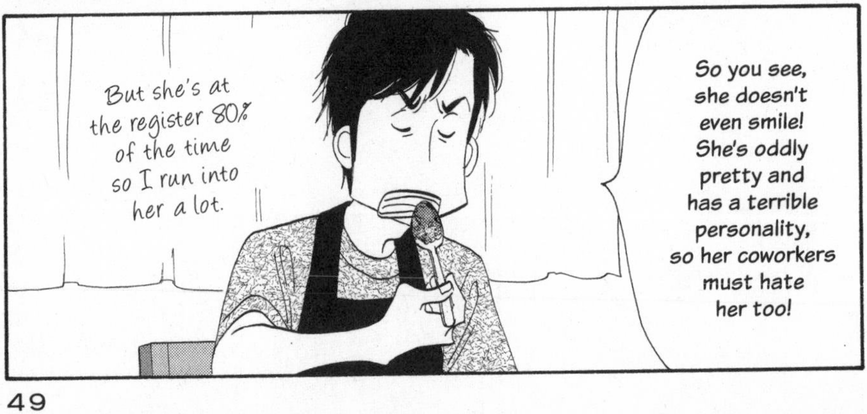
So you see, she doesn't even smile! She's oddly pretty and has a terrible personality, so her coworkers must hate her too!
But she's at the register 80% of the time so I run into her a lot.

Okay, but it won't taste exactly the same.

Make this again ♡

Eel sauce, ichimi, I just throw in whatever I have then.

Huh, really?

Heheh, Shiro, this avocado salad. The wasabi tastes great. I love tonight's dinner ♡

Oh really, is that so ♡

Ooh, the curry too, so many summer vegetables, and the roux has so much depth, it's just great!!

Gets so happy when Shiro runs women down.

Mm, mornin'.

Good morning.

CHIRP CHIRP CHIRP

No Thursday skim milk sale this week either...

Ahh...

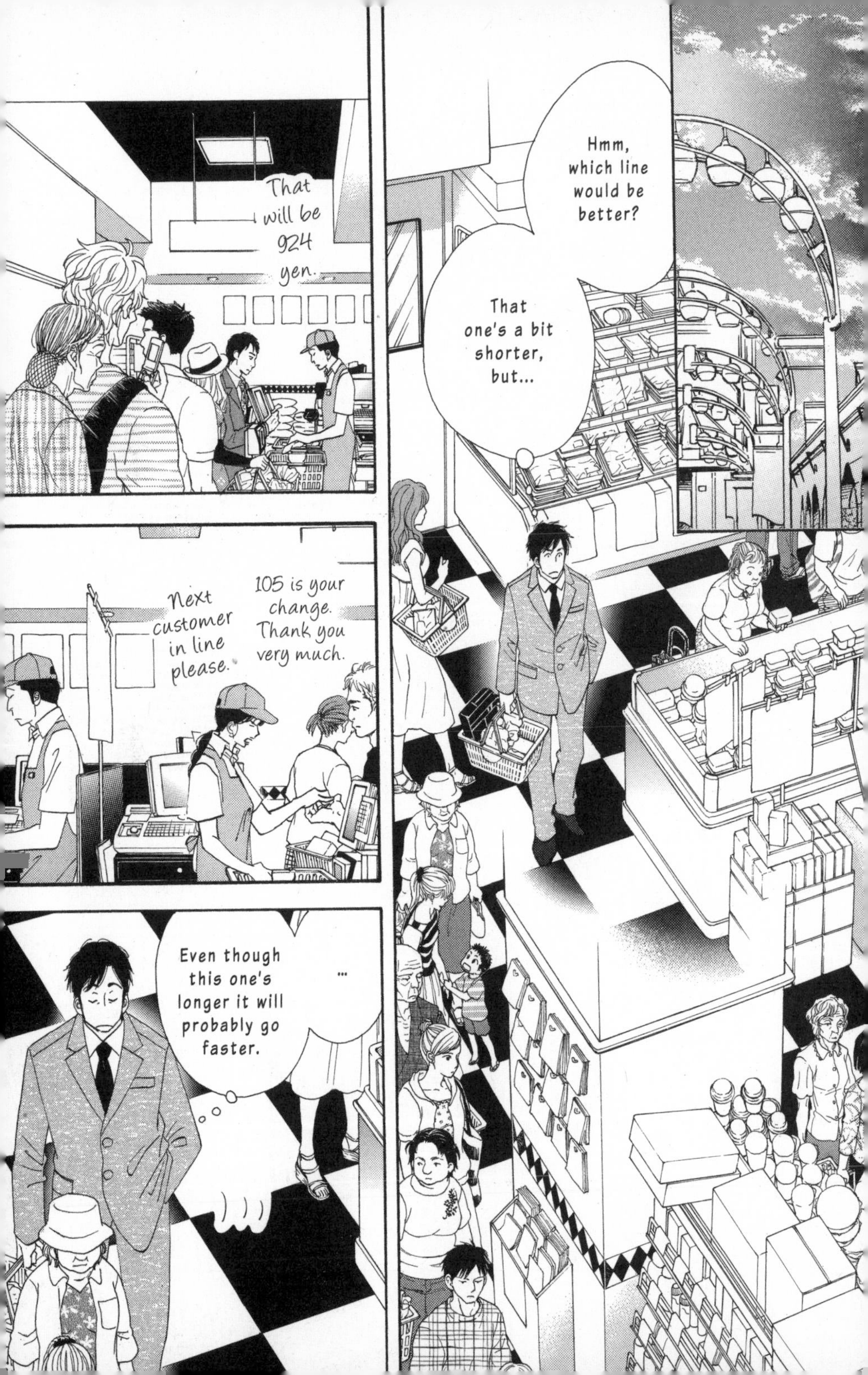
Hmm, which line would be better?
That one's a bit shorter, but...
That will be 924 yen.
105 is your change. Thank you very much.
Next customer in line please.
Even though this one's longer it will probably go faster.
...

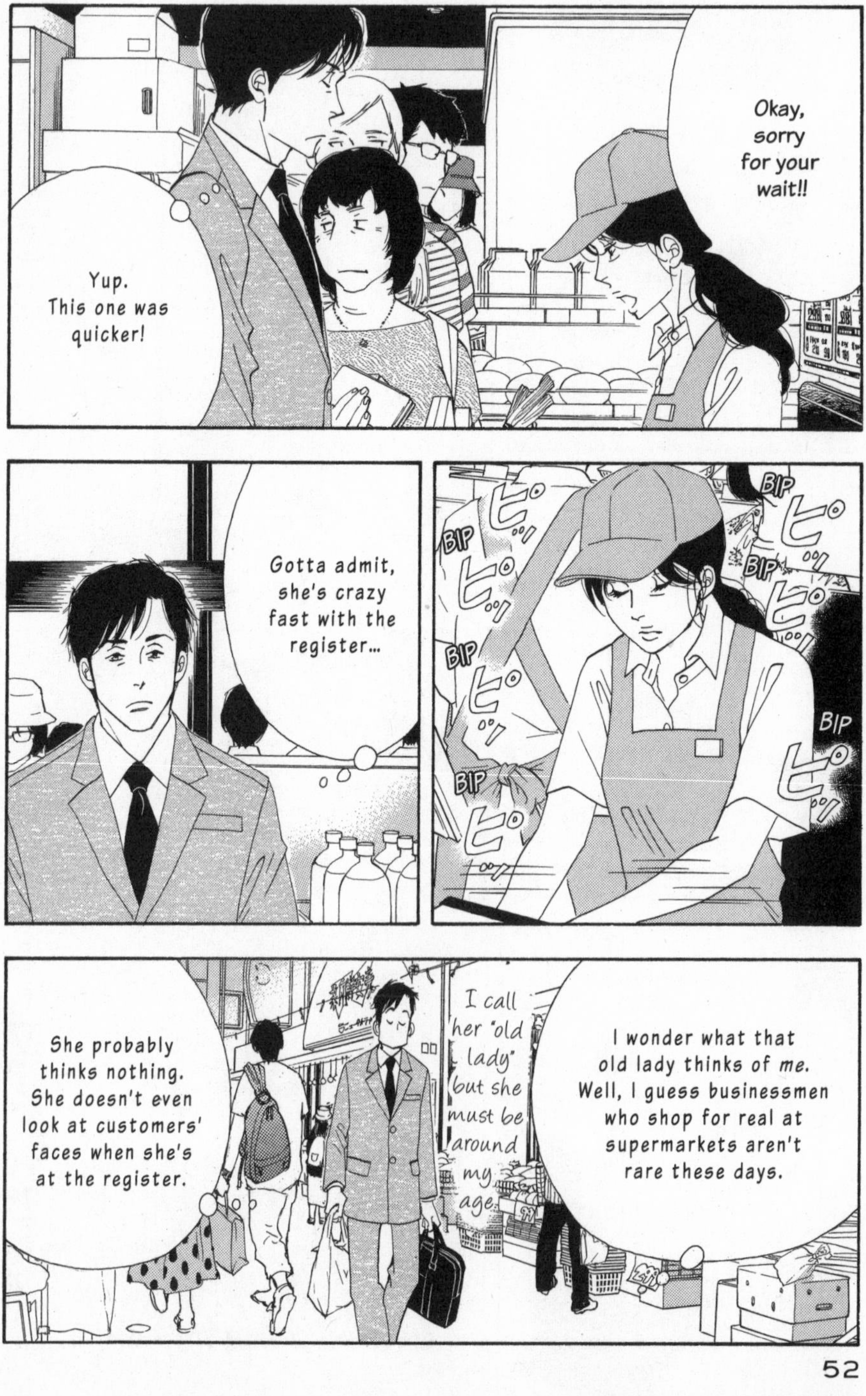
Okay, sorry for your wait!!
Yup. This one was quicker!
BIP
BIP
BIP
BIP
BIP
BIP
Gotta admit, she's crazy fast with the register...
I wonder what that old lady thinks of *me*. Well, I guess businessmen who shop for real at supermarkets aren't rare these days.
I call her "old lady" but she must be around my age.
She probably thinks nothing. She doesn't even look at customers' faces when she's at the register.

Whuh?!

All right, *natto* and ground pork today...

2008 yen thank you.

That would be 1598 yen altogether!

All the lines...

Won't make any difference whichever line I pick.

Aah...

I apologize for the long wait.

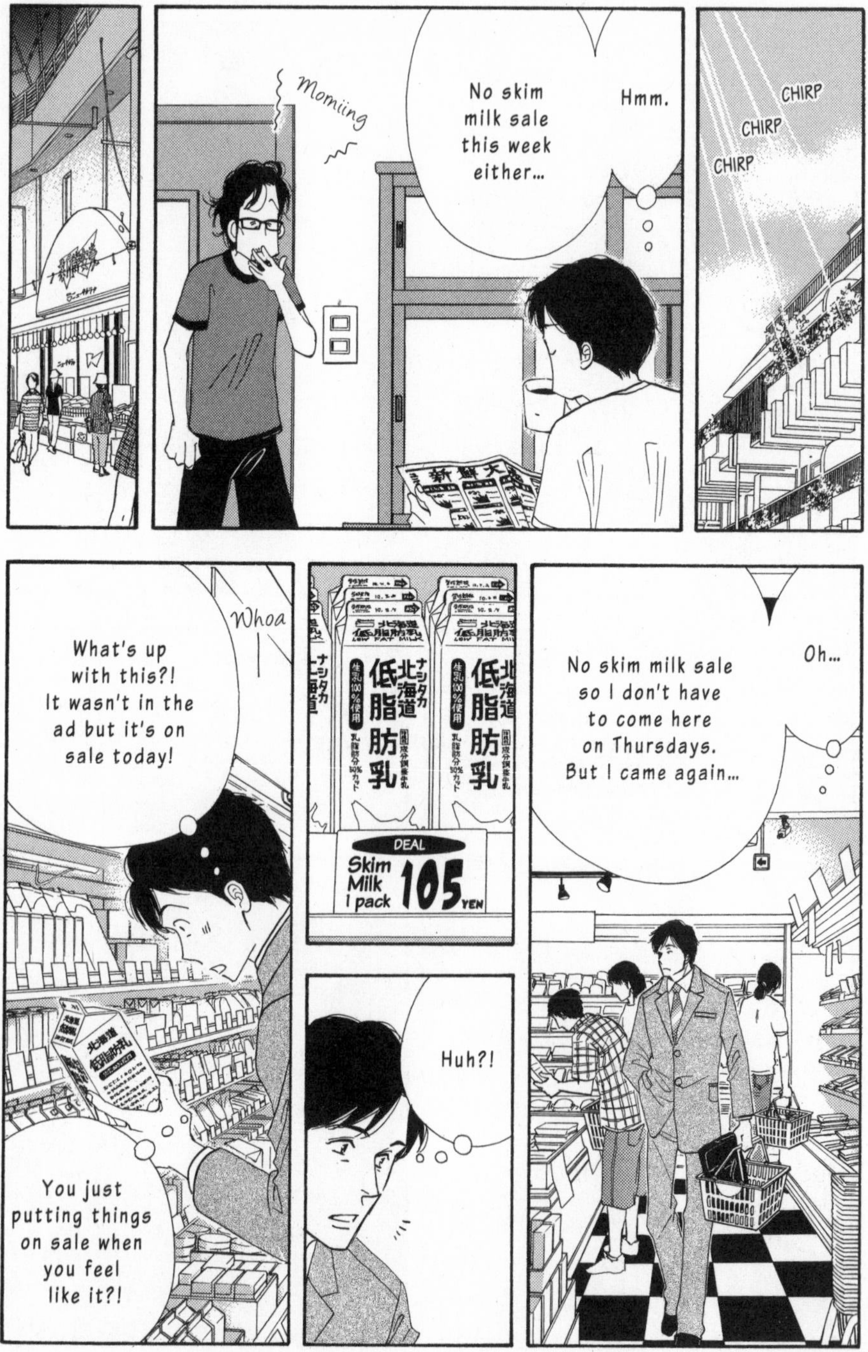
CHIRP
CHIRP
CHIRP
Hmm.
No skim milk sale this week either...
Momiing
Oh...
No skim milk sale so I don't have to come here on Thursdays. But I came again...
DEAL
Skim Milk 1 pack
105 YEN
Huh?!
Whoa
What's up with this?! It wasn't in the ad but it's on sale today!
You just putting things on sale when you feel like it?!

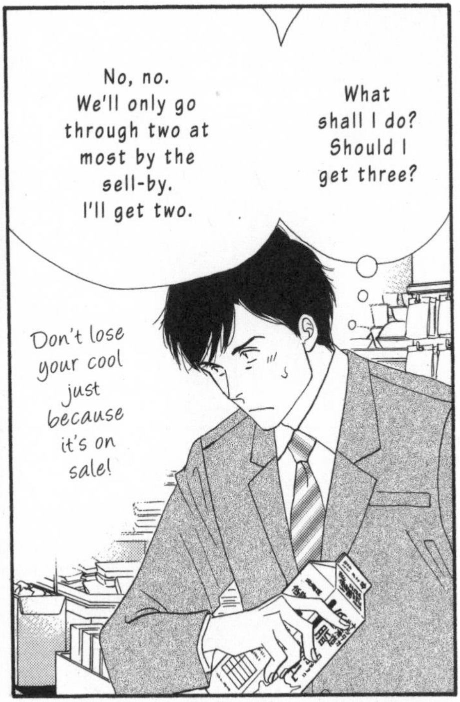
What shall I do? Should I get three?
No, no. We'll only go through two at most by the sell-by. I'll get two.
Don't lose your cool just because it's on sale!
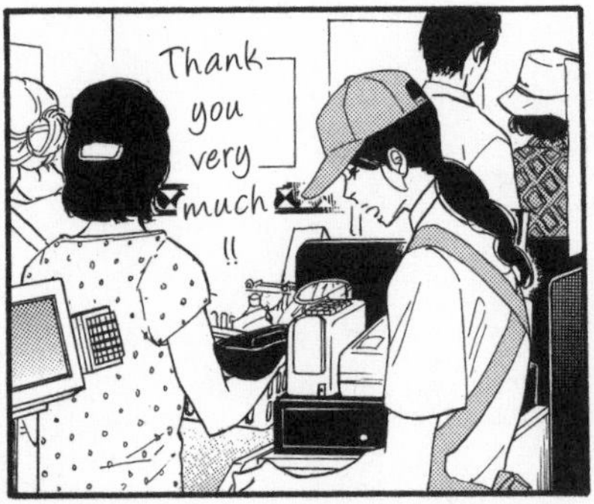
Thank you very much !!
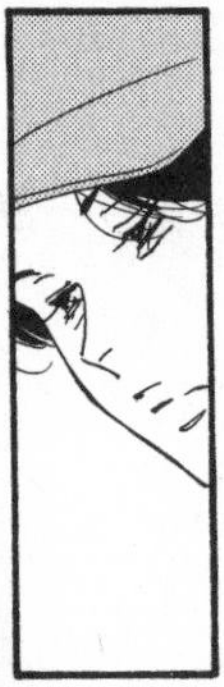
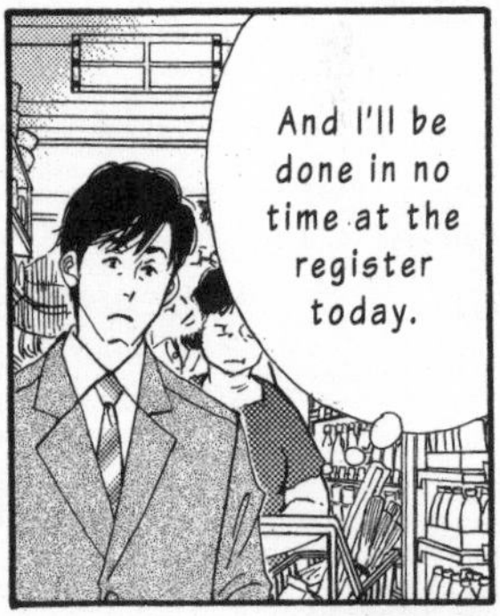
And I'll be done in no time at the register today.
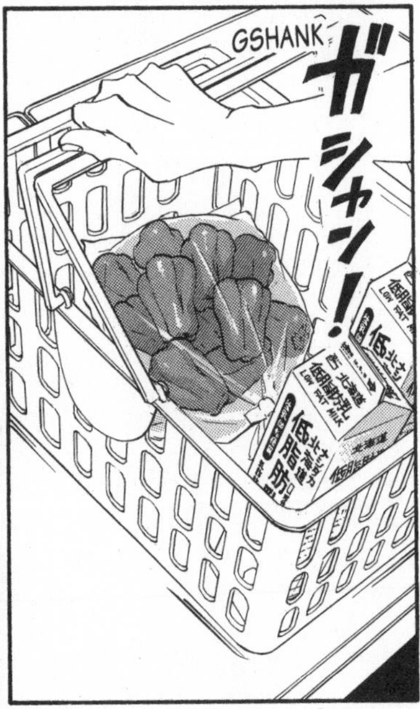
GSHANK
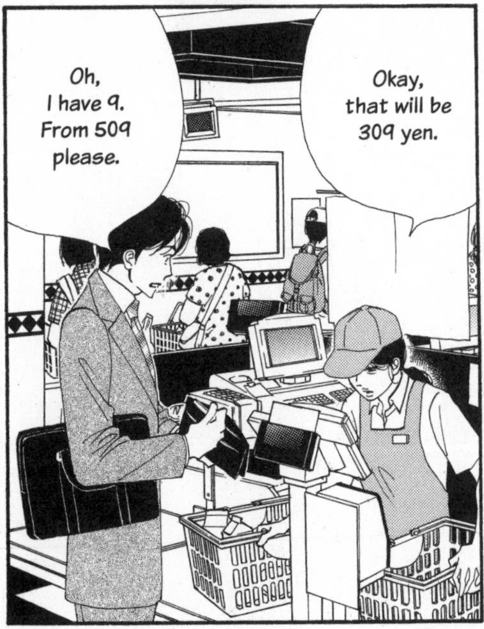
Okay, that will be 309 yen.
Oh, I have 9. From 509 please.

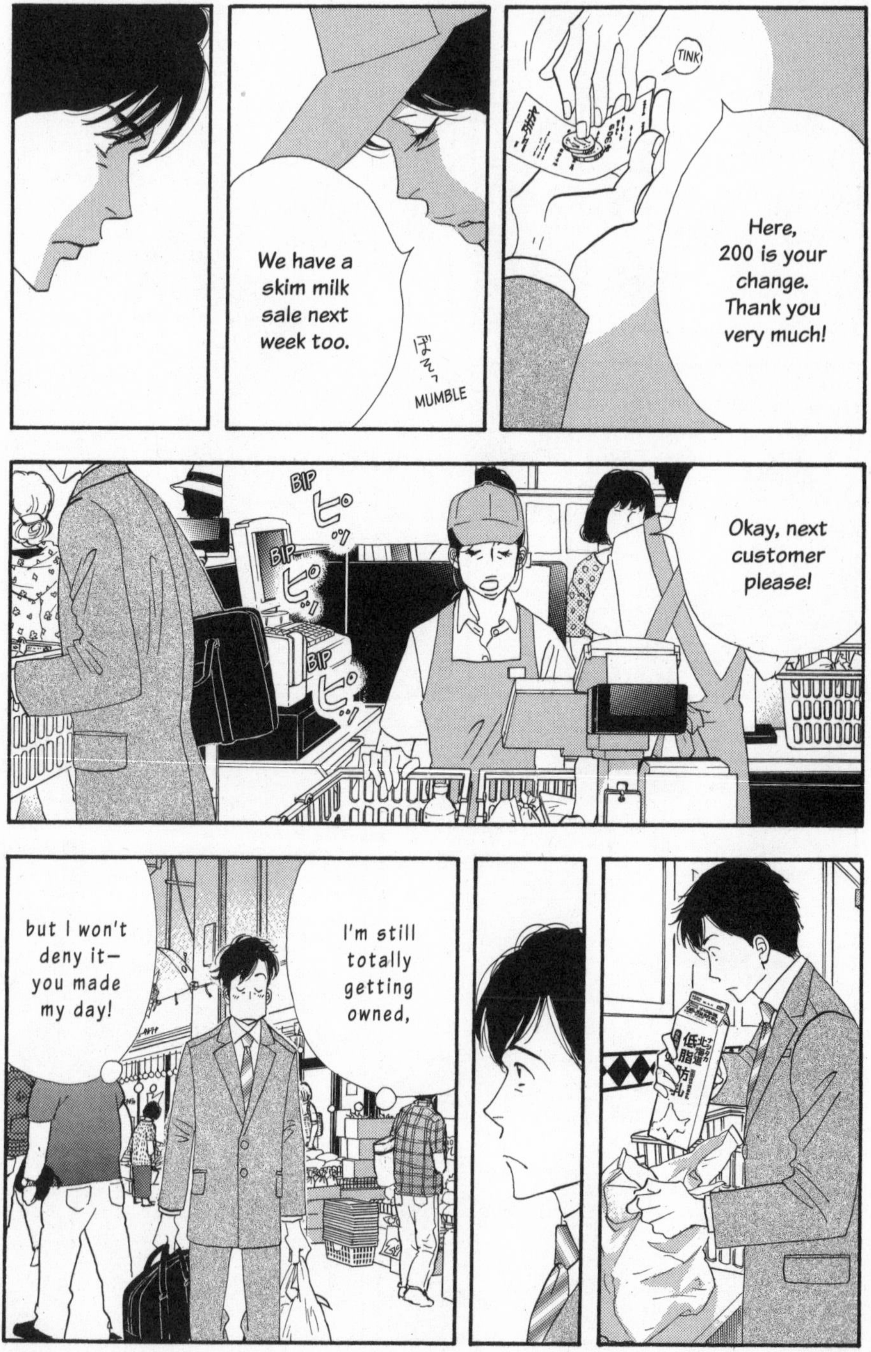
TINK
Here, 200 is your change. Thank you very much!
We have a skim milk sale next week too.
ぼそっ
MUMBLE
Okay, next customer please!
BIP
ピッ
BIP
ピッ
BIP
ピッ
I'm still totally getting owned,
but I won't deny it— you made my day!

#35 END

Summer veggie curry

You can add volume by
adding *kabocha*, too.
Zucchinis work too if you have any.

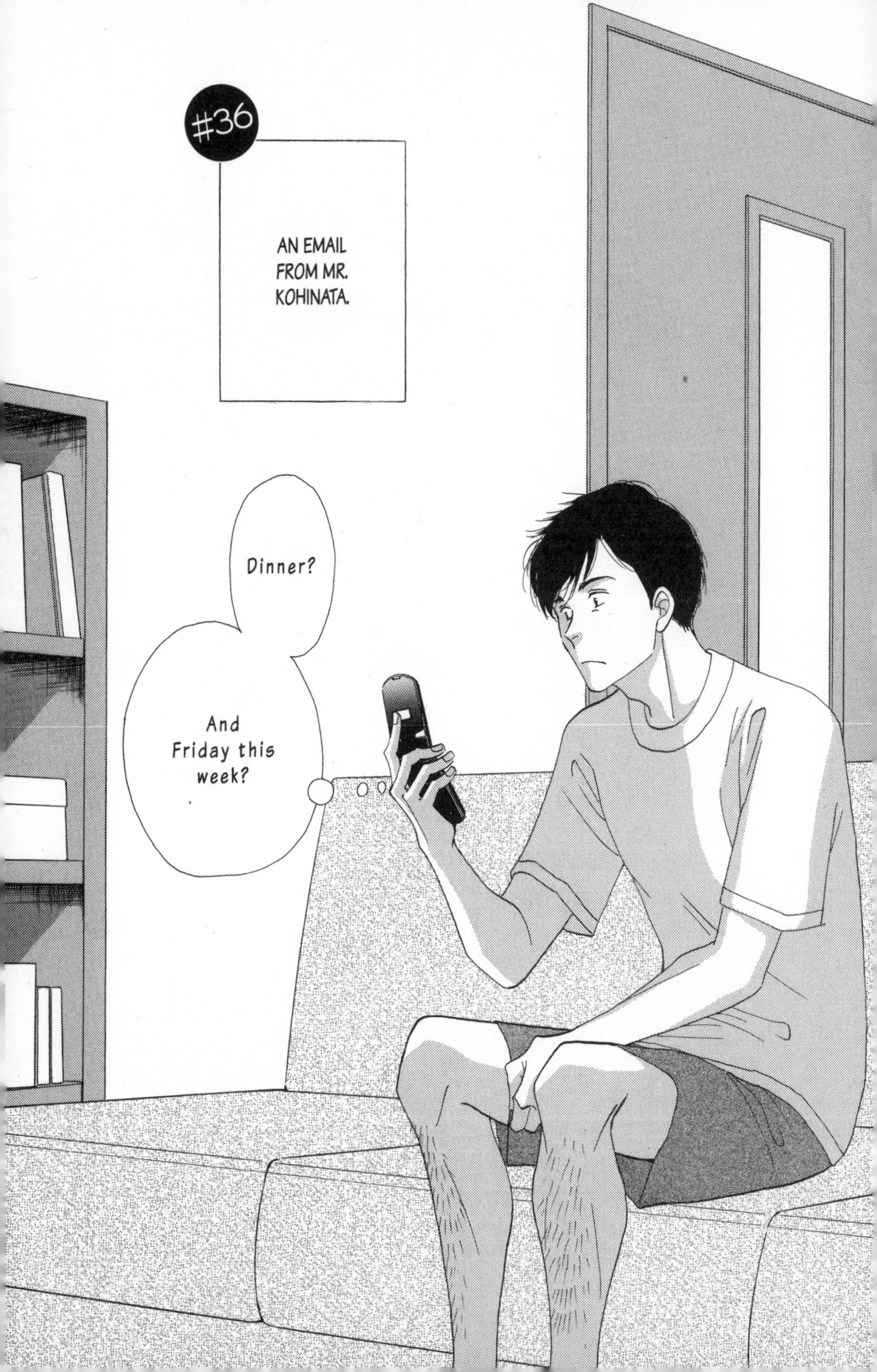
#36
AN EMAIL FROM MR. KOHINATA.
Dinner?
And Friday this week?

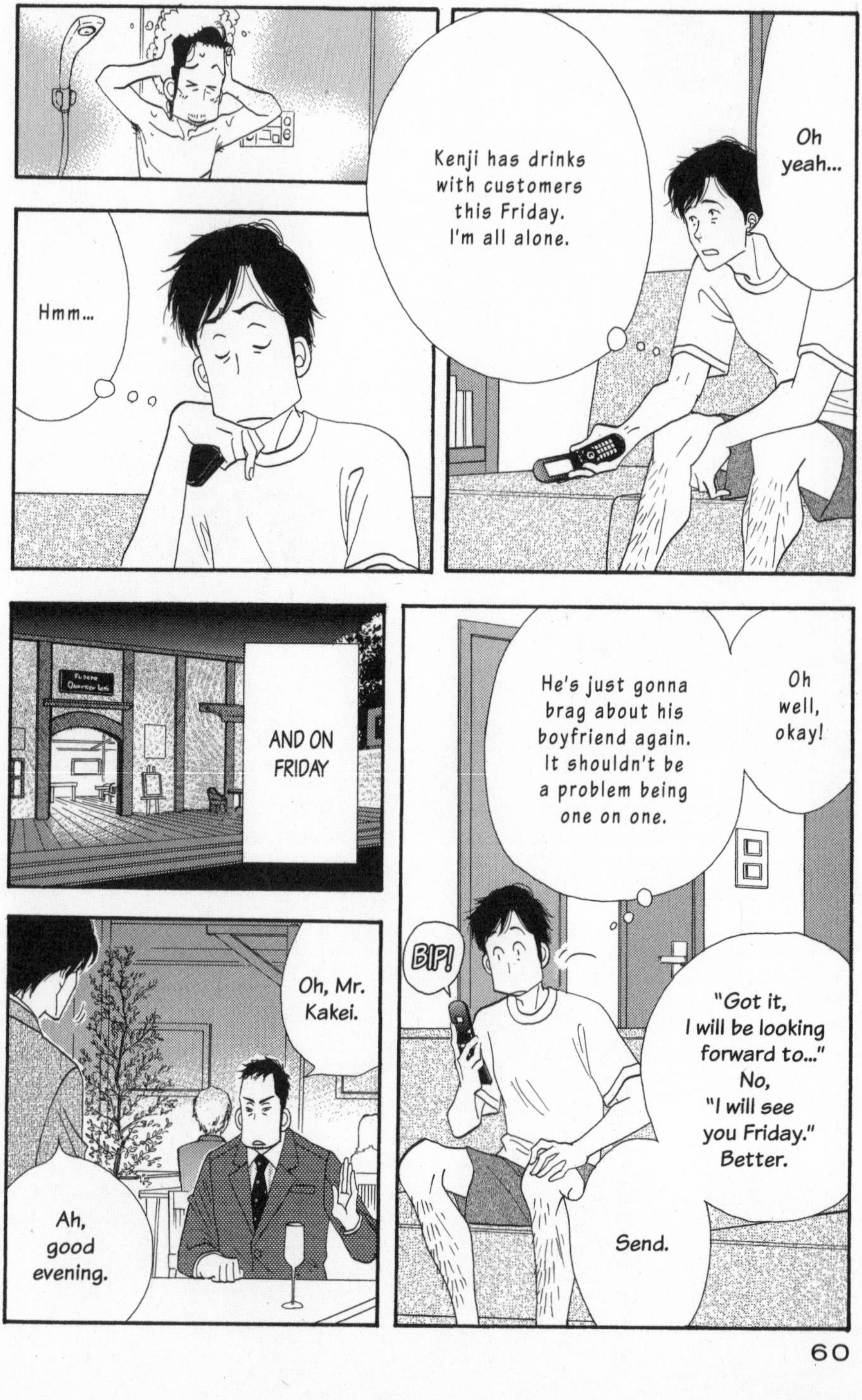
Oh yeah...
Kenji has drinks with customers this Friday. I'm all alone.
Hmm...
Oh well, okay!
He's just gonna brag about his boyfriend again. It shouldn't be a problem being one on one.
BIP!
"Got it, I will be looking forward to..." No, "I will see you Friday." Better.
Send.
AND ON FRIDAY
Oh, Mr. Kakei.
Ah, good evening.

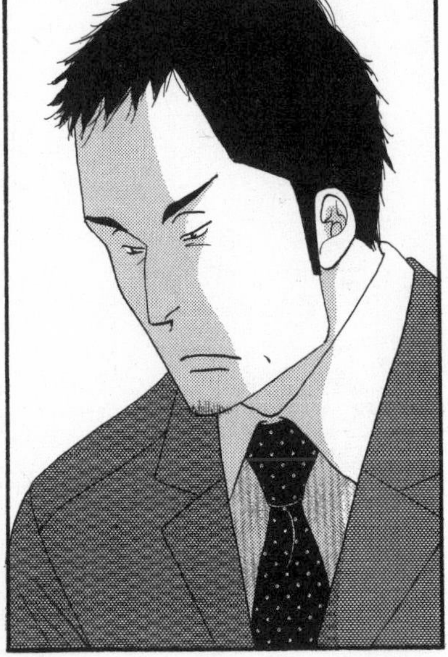
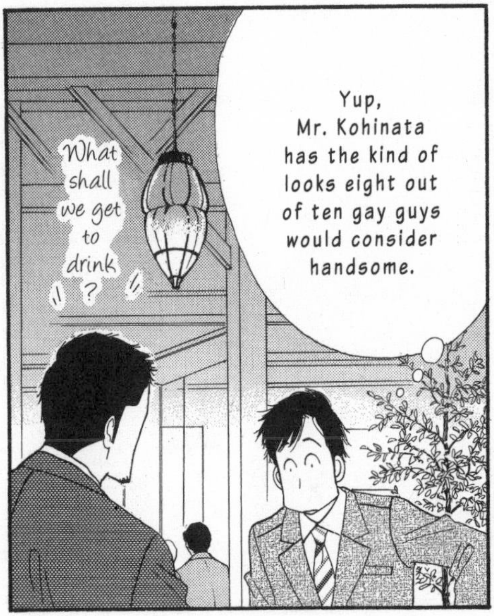
Yup, Mr. Kohinata has the kind of looks eight out of ten gay guys would consider handsome.
What shall we get to drink ?
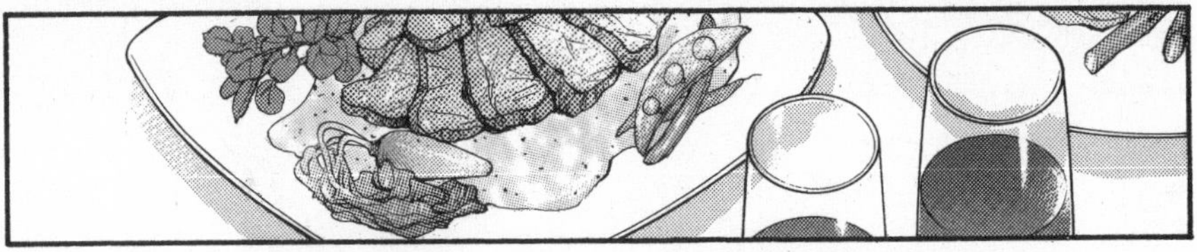
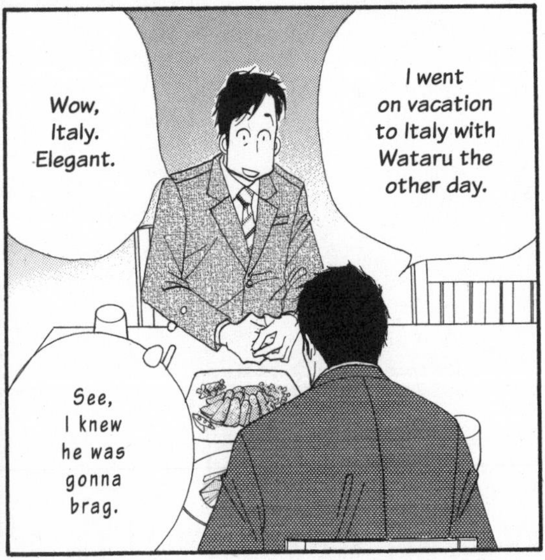
I went on vacation to Italy with Wataru the other day.
Wow, Italy. Elegant.
See, I knew he was gonna brag.
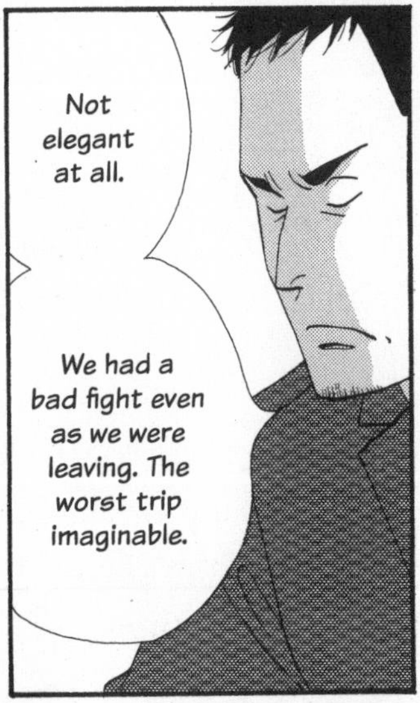
Not elegant at all.
We had a bad fight even as we were leaving. The worst trip imaginable.

I asked him a few times if he didn't need to, but he'd just say, "Oh, it's okay," or "Not today."

He took clothes for cleaning because we were going on a trip. But he never went to get them.

I think at that point he was already hoping I'd buckle and go get them for him.

He'll only get in a worse mood if I tell him that I told him.

Hey!! Dai!!

And the morning of our departure date, just as I feared...

Aaaah! I forgot to go get my clothes from the cleaners!

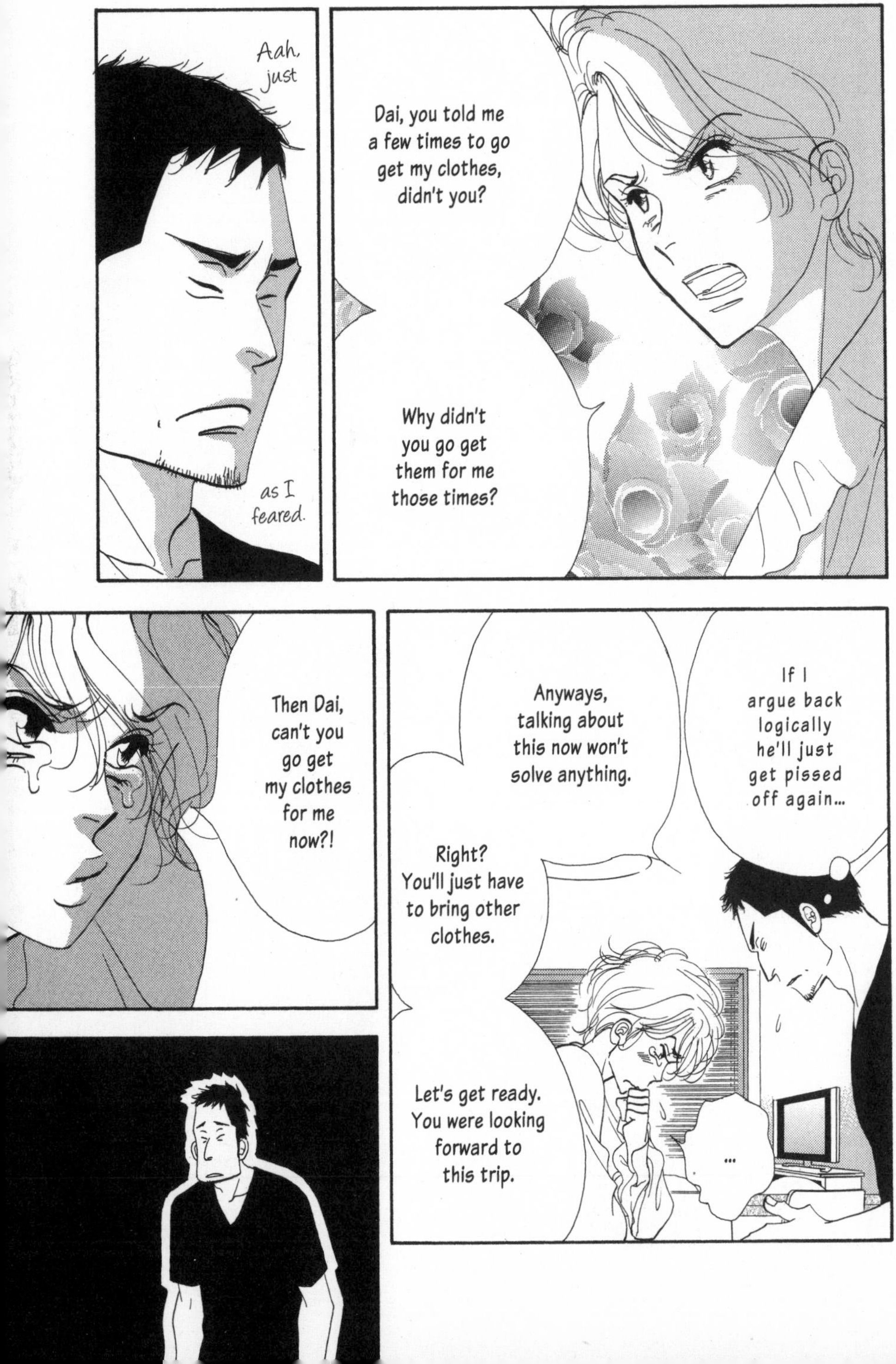
Dai, you told me a few times to go get my clothes, didn't you?
Why didn't you go get them for me those times?
Aah, just
as I feared.
Then Dai, can't you go get my clothes for me now?!
If I argue back logically he'll just get pissed off again...
Anyways, talking about this now won't solve anything.
Right? You'll just have to bring other clothes.
Let's get ready. You were looking forward to this trip.
...

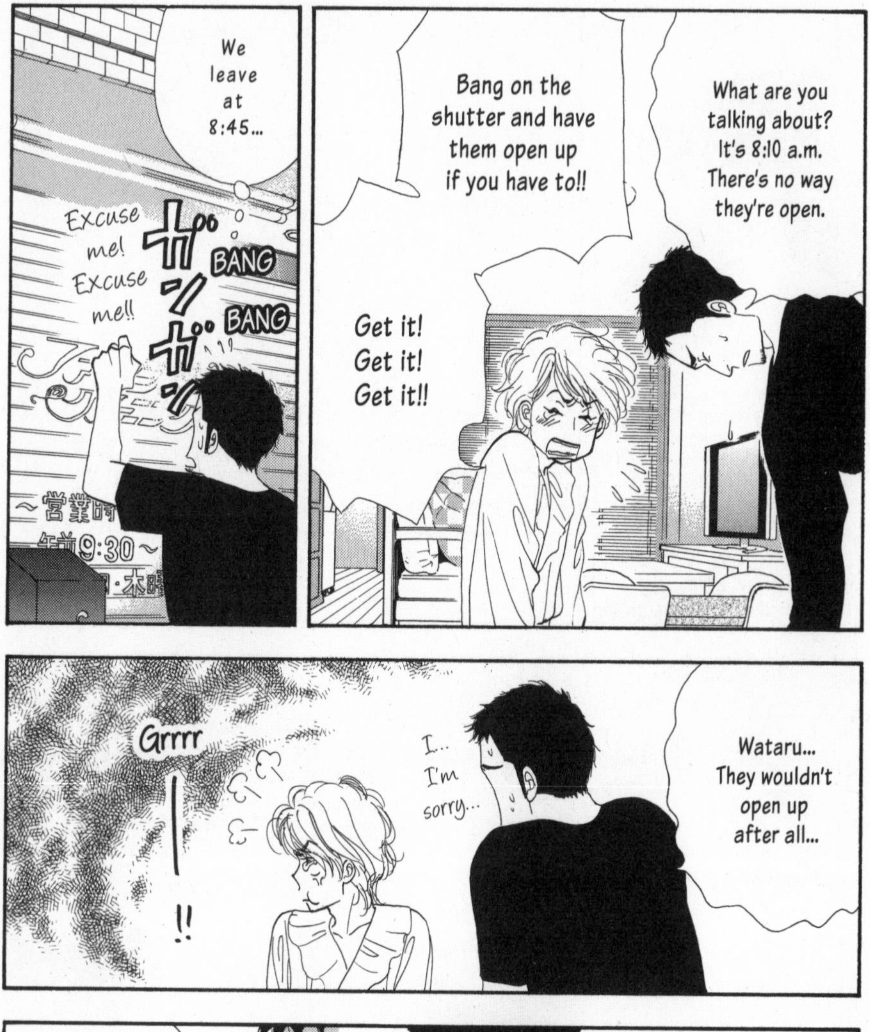
What are you talking about? It's 8:10 a.m. There's no way they're open.
Bang on the shutter and have them open up if you have to!!
Get it! Get it! Get it!!
We leave at 8:45...
Excuse me! Excuse me!!
BANG
BANG
Wataru... They wouldn't open up after all...
I... I'm sorry...
Grrrr
!!
And so I had to try to make Wataru feel better. He was so angry. I managed to get him on the Narita Express...
I asked myself what the hell I was doing even as I apologized to Wataru...

65

HUH?

Ahhh, good evening, I'm Wataru. Nice to meet you.

So, I wanted to introduce you to Wataru today. This is Wataru Inoue, my boyfriend.

* T-Shirt text: "Elephant"

And I told you he used to work at a company. How would he actually be a boy?

I meant that he's like Gilbert to me!

Didn't you say a beautiful boy like Gilbert?!

Mr. Kohinata.

?

No matter how you look at it he looks like an ordinary young man!

I don't even know where to begin with you!!

What sorta absurd hoops do you put Mr. Kohinata through with an affable mug like yours?!

What kinda clothes do you take to the cleaners when you dress as you do?!

And he seems like a total sweetheart. He doesn't seem to care about clothes at all...

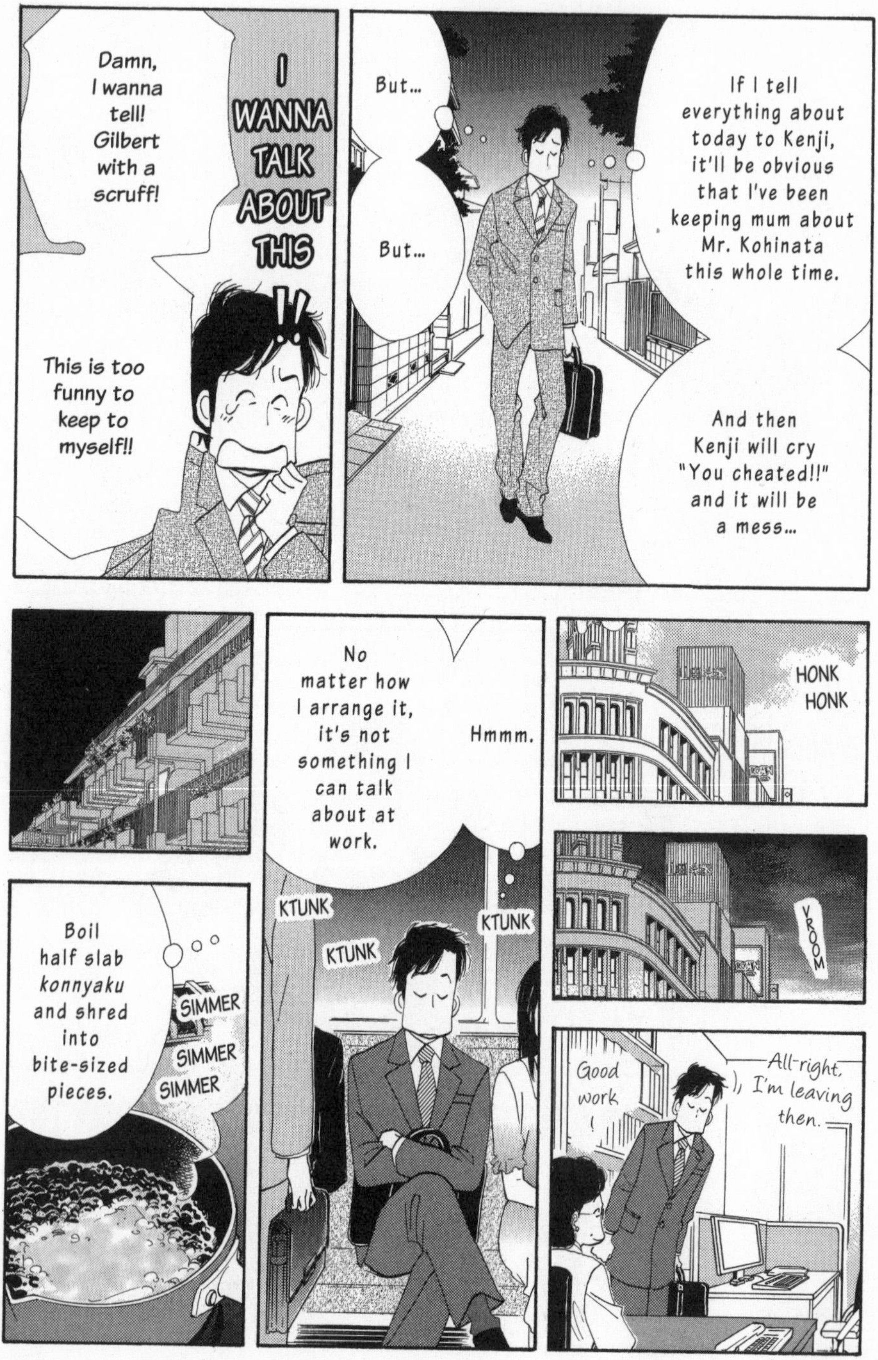
If I tell everything about today to Kenji, it'll be obvious that I've been keeping mum about Mr. Kohinata this whole time.
And then Kenji will cry "You cheated!!" and it will be a mess...
But...
But...
Damn, I wanna tell! Gilbert with a scruff!
I WANNA TALK ABOUT THIS !!
This is too funny to keep to myself!!
HONK HONK
VROOM
All-right, I'm leaving then.
Good work!
Hmmm.
No matter how I arrange it, it's not something I can talk about at work.
KTUNK
KTUNK
KTUNK
Boil half slab konnyaku and shred into bite-sized pieces.
SIMMER
SIMMER
SIMMER

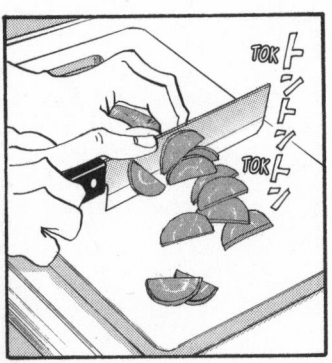

TOK
TOK
About 7 oz pork.
Tonight we're doing pork miso soup.
Fry the sliced pork belly in our biggest pot with a little vegetable oil,
SZZ
and once the color changes, fry it with 2/3 of a stick of half-mooned carrots.
Lower the heat so it won't burn, and put a lid on it and stir sometimes.
Meanwhile shred half a burdock root...
Chop 1/3 *daikon* into quarters.
Add the burdock root and *daikon* in the fry and replace lid.

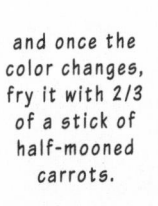

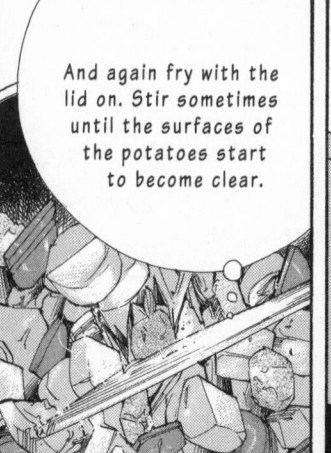

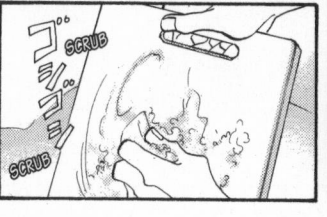

I feel like the flavor sinks in better and it's less likely to fall apart during the boiling stage if I steam and fry it like this with the lid on.
Now cut 2 potatoes into bite-sized pieces and toss into the pot with the *konnyaku*...
And again fry with the lid on. Stir sometimes until the surfaces of the potatoes start to become clear.
SCRUB
SCRUB
In the meantime, finely chop the scallion that goes on top of the soup.
TOK
TOK
Once the ingredients are well cooked, add in half a sheet of sliced fried tofu, a lot of water, and a little rice wine. Start off with high heat, and once it comes to a boil, lower to medium low and keep boiling.

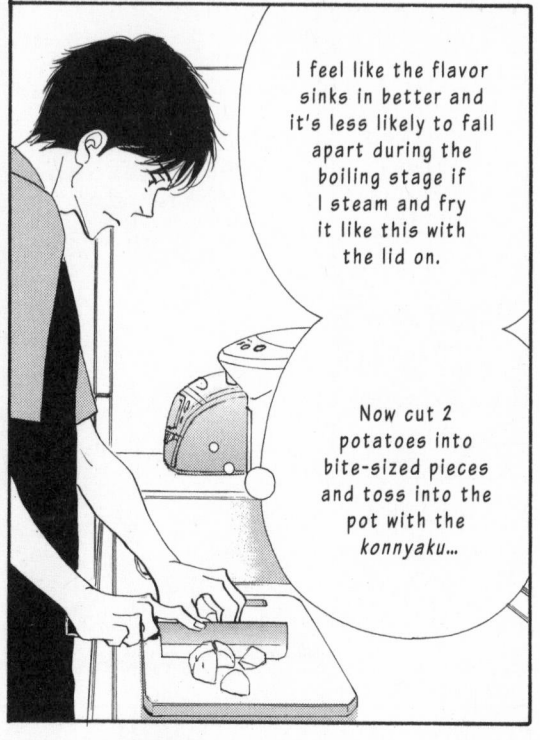

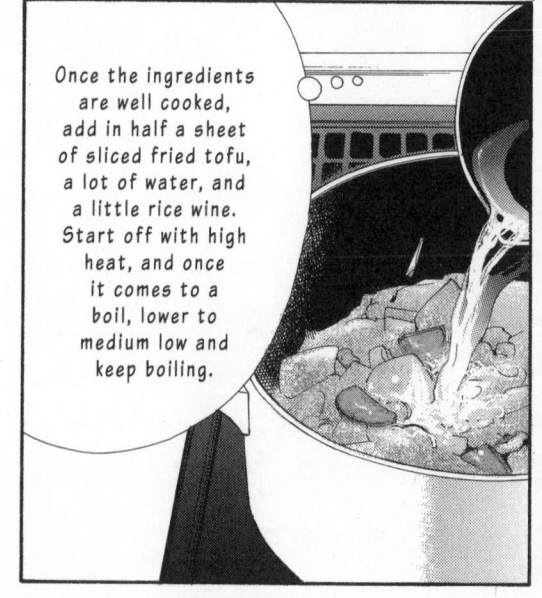

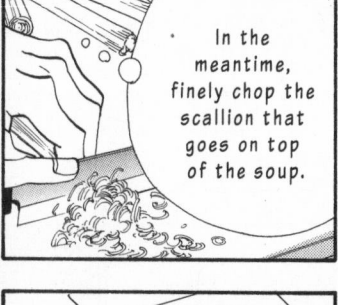

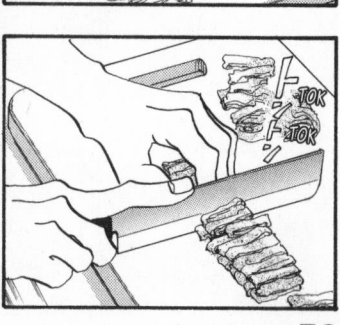

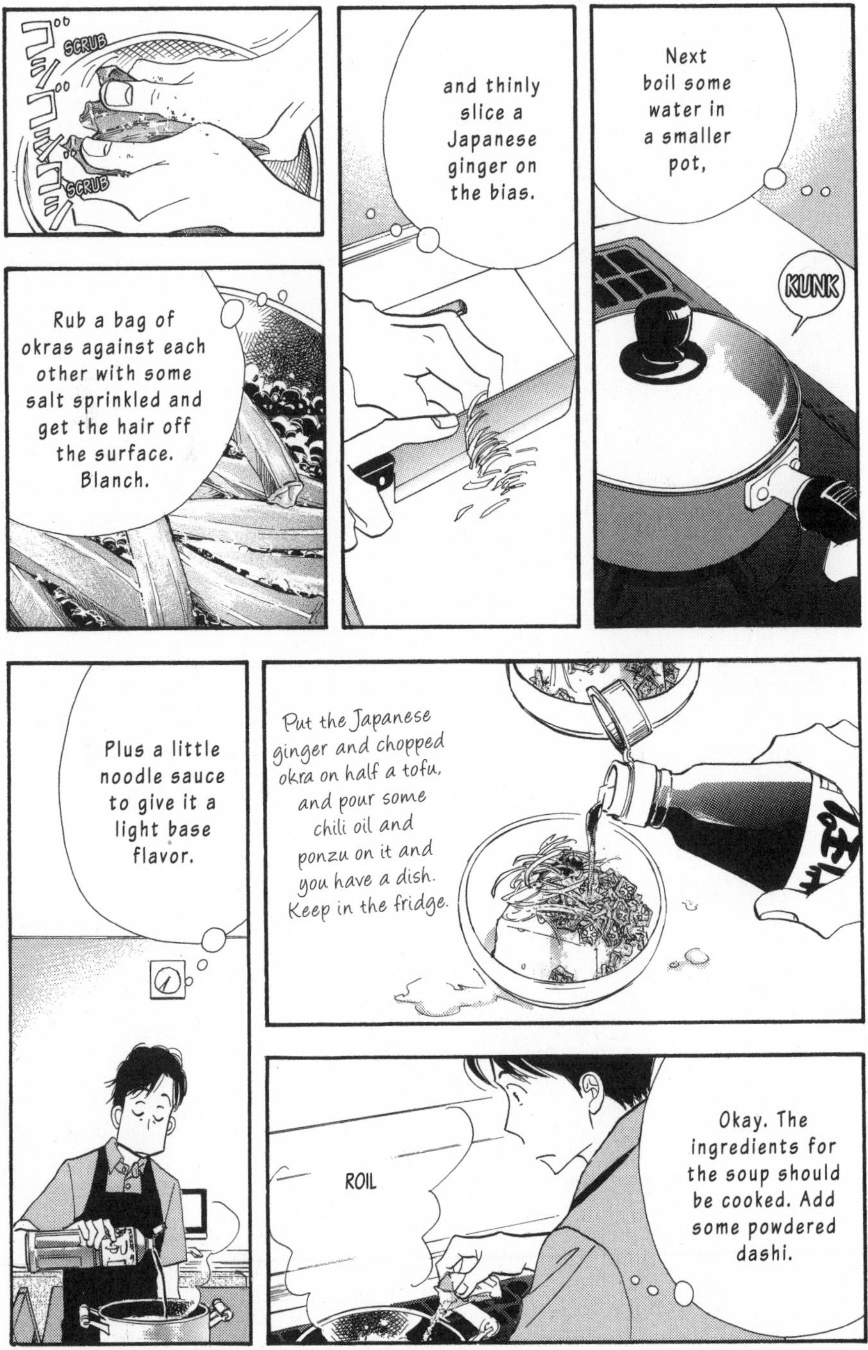
Next boil some water in a smaller pot,
KUNK
SCRUB
SCRUB
Rub a bag of okras against each other with some salt sprinkled and get the hair off the surface. Blanch.
and thinly slice a Japanese ginger on the bias.
Put the Japanese ginger and chopped okra on half a tofu, and pour some chili oil and ponzu on it and you have a dish. Keep in the fridge.
Okay. The ingredients for the soup should be cooked. Add some powdered dashi.
ROIL
Plus a little noodle sauce to give it a light base flavor.

Pork soups have a deeper flavor when you give it a little base flavor first with soy sauce and mirin before adding in the miso.

But it's a drag so we're just gonna use noodle sauce.

And next, we fry a can of corn minus the liquid and add a cube of butter.

CLICK

And let's turn on the fish cooker grill now.

Drizzle in soy sauce.

Turn off heat on the pork soup and dissolve miso into it.

Very easy.

Sprinkle black pepper and we have corn fried in soy sauce and butter.

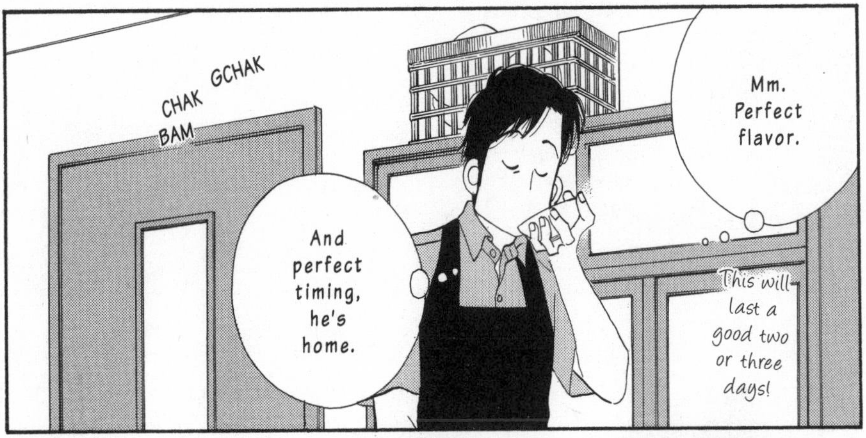
Mm. Perfect flavor.
This will last a good two or three days!
And perfect timing, he's home.
GCHAK
CHAK
BAM

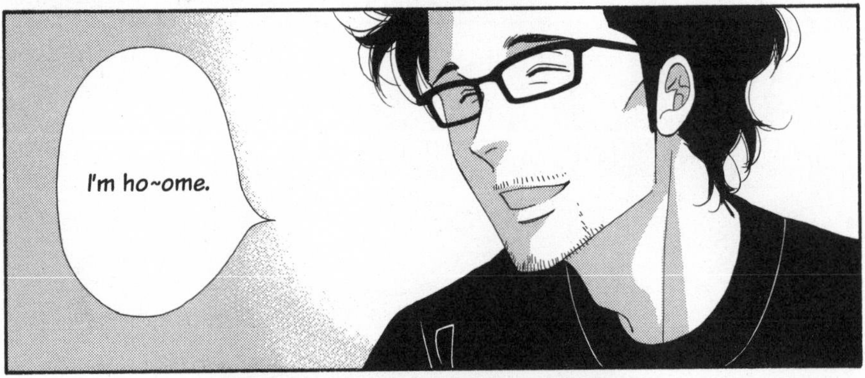
I'm ho~ome.

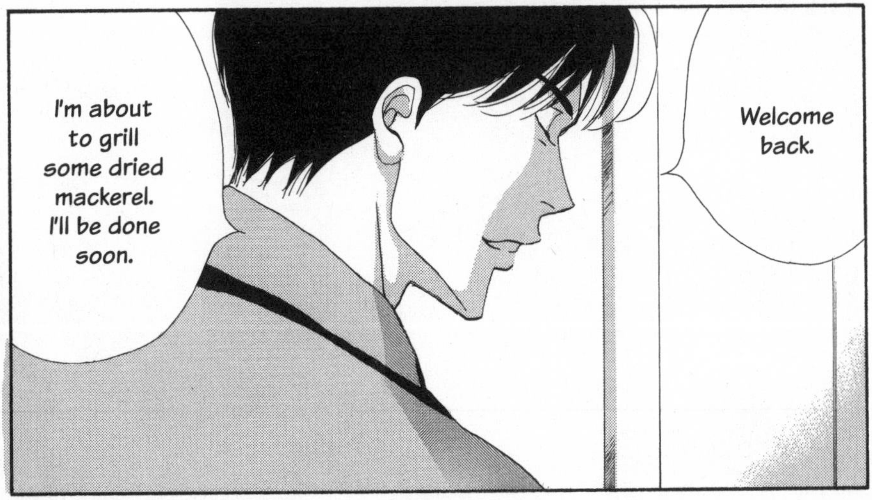
Welcome back.
I'm about to grill some dried mackerel. I'll be done soon.

Whee!
The pork soup
looks good.
Thank you!!

Pour generous
amount of the
pork soup in
a big bowl and
put a bunch
of scallions
on top...

SHHH

• Pork soup
• Dried mackerel
• Corn fried in soy sauce
  and butter
• Spicy tofu with okra

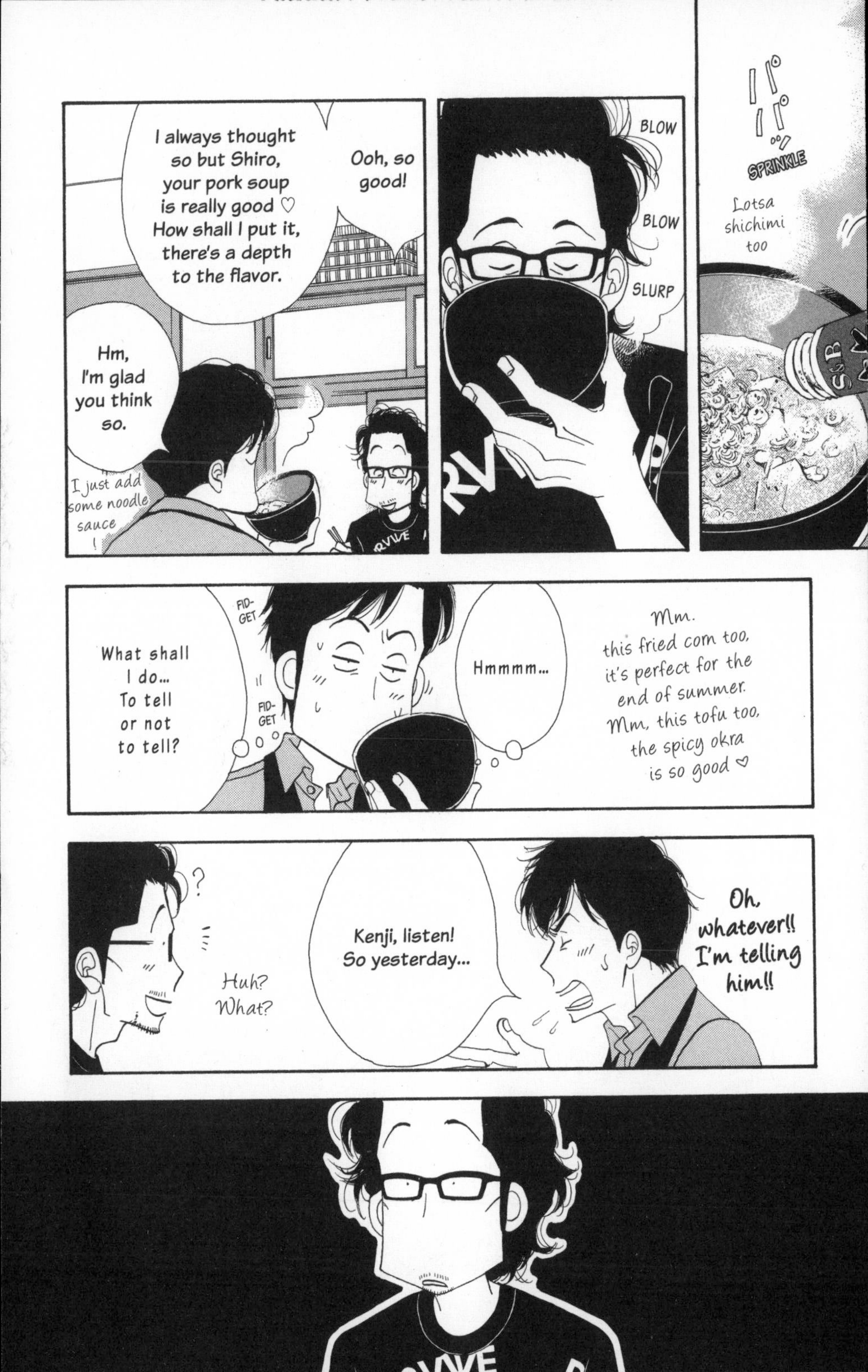
SPRINKLE
Lotsa shichimi too
BLOW
BLOW
SLURP
Ooh, so good!
I always thought so but Shiro, your pork soup is really good ♡ How shall I put it, there's a depth to the flavor.
Hm, I'm glad you think so.
I just add some noodle sauce!
Mm. this fried corn too, it's perfect for the end of summer. Mm, this tofu too, the spicy okra is so good ♡
Hmmmm...
FID-GET
FID-GET
What shall I do... To tell or not to tell?
Oh, whatever!! I'm telling him!!
Kenji, listen! So yesterday...
Huh? What?
?

A Gilbert with scruff and bed head? That's not a Gilbert at all...

What...

PFFT

Not surprisingly, Kenji got The Song of the Wind and Trees reference.

I wanna meet them tooo!

Hey, I won't mention you so can I talk about this at my salon?!

Ahahaha! That's too funny. Too weird!! I wanna tell someone!!

Right?! Right?!

Yes!! The funny factor squelched the cheating accusation!

#36 END

Canned corn

Also good boiled with the liquid,
with some butter tossed in,
and served sprinkled with black pepper.

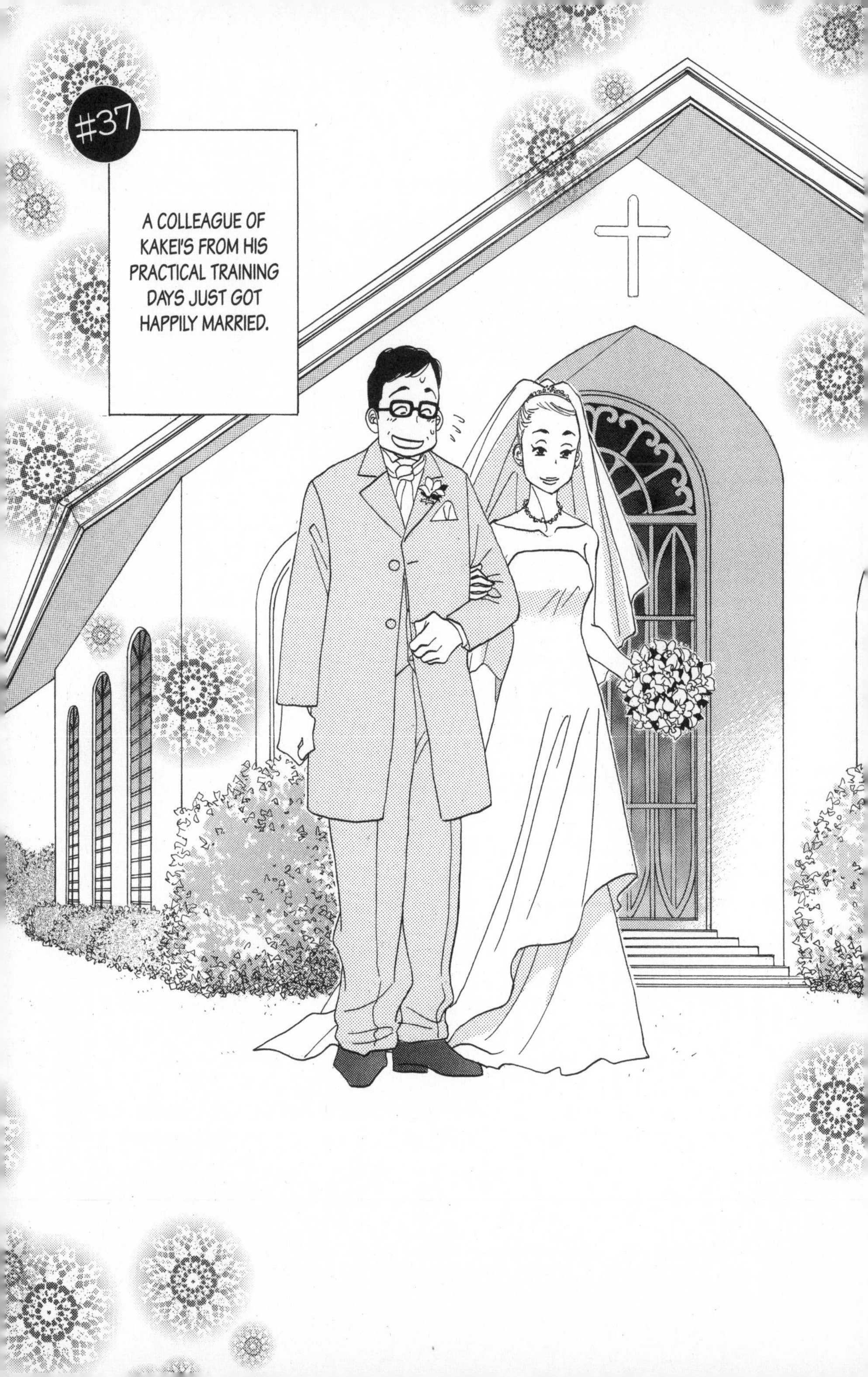
#37
A COLLEAGUE OF KAKEI'S FROM HIS PRACTICAL TRAINING DAYS JUST GOT HAPPILY MARRIED.

SINCE MOST OF THE GROOM'S FRIENDS WERE MARRIED, KAKEI, SINGLE AND IN SHAPE AND NOT ALL OVER THE WOMEN, NATURALLY BECAME THE TARGET OF ALL THE LADIES.

AND THE AFTER-PARTY.

Yes, we were the same year for our practical.

Oh, so you're a friend of Koichi, the groom!

Huh?! Um, excuse me, but if you were the same year as Koichi, your age...

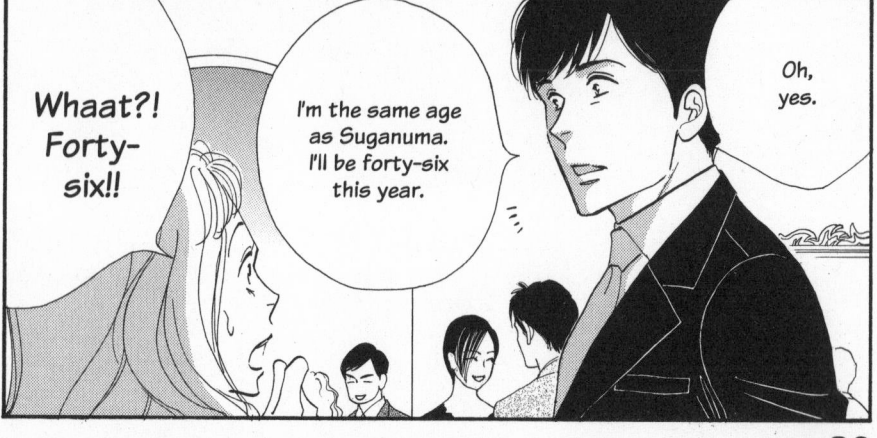

Whaat?! Forty-six!!

I'm the same age as Suganuma. I'll be forty-six this year.

Oh, yes.

The fortyish ladies who thought Kakei was in his thirties and had stayed away.

GLARE

Ughh. There's no place like a wedding after-party that makes me wish I had a ring on my ring finger!!

I'm in general affairs at Mr. Suganuma's office...

Oh hello, I'm the bride Megumi's boss at her company.

You birthday's coming up, right? What if I get matching rings for us?

Hey, Kenji.

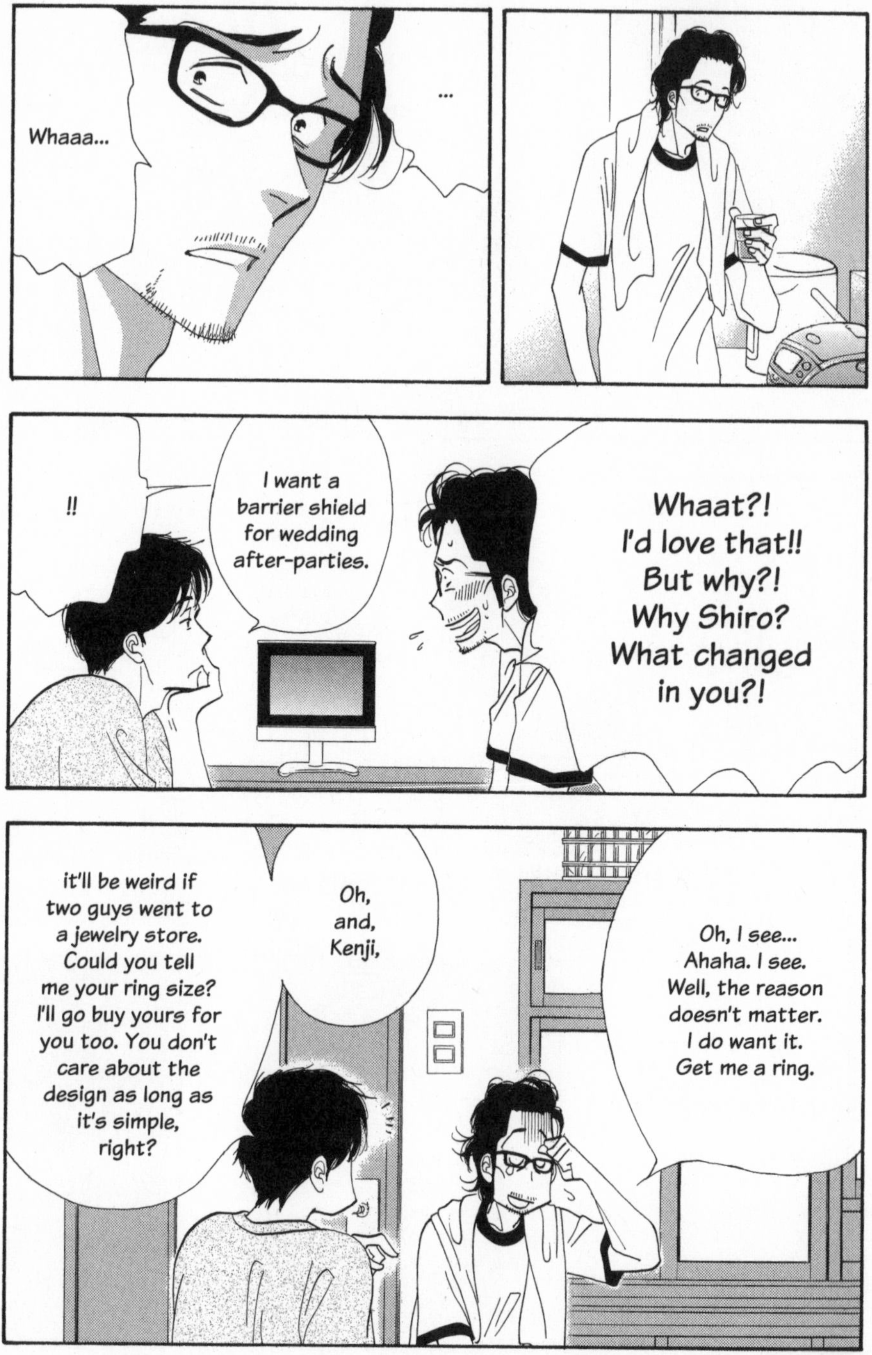
...
Whaaa...
I want a barrier shield for wedding after-parties.
Whaat?! I'd love that!! But why?! Why Shiro? What changed in you?!
!!
Oh, and, Kenji,
it'll be weird if two guys went to a jewelry store. Could you tell me your ring size? I'll go buy yours for you too. You don't care about the design as long as it's simple, right?
Oh, I see... Ahaha. I see. Well, the reason doesn't matter. I do want it. Get me a ring.

Do you know yours, Shiro?

Huh?! Really?!

Huh? But I don't know what my ring size is.

I haven't a clue...

And you have skinny fingers. If you wear mine it'll definitely be loose.

Shiro, rings aren't like clothes. Sizes completely differ from person to person. It doesn't work like "about 13."

Ah, you could just go to a store alone and get one ring! And I'll just borrow it...

Didn't you want a barrier at after-parties? It wouldn't mean anything if the ring doesn't fit!

Uh-uh, that won't work!

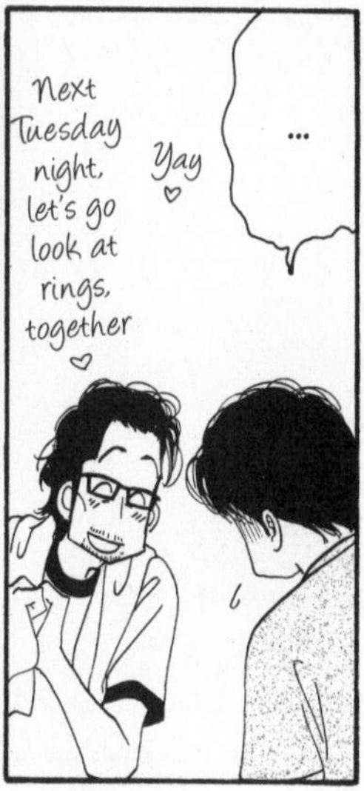
...
Next Tuesday night, let's go look at rings, together ♡
Yay ♡

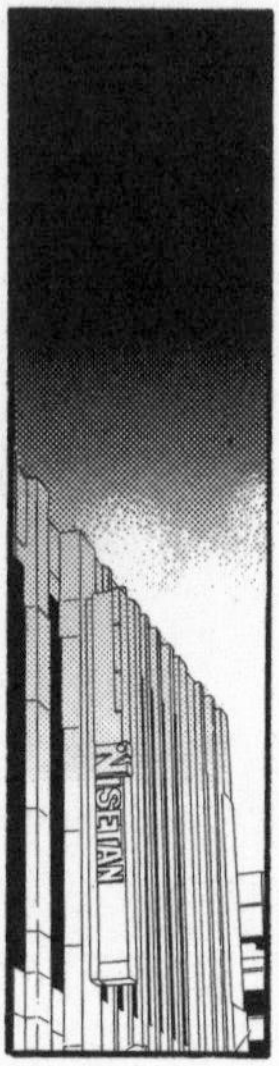

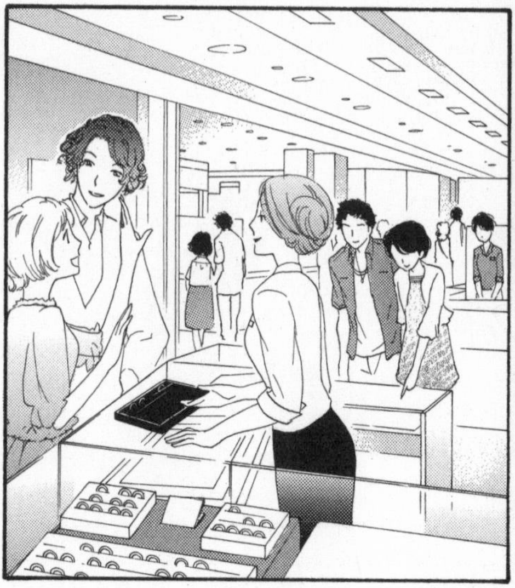

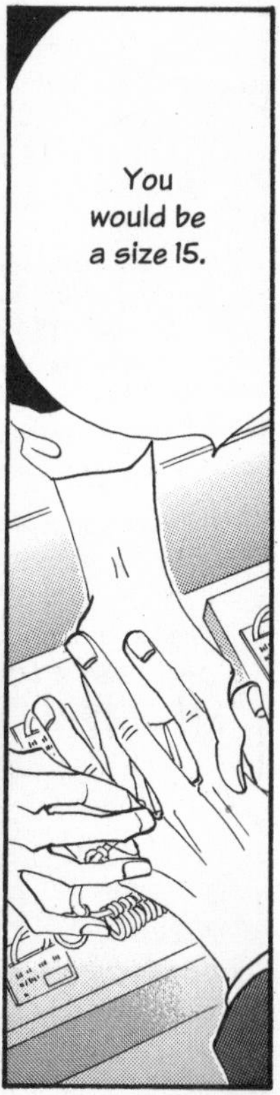
You would be a size 15.

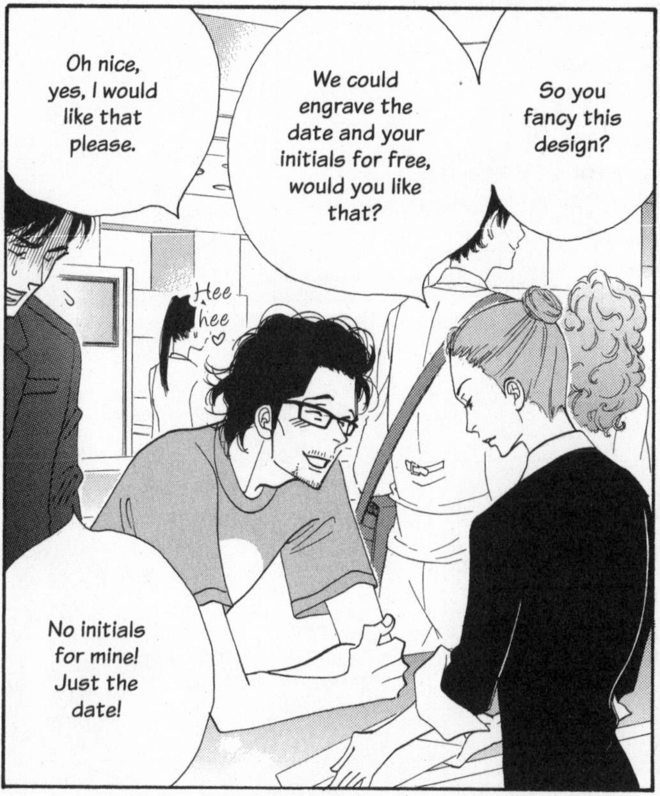
So you fancy this design?
We could engrave the date and your initials for free, would you like that?
Oh nice, yes, I would like that please.
Hee hee ♡
No initials for mine! Just the date!

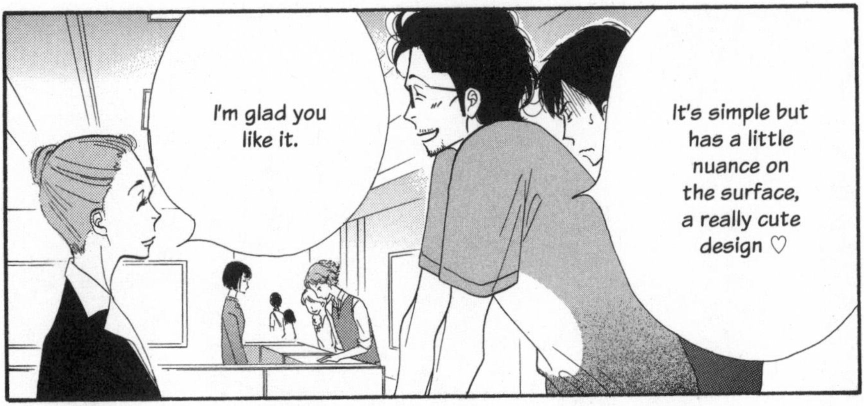
It's simple but has a little nuance on the surface, a really cute design ♡
I'm glad you like it.
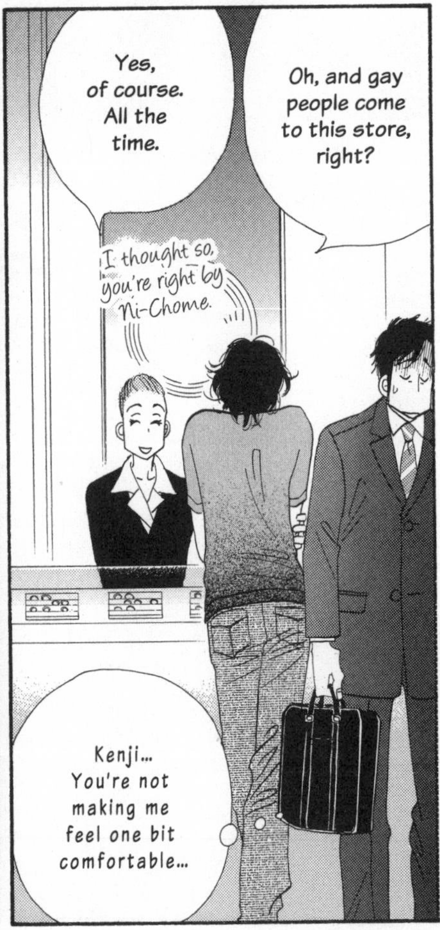
Oh, and gay people come to this store, right?
Yes, of course. All the time.
I thought so, you're right by Ni-Chome.
Kenji... You're not making me feel one bit comfortable...
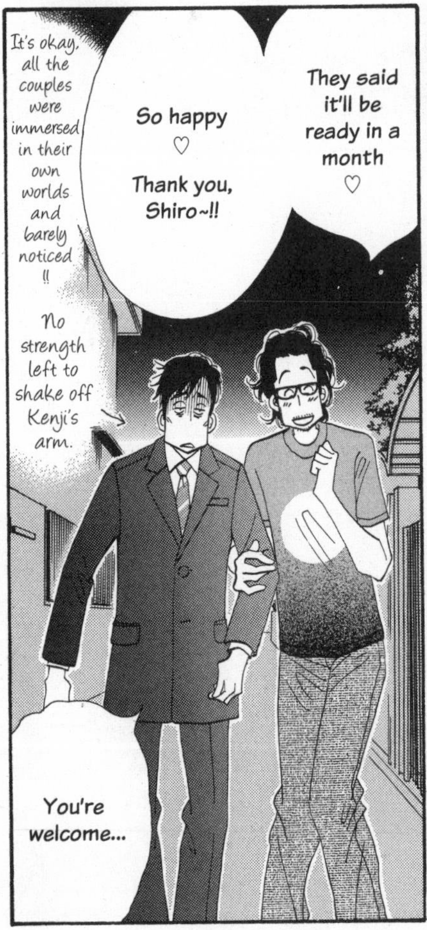
They said it'll be ready in a month ♡
So happy ♡ Thank you, Shiro~!!
It's okay, all the couples were immersed in their own worlds and barely noticed !!
No strength left to shake off Kenji's arm.
You're welcome...

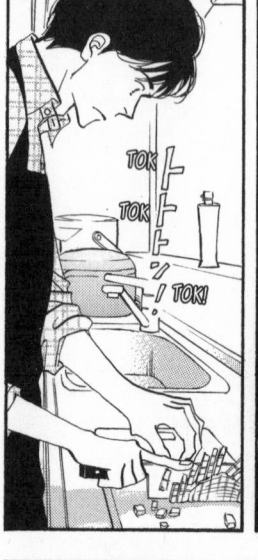

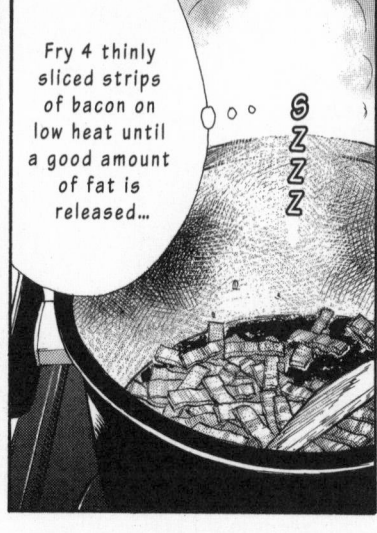

Fry 4 thinly sliced strips of bacon on low heat until a good amount of fat is released...
SZZZ
TOK トTOK トトン! TOK!
Add in a big onion cut into half-inch cubes, lightly fry, then lid.
FZZZZ ジュウウ
カポ CLOP
Roughly mince a nub of garlic, chop one carrot into quarter-inch cubes, and finely slice the leaves of a sack of celery...
FZZZZ ジュ～～～ッ

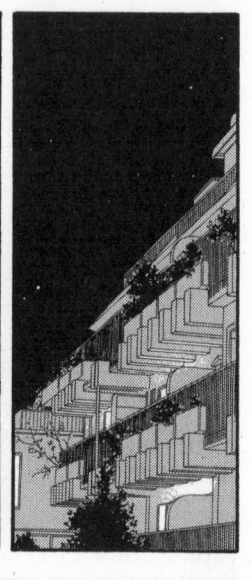

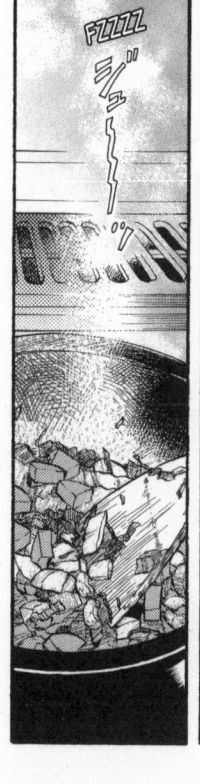

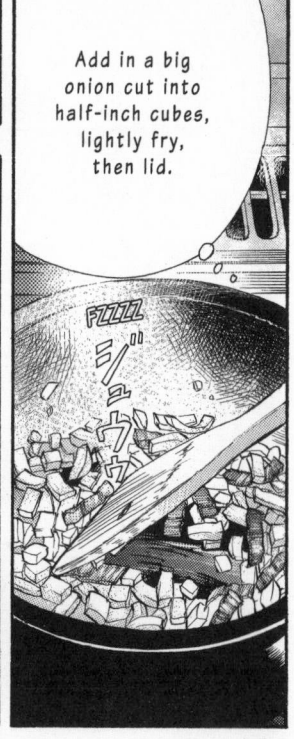

More and more ingredients.

Then chop 1/6-1/4 of a cabbage into fairly small chunks, and throw in the pot too.

SZZZ ジャアアアア

The timing works better if you don't put all the vegetables in at once but cut them in order and throw them in the pot, putting the lid on each time.

Like we did for the pork soup.

Put the lid back on after you throw that in.

CLOP

With a lid on, a lot of water comes out from the vegetables, so raise the heat to medium low.

Next cut two small potatoes a little bigger than the carrots and throw it in the pot.

Now add two cubes of consommé and about a quart of water.

And finally, chop two tomatoes and cook until they lose shape.

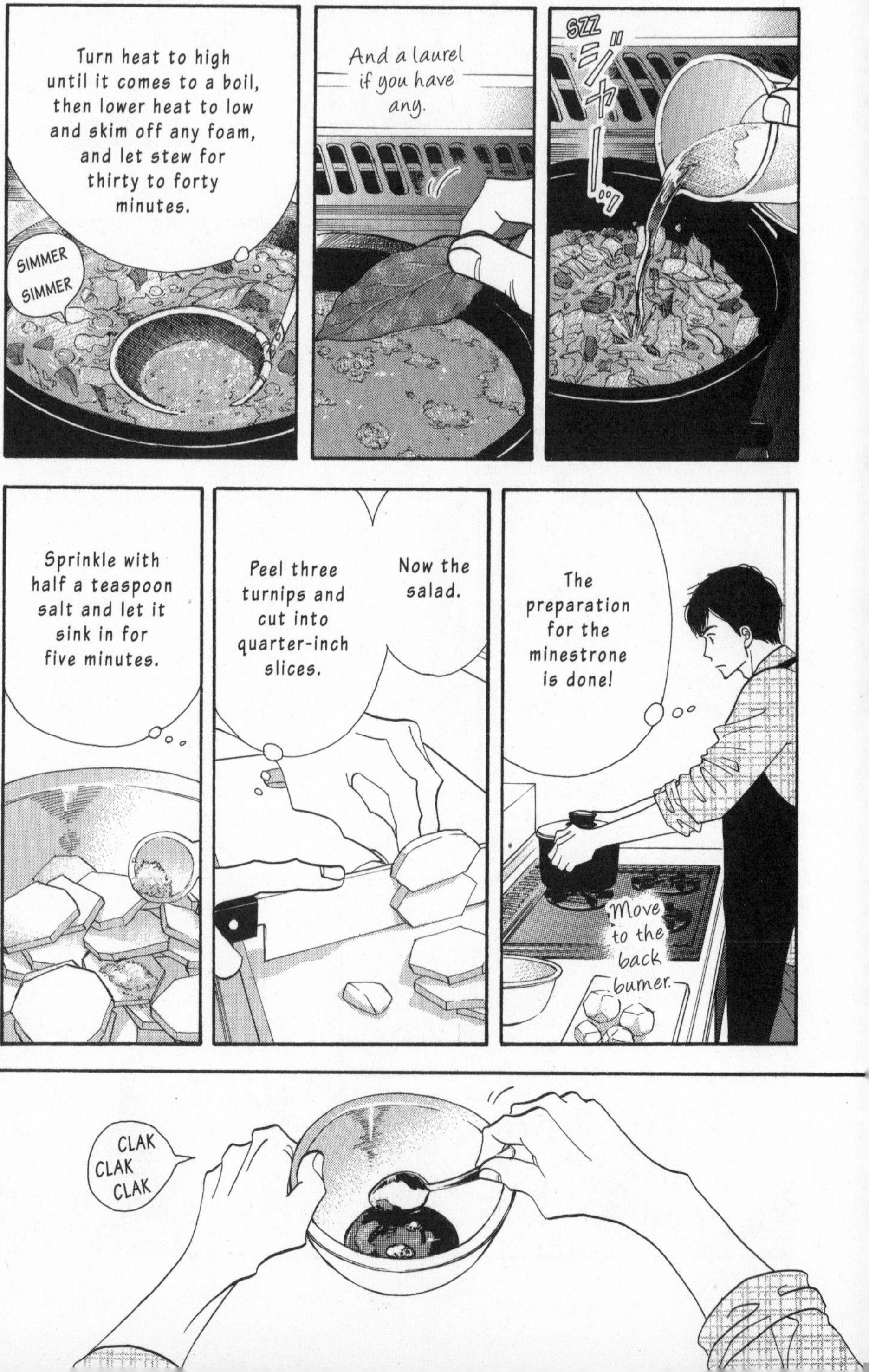
SZZ
And a laurel if you have any.
Turn heat to high until it comes to a boil, then lower heat to low and skim off any foam, and let stew for thirty to forty minutes.
SIMMER SIMMER
The preparation for the minestrone is done!
Move to the back burner.
Now the salad.
Peel three turnips and cut into quarter-inch slices.
Sprinkle with half a teaspoon salt and let it sink in for five minutes.
CLAK CLAK CLAK

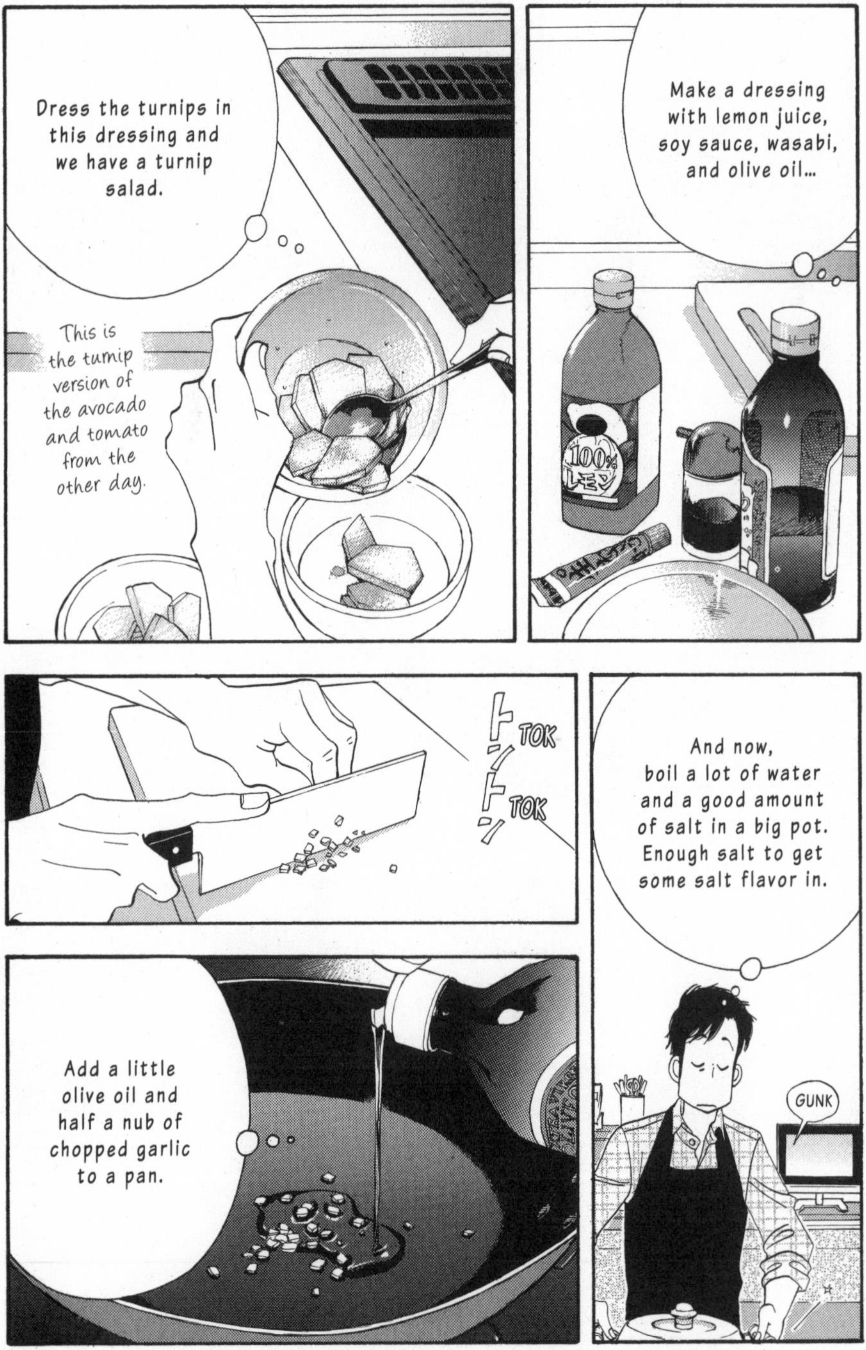
Make a dressing with lemon juice, soy sauce, wasabi, and olive oil...
100% レモン
Dress the turnips in this dressing and we have a turnip salad.
This is the turnip version of the avocado and tomato from the other day.
And now, boil a lot of water and a good amount of salt in a big pot. Enough salt to get some salt flavor in.
GUNK
TOK
TOK
Add a little olive oil and half a nub of chopped garlic to a pan.

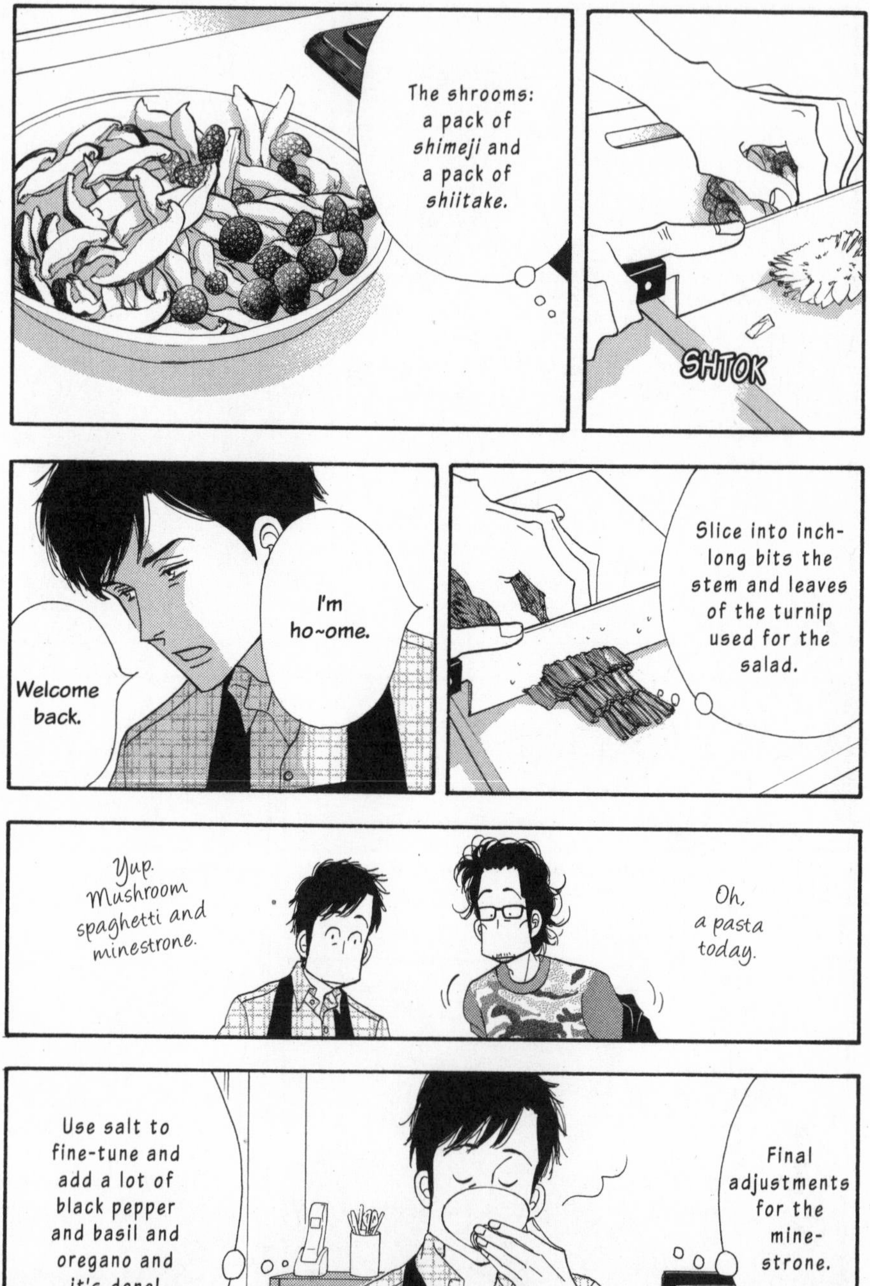
SHTOK
The shrooms: a pack of shimeji and a pack of shiitake.
Slice into inch-long bits the stem and leaves of the turnip used for the salad.
I'm ho~ome.
Welcome back.
Oh, a pasta today.
Yup. Mushroom spaghetti and minestrone.
Final adjustments for the mine-strone.
Use salt to fine-tune and add a lot of black pepper and basil and oregano and it's done!

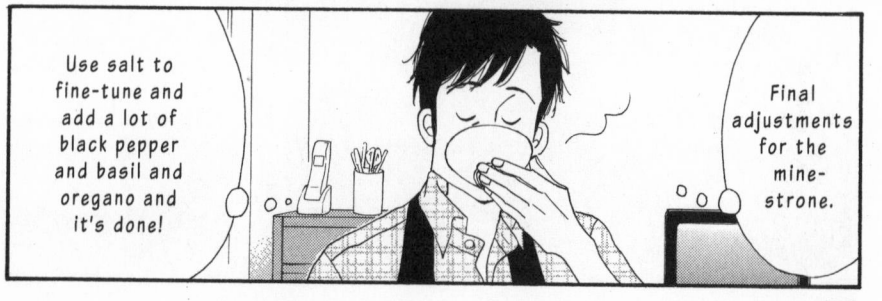

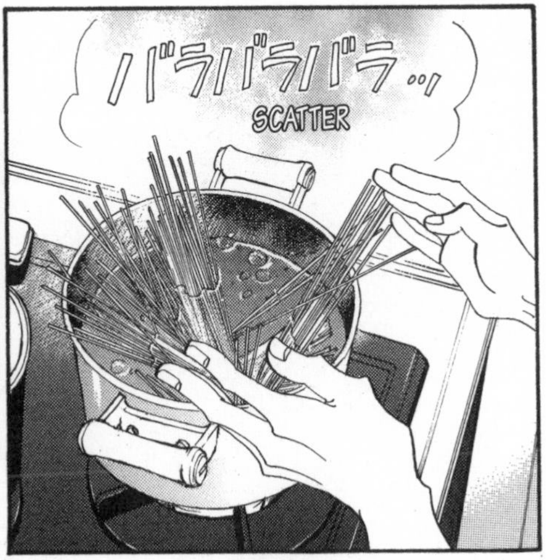
バラバラバラ…
SCATTER

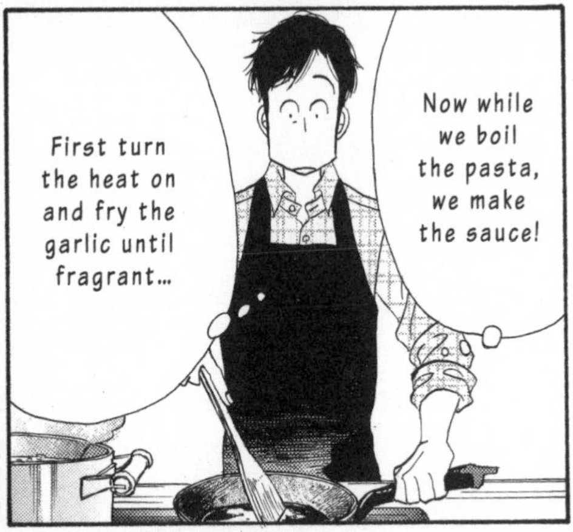
Now while we boil the pasta, we make the sauce!
First turn the heat on and fry the garlic until fragrant...

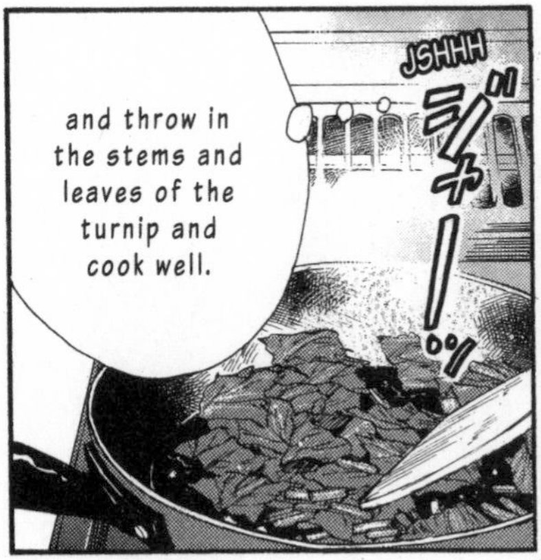
and throw in the stems and leaves of the turnip and cook well.
ジャー…
JSHHH

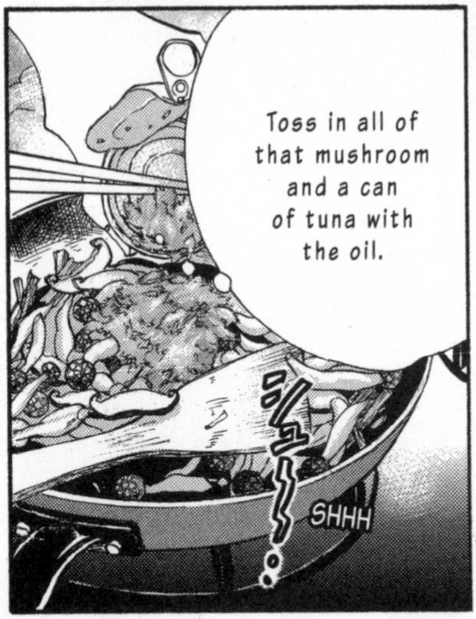
Toss in all of that mushroom and a can of tuna with the oil.
シュ〜〜…
SHHH

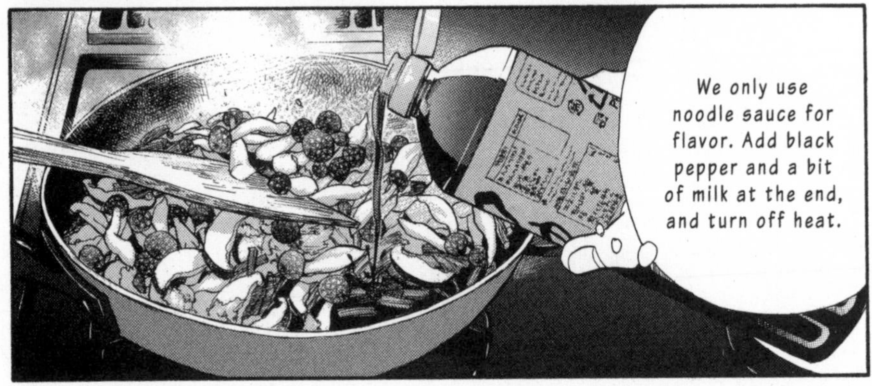
We only use noodle sauce for flavor. Add black pepper and a bit of milk at the end, and turn off heat.

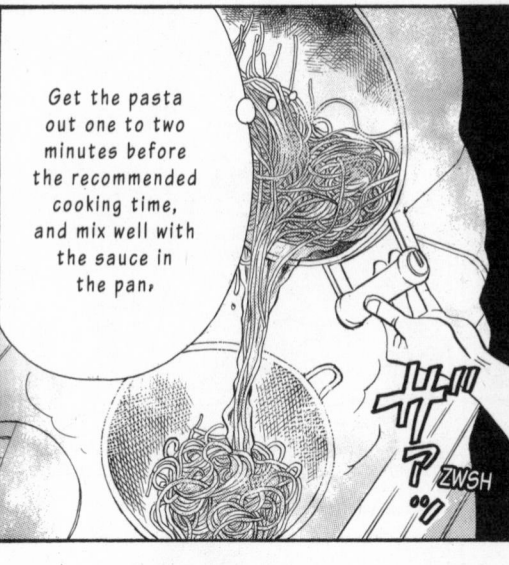

Set the table before the pasta is done.
Put out what I can.
Get the pasta out one to two minutes before the recommended cooking time, and mix well with the sauce in the pan.
ZWSH
Kenji, could you pour the minestrone?
Yu~p
Cook the pasta until the sauce's moisture is gone...
FZZZ
Mm. Perfect flavor and boil time.
SLURP
BWUSH

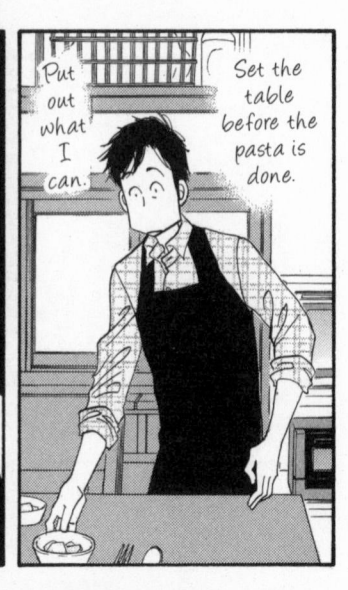

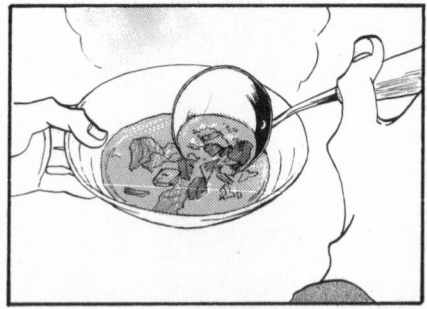

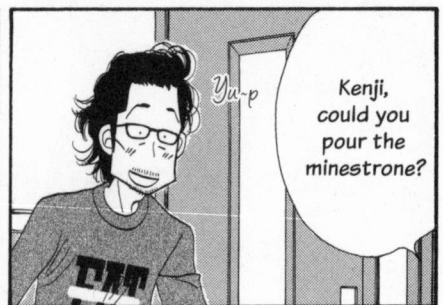

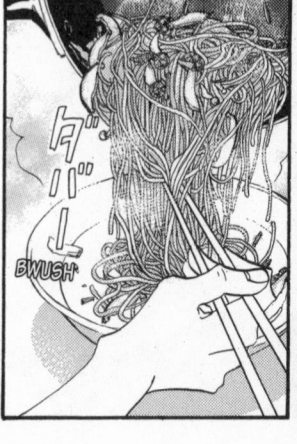

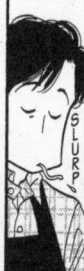

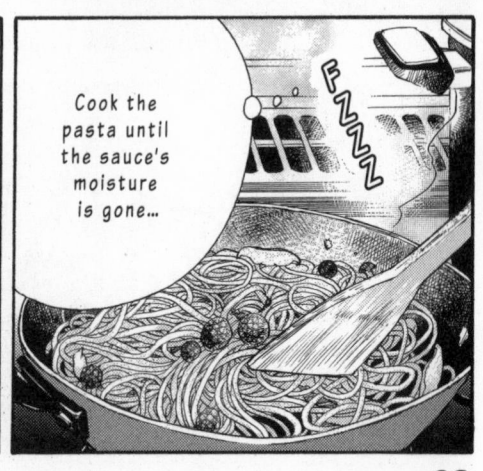

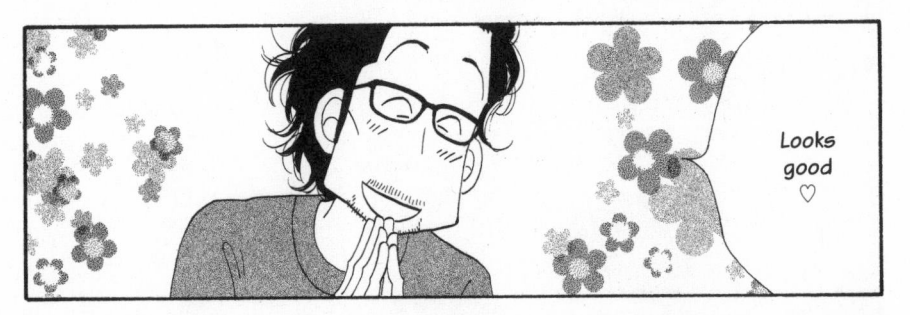

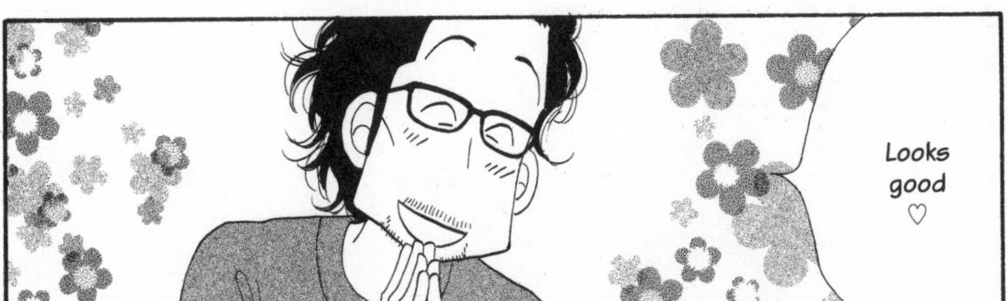
Looks good ♡

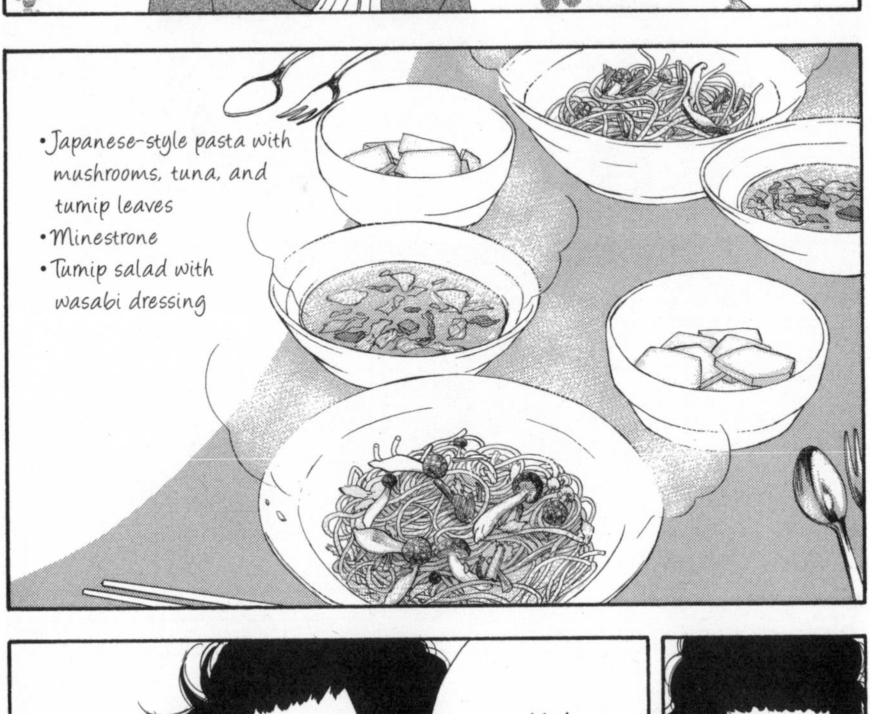
•Japanese-style pasta with mushrooms, tuna, and turnip leaves
•Minestrone
•Turnip salad with wasabi dressing

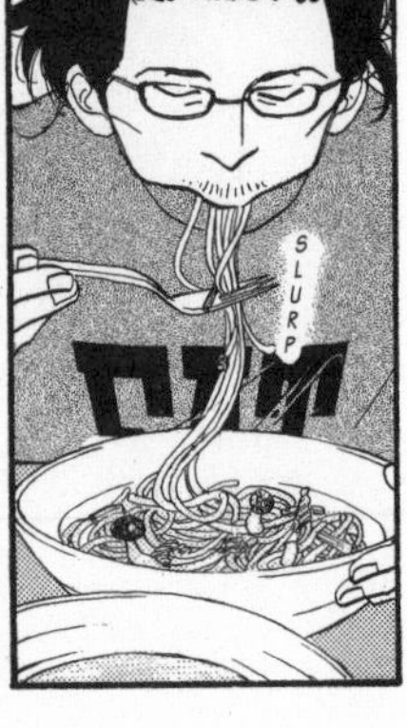
SLURP

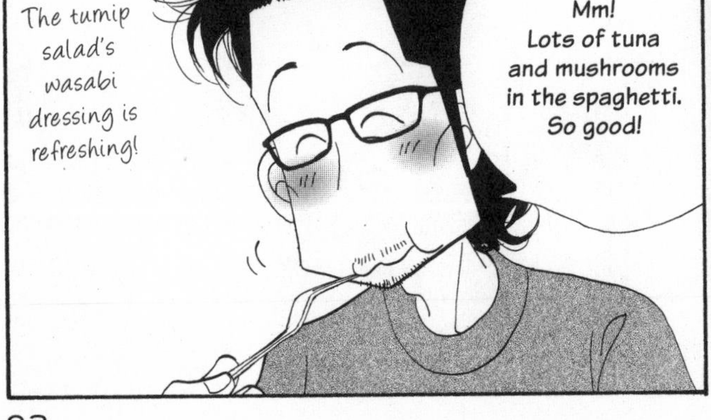
Mm! Lots of tuna and mushrooms in the spaghetti. So good!
The turnip salad's wasabi dressing is refreshing!

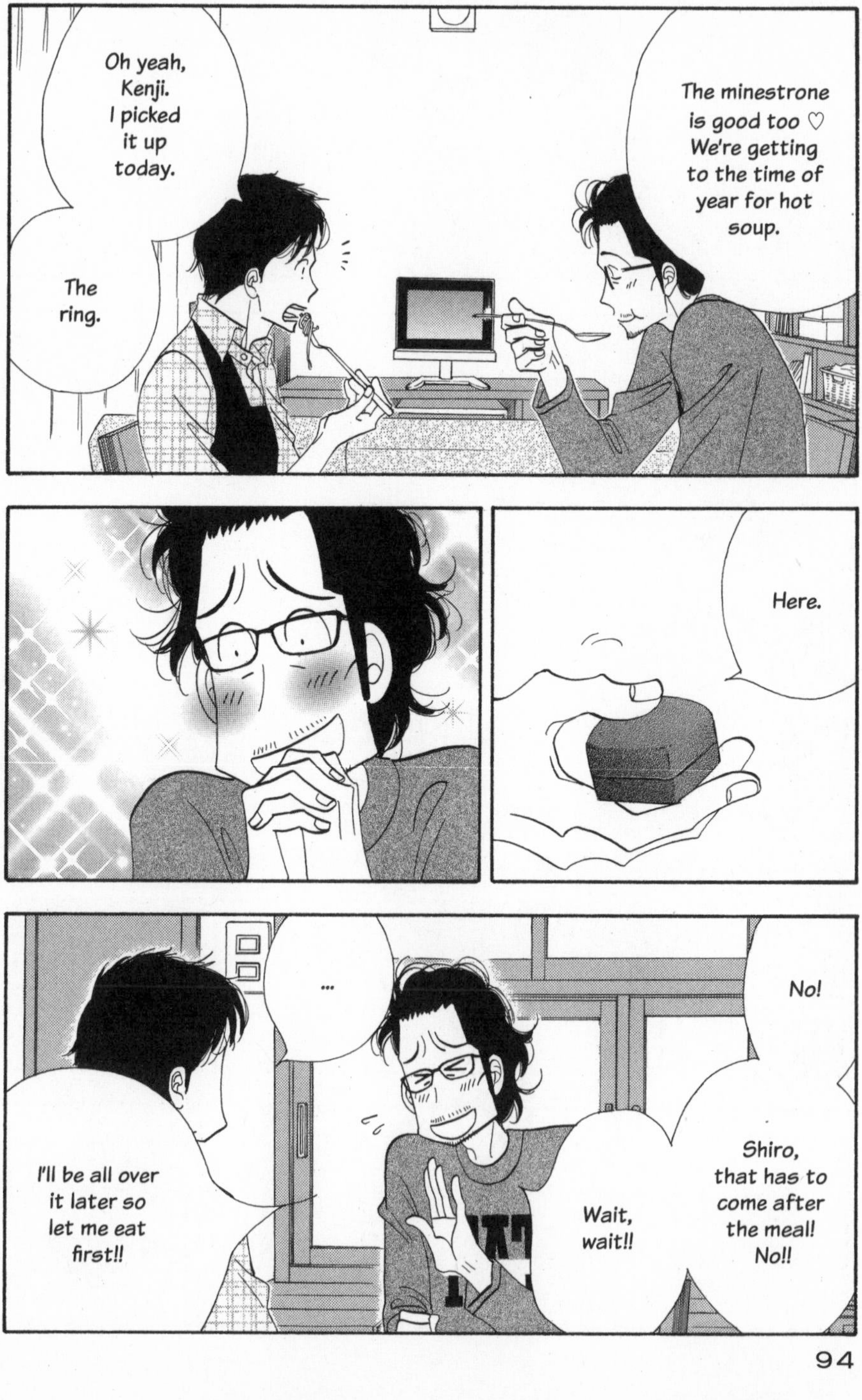
The minestrone is good too ♡ We're getting to the time of year for hot soup.
Oh yeah, Kenji. I picked it up today.
The ring.
Here.
No!
...
Shiro, that has to come after the meal! No!!
Wait, wait!!
I'll be all over it later so let me eat first!!

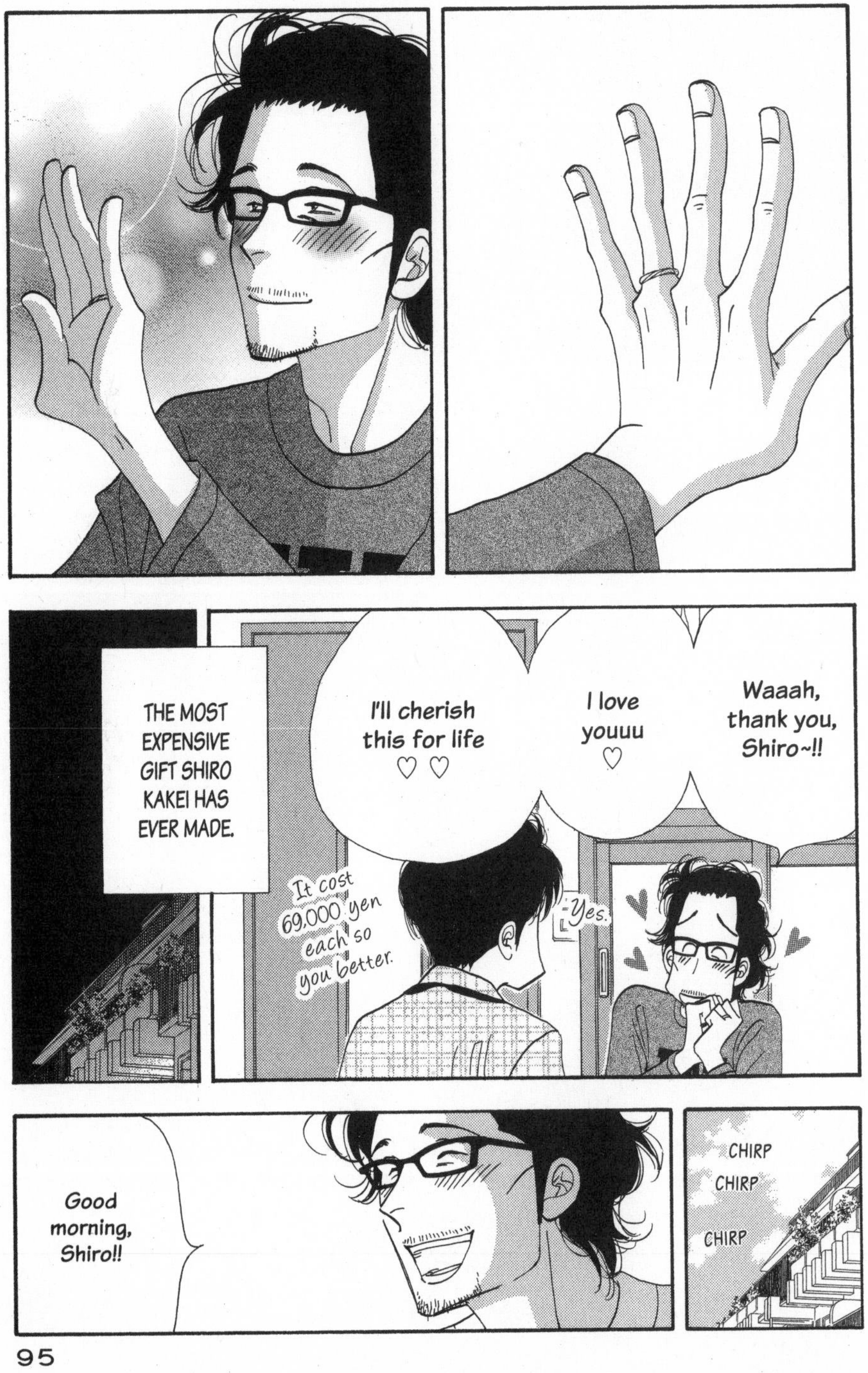
Waaah, thank you, Shiro~!!
I love youuu ♡
I'll cherish this for life ♡ ♡
-Yes.
It cost 69,000 yen each so you better.
THE MOST EXPENSIVE GIFT SHIRO KAKEI HAS EVER MADE.
CHIRP
CHIRP
CHIRP
Good morning, Shiro!!

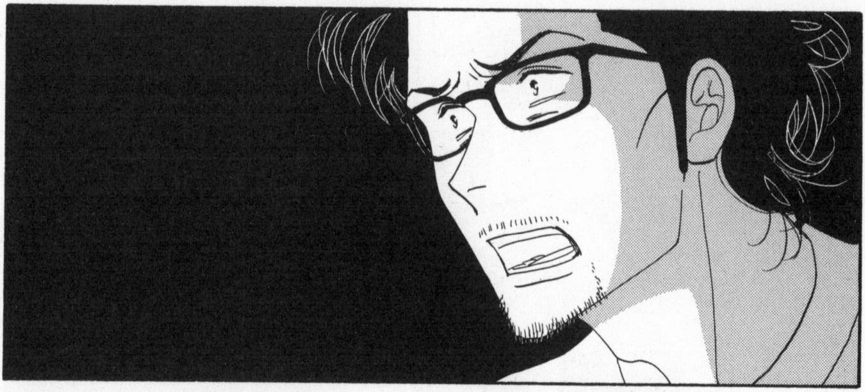

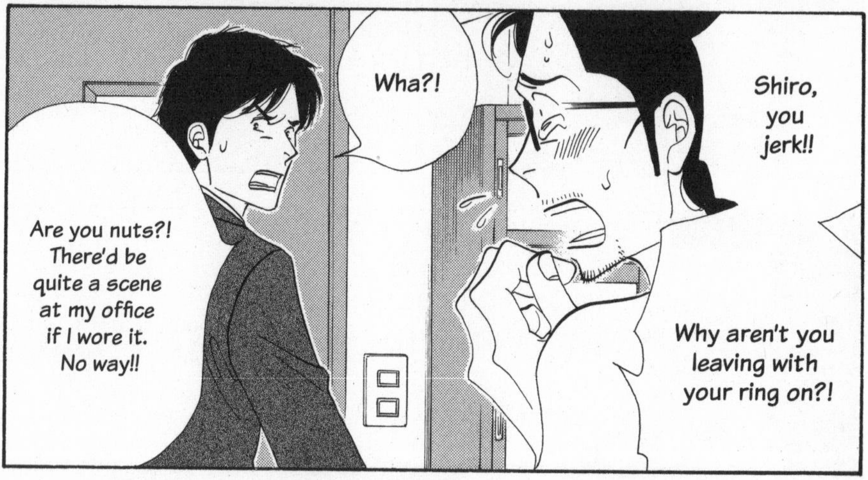
Shiro, you jerk!!
Why aren't you leaving with your ring on?!
Wha?!
Are you nuts?! There'd be quite a scene at my office if I wore it. No way!!

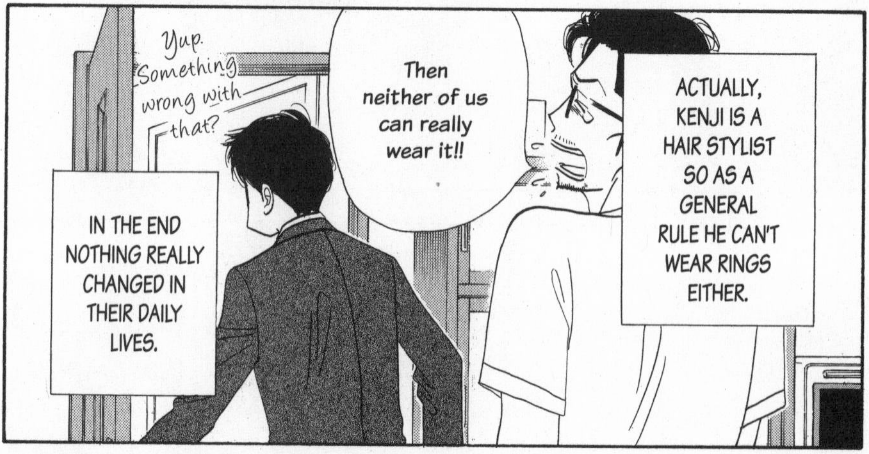
ACTUALLY, KENJI IS A HAIR STYLIST SO AS A GENERAL RULE HE CAN'T WEAR RINGS EITHER.
Then neither of us can really wear it!!
Yup. Something wrong with that?
IN THE END NOTHING REALLY CHANGED IN THEIR DAILY LIVES.

#37 **END**

Minestrone

Use canned tomatoes instead
of raw tomatoes and it'll still
come out fine.
In either case, frying until the
tomatoes lose shape and then
boiling in water will remove some
of the tartness and make the soup mild.

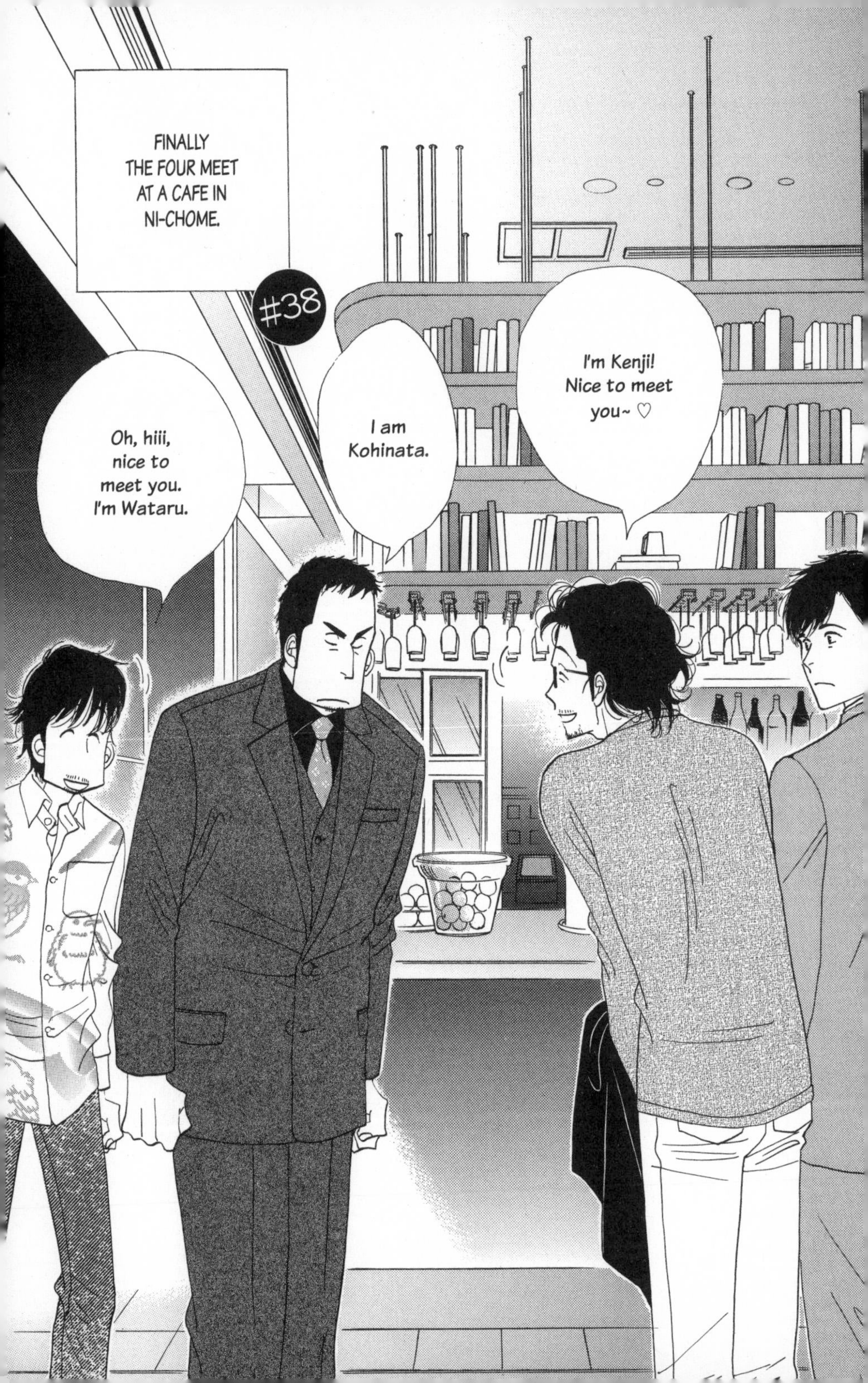
FINALLY THE FOUR MEET AT A CAFE IN NI-CHOME.
#38
I'm Kenji! Nice to meet you~ ♡
I am Kohinata.
Oh, hiii, nice to meet you. I'm Wataru.

I actually do this for a living.

Moripro Inc.
First Management Office
Production Department
Group Leader
Daisaku Kohinata
Tokyo

Tel. (03) XXXX-XXXX Fax (03) XXXX-XXXX
Cell. 090.
E-Mail kohinata@XXXXXX
URL http://www.XXXXXX.com

I didn't know...

Oh wow, you work for a talent agency?

Must be hectic!

Well, not really these days.

Until I was in my mid-thirties I managed individual celebrities so I was pretty busy, but I'm a group leader now.

Now my main job is producing and scheduling for those names on the back of the card.

I only travel when they start filming. The rest is having drinks with big shots from TV and movie production companies. It's all good times.

He must be tough.

I see, he used to manage celebrities. No wonder he can endure his boyfriend's absurd antics.

For real?!

I see names like Hiroko Matsuura and Kaho Yoshino and Mami Mitsuya on the back of your card...

Mr. Kohinata...

Uh, yes? I used to be the manager for all of them.

And Kaho Yoshino! I was just watching that drama *Face* and was thinking a really fine and cute actress has come along!!

Hiroko Matsuura!! I've followed her since her debut in *Yo-Yo Detective* when she had that cute pony tail with that loose lock!!

I-I...!! I don't really watch TV, but!!

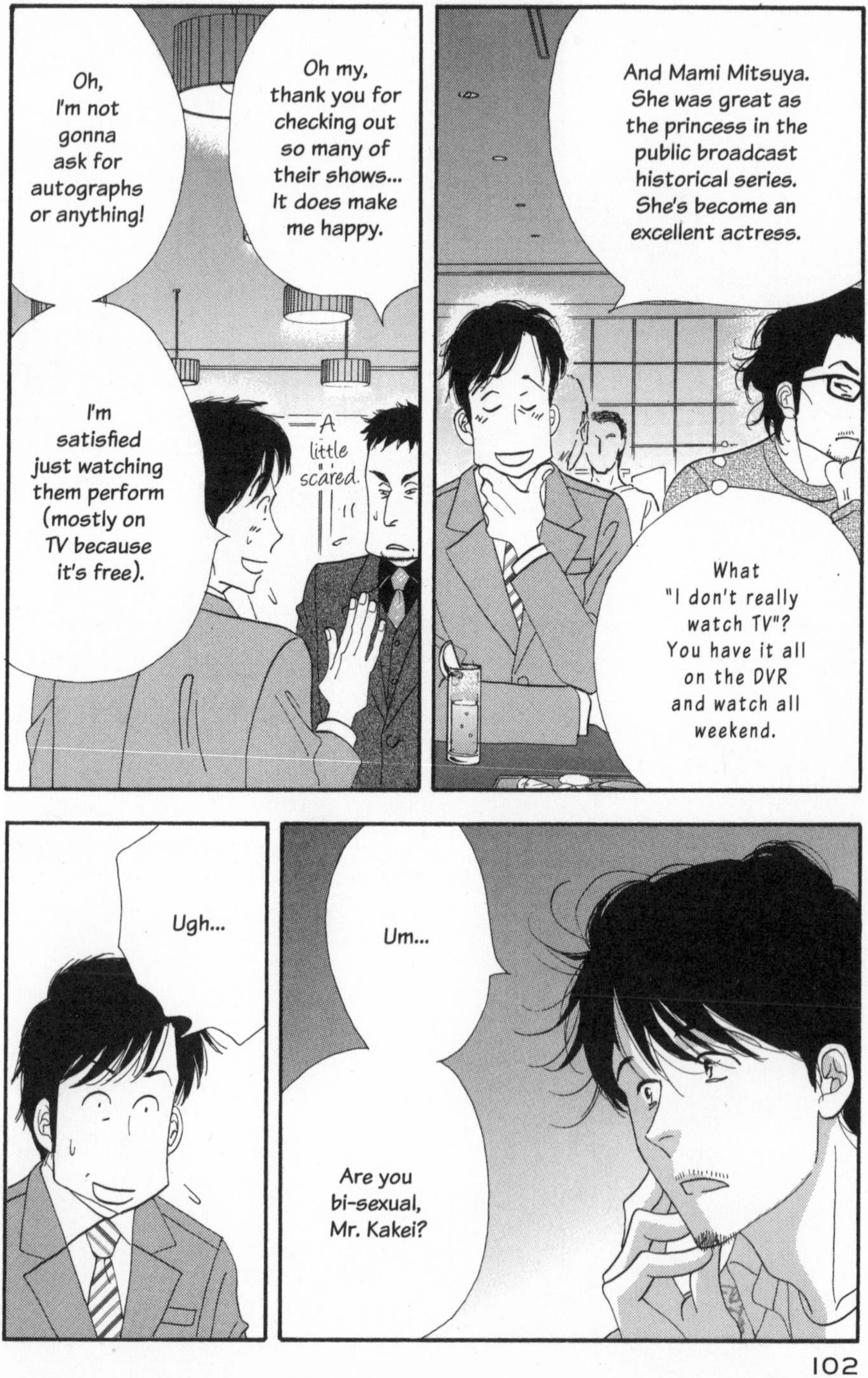
And Mami Mitsuya. She was great as the princess in the public broadcast historical series. She's become an excellent actress.
What "I don't really watch TV"? You have it all on the DVR and watch all weekend.
Oh my, thank you for checking out so many of their shows... It does make me happy.
Oh, I'm not gonna ask for autographs or anything!
I'm satisfied just watching them perform (mostly on TV because it's free).
A little scared.
Um...
Are you bi-sexual, Mr. Kakei?
Ugh...

You yourself said once, Kenji, that a lot of gay guys have female idols that they love!

No, listen. That's not true!

Right?! Don't you think so, Wataru?!

I'm a minority within a minority.

I...know I don't fit in the gay mainstream.

They're all idols straight guys your age loved.

Sure, but the types of women you seem to like are a bit different from the idols gay guys tend to like.

Oh, but Mr. Kakei.

But some straight guys like all the idols gay guys love. So I guess the opposite pattern isn't out of the question.

103

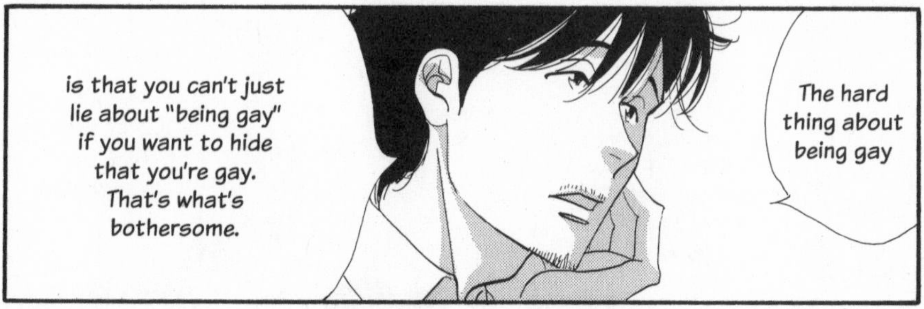
The hard thing about being gay
is that you can't just lie about "being gay" if you want to hide that you're gay. That's what's bothersome.
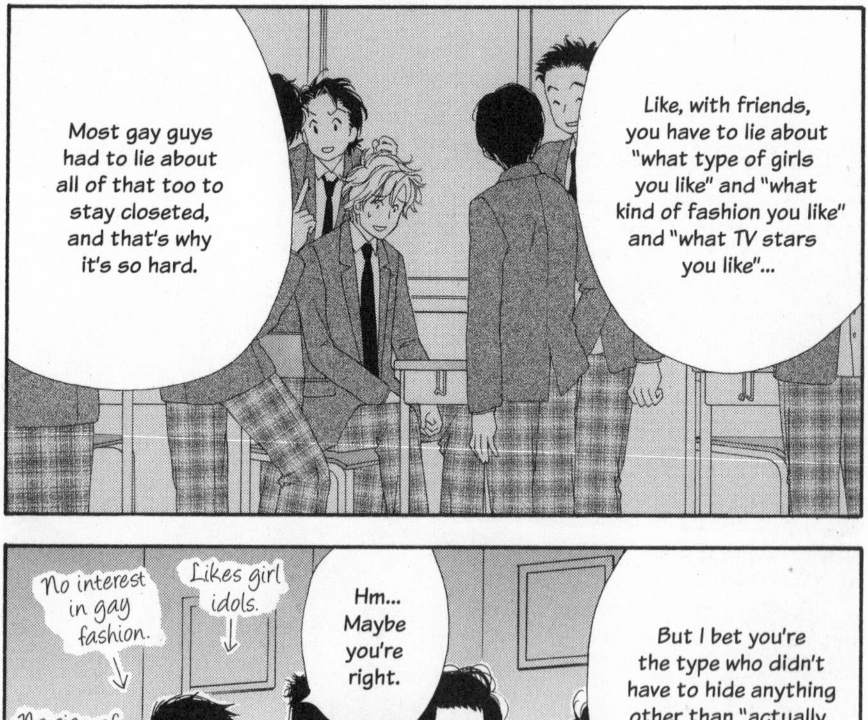
Like, with friends, you have to lie about "what type of girls you like" and "what kind of fashion you like" and "what TV stars you like"...
Most gay guys had to lie about all of that too to stay closeted, and that's why it's so hard.
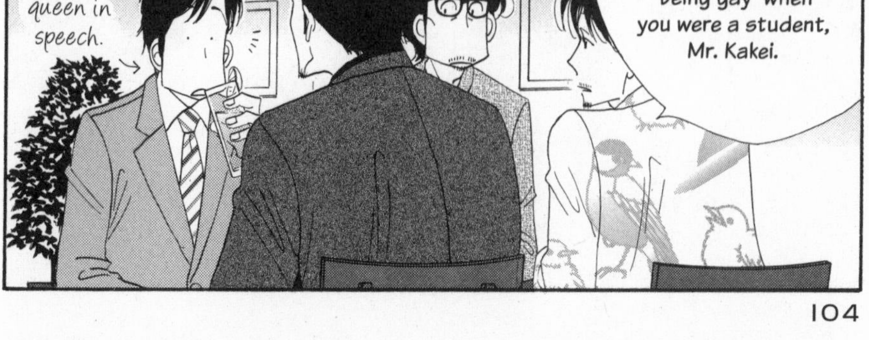
But I bet you're the type who didn't have to hide anything other than "actually being gay" when you were a student, Mr. Kakei.
Hm... Maybe you're right.
Likes girl idols.
No interest in gay fashion.
No sign of queen in speech.

What? But you don't hide a damn thing!

Likes boy idols.

Loves pink.

Queen speech.

Come to think of it, it's not fair, Shiro~

Ugh...

Wataru!

Still closeted at workplace.

But it's types like Mr. Kakei who face the highest hurdles as a result when they decide to come out.

Ah, true.

Oh, but Shiro!

That Gilbert with a scruff... He's not the easiest guy.

You gave them a small cake you made, didn't you? I'm surprised!

Your present!

Huh? Really?!

Well, I tried to learn from you— bringing something modest as a sign of friendship... Was it weird?

I don't dislike guys like Wataru.

Really? I had fun ♡

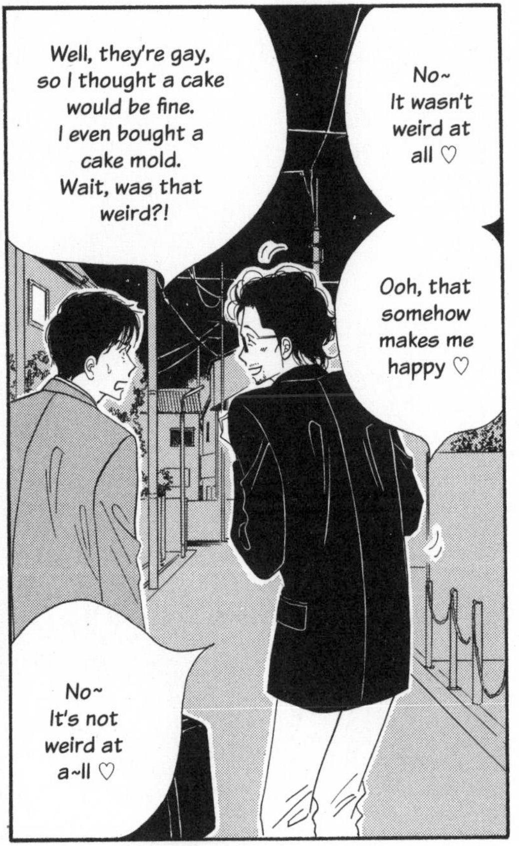
Well, they're gay, so I thought a cake would be fine. I even bought a cake mold. Wait, was that weird?!
No~ It wasn't weird at all ♡
Ooh, that somehow makes me happy ♡
No~ It's not weird at a~ll ♡

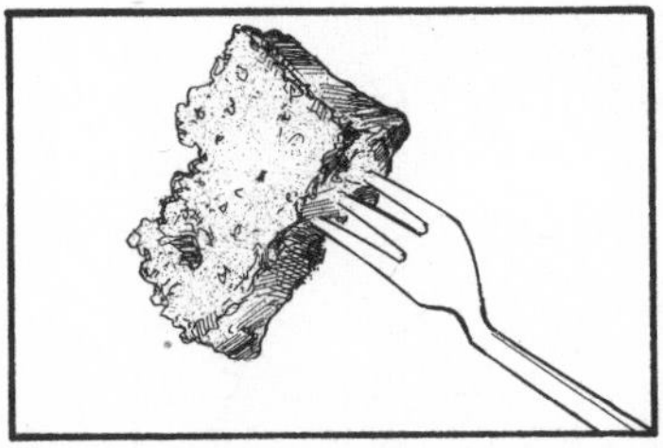

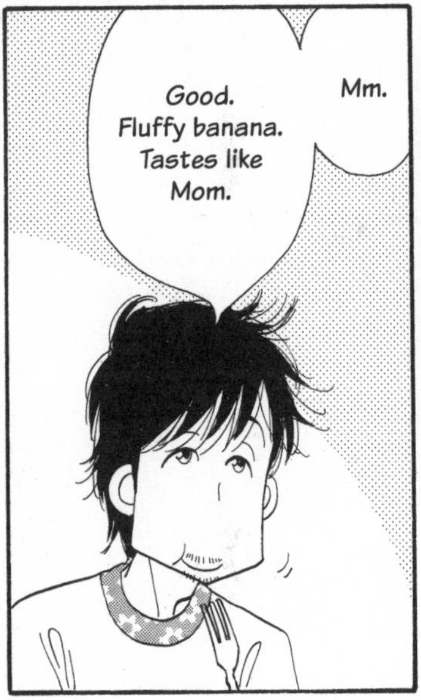
Mm.
Good. Fluffy banana. Tastes like Mom.

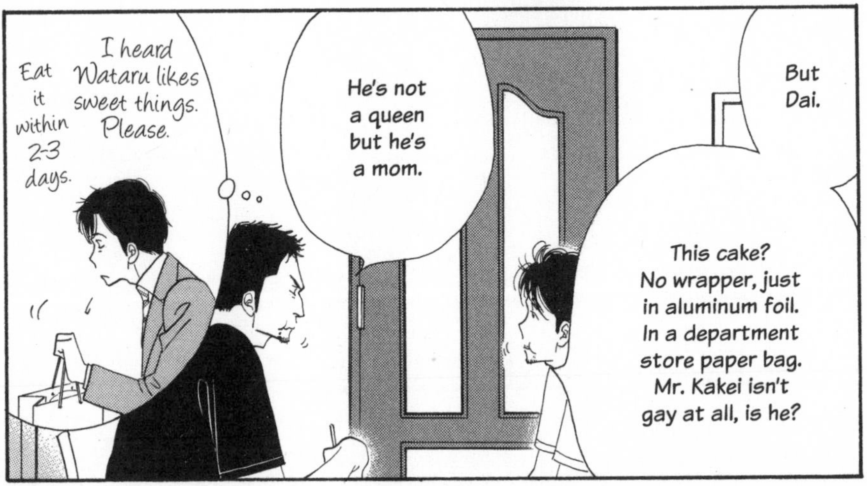
But Dai.
This cake? No wrapper, just in aluminum foil. In a department store paper bag. Mr. Kakei isn't gay at all, is he?
He's not a queen but he's a mom.
I heard Wataru likes sweet things. Please.
Eat it within 2-3 days.

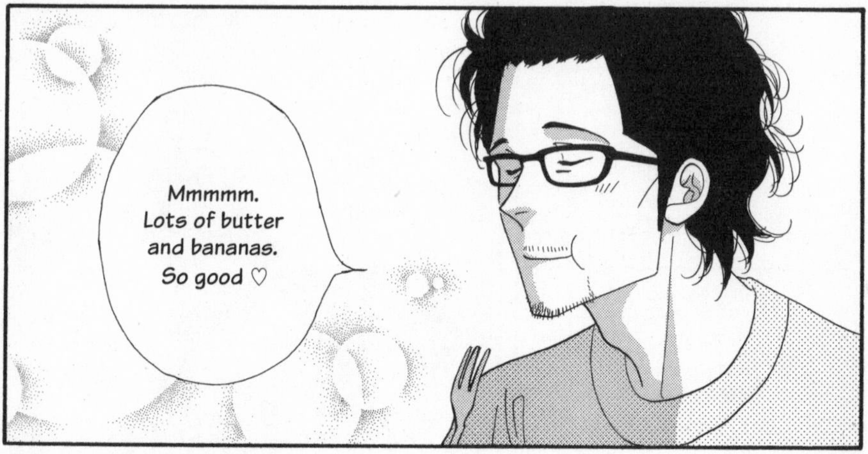
Mmmmm. Lots of butter and bananas. So good ♡

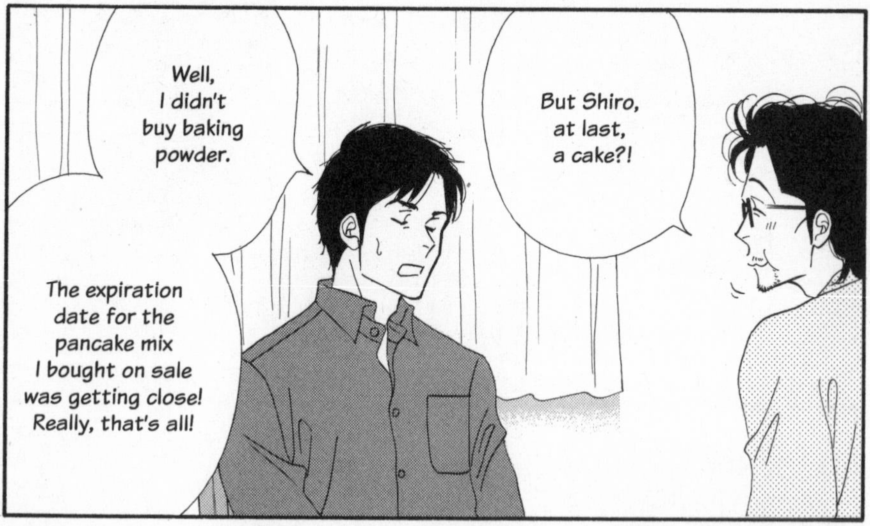
But Shiro, at last, a cake?!
Well, I didn't buy baking powder.
The expiration date for the pancake mix I bought on sale was getting close! Really, that's all!

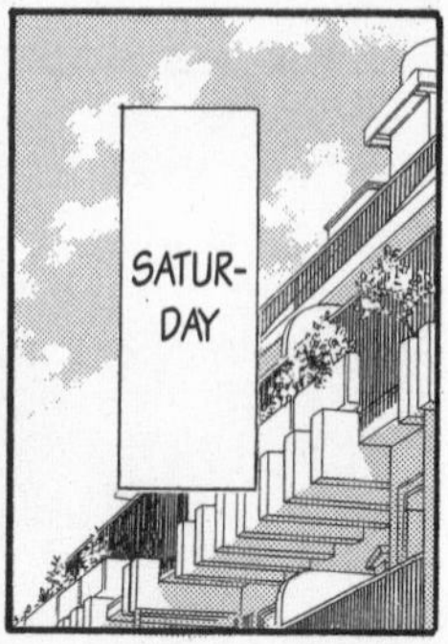
SATUR-DAY

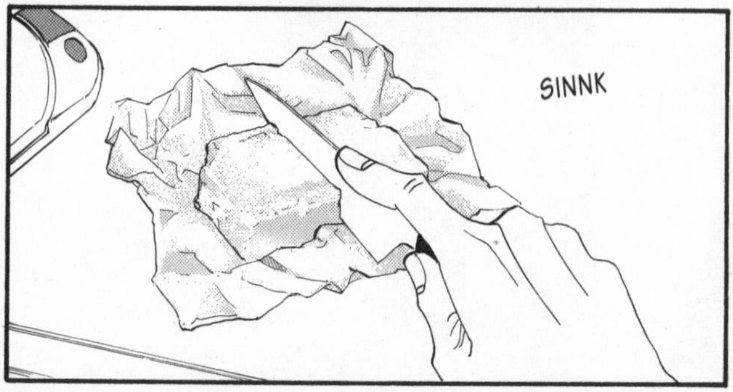
SINNK

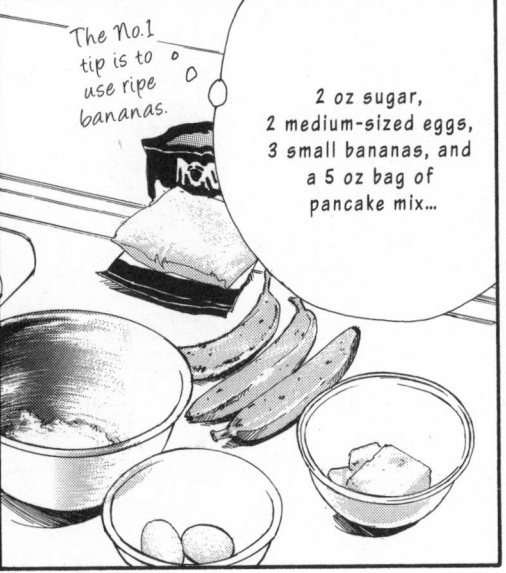

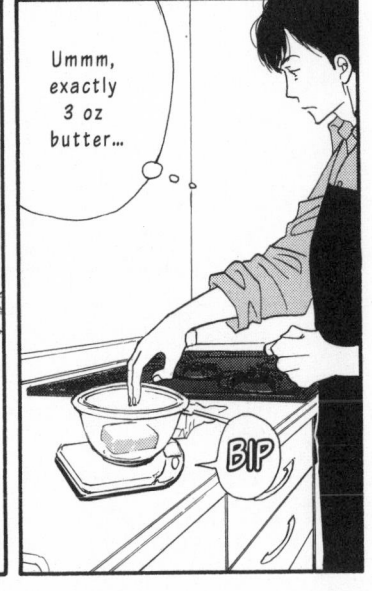

Ummm, exactly 3 oz butter...
BIP
The No.1 tip is to use ripe bananas.
2 oz sugar, 2 medium-sized eggs, 3 small bananas, and a 5 oz bag of pancake mix...
MICROWAVE
SETTING 85°F
BIP
BIP
I wanna make the butter soft enough to push in with a finger, so put it in a heat-resistant bowl and microwave at 85°F...
VMMMM
If it's still hard, turn it over and microwave again at 85 degrees.
Here we go.
The second tip is not to melt the butter to a liquid.
Once it's soft, mix it with the sugar and stir well until white-ish with a whisk.

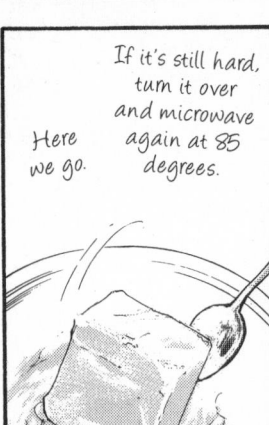

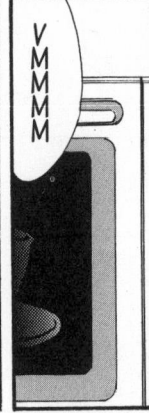

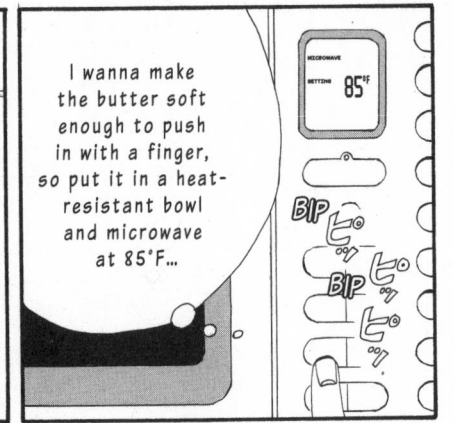

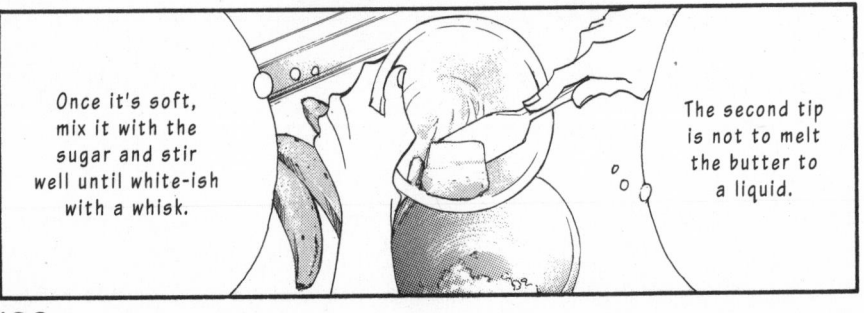

Once the butter and sugar are completely mixed and white-ish...

KSH
KSH
KSH
KSH
KSH

KSH
KSH
KSH
KSH

pour in 2 beaten eggs little by little and mix well.

GSH GSH GSH GSH

PRESS

PRESS

And heat the oven to 360°F around now.

SETTING 360°

WARM START

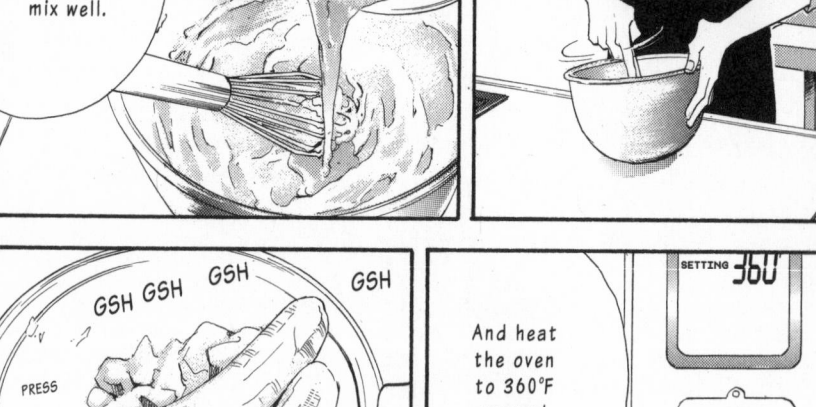

Crush the banana using a fork so that no liquid comes out, add to bowl with the egg, butter, and sugar, then lightly mix up with a spatula this time.

And don't knead this either. Mix it with a spatula like you're lightly cutting it...

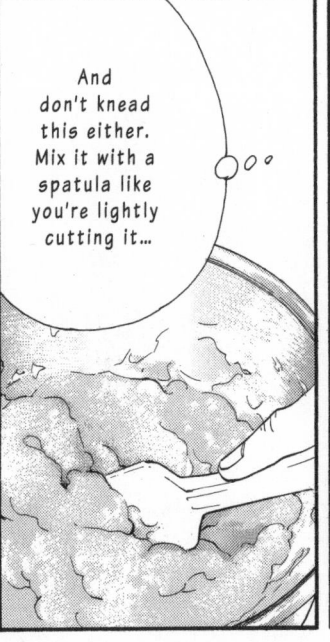

— Unlike normal flour, no need to sift!

Finally, pour in all 5 oz of the pancake mix.

BEEP BEEP BEEP

Pour evenly into two 7" x 2" x 2" pans, and smooth out the surface with the spatula.

We have a teflon so it went in directly, but if not, use separately melted butter and sprinkle with cake flour and get rid of the excess powder. It'd be even easier with one of those dollar-shop paper molds.

Oh, the pre-heat is done.

It's convenient if you have two molds, you could use one to gift to someone.

You could of course just put it in one larger mold.

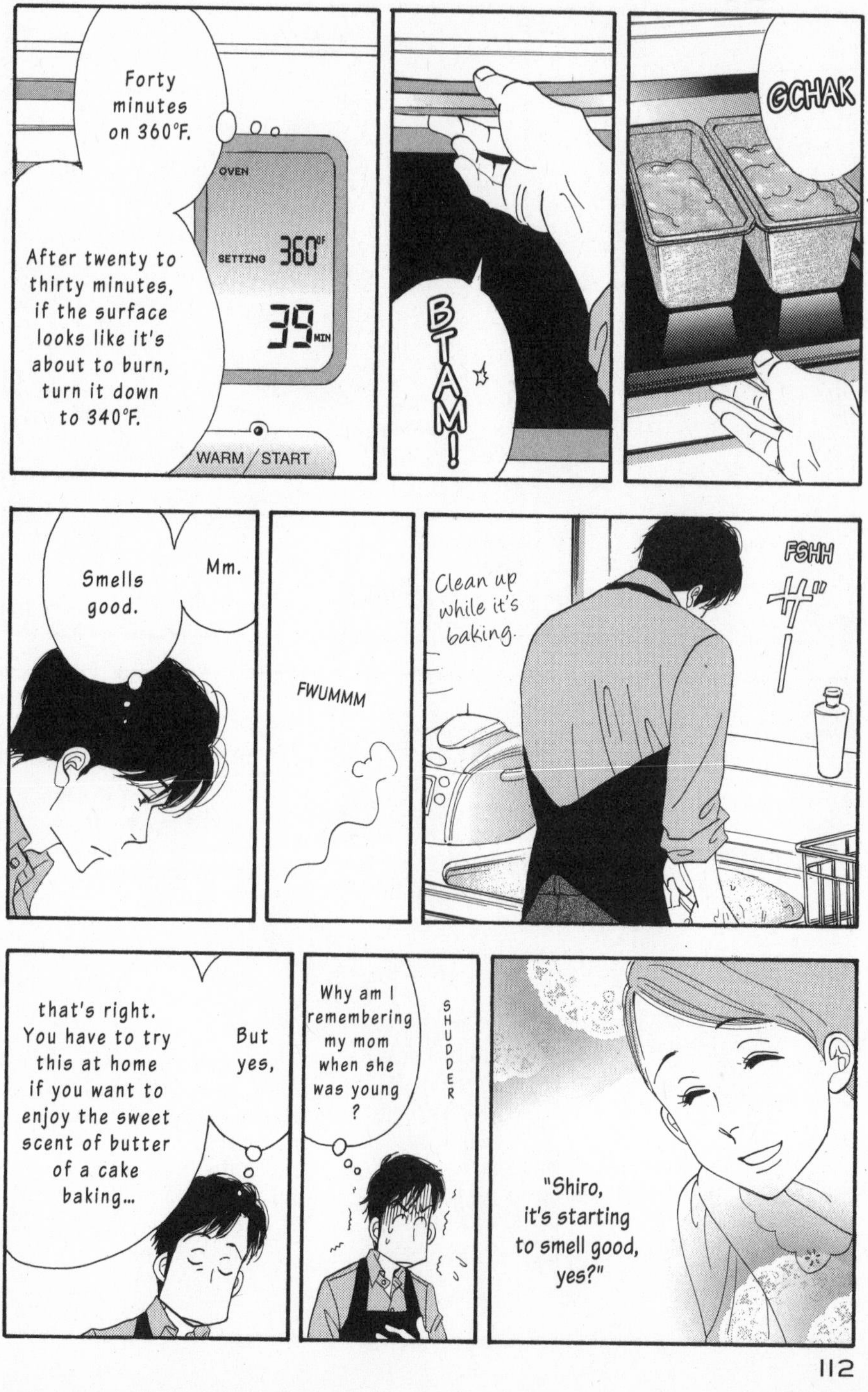
GCHAK
BTAM!
Forty minutes on 360°F.
After twenty to thirty minutes, if the surface looks like it's about to burn, turn it down to 340°F.
OVEN
SETTING 360°F
39 MIN
WARM / START
FSHH
Clean up while it's baking.
FWUMMM
Mm.
Smells good.
"Shiro, it's starting to smell good, yes?"
SHUDDER
Why am I remembering my mom when she was young?
But yes,
that's right. You have to try this at home if you want to enjoy the sweet scent of butter of a cake baking...

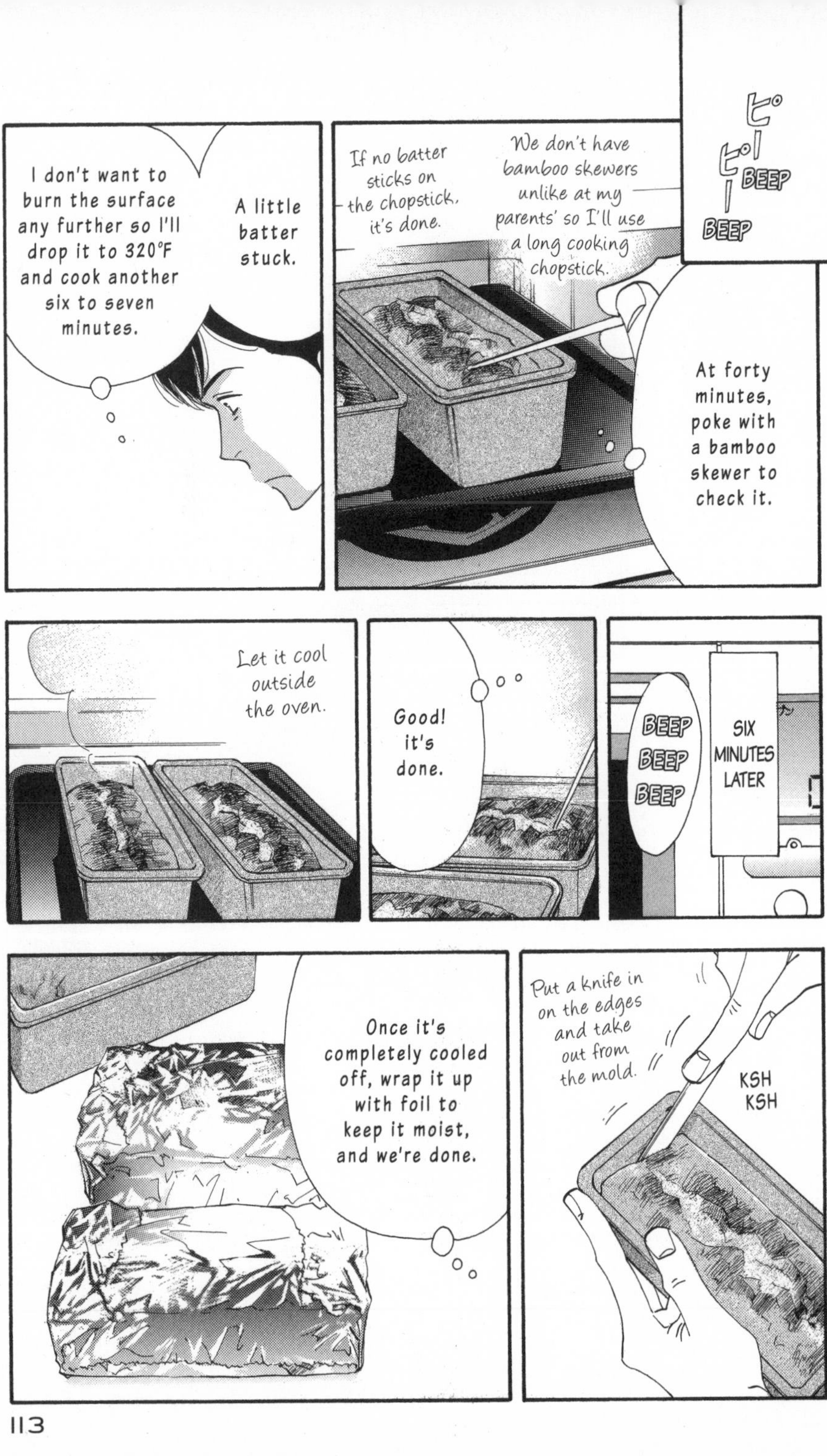
ピ ピ
BEEP BEEP
At forty minutes, poke with a bamboo skewer to check it.
We don't have bamboo skewers unlike at my parents' so I'll use a long cooking chopstick.
If no batter sticks on the chopstick, it's done.
A little batter stuck.
I don't want to burn the surface any further so I'll drop it to 320°F and cook another six to seven minutes.
SIX MINUTES LATER
BEEP BEEP BEEP
Good! it's done.
Let it cool outside the oven.
Put a knife in on the edges and take out from the mold.
KSH KSH
Once it's completely cooled off, wrap it up with foil to keep it moist, and we're done.

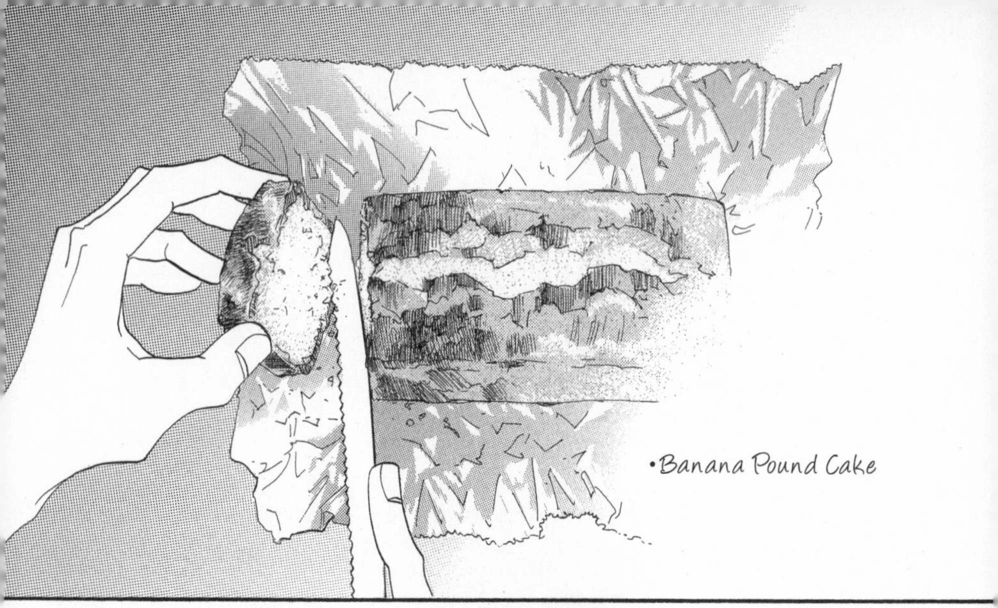
•Banana Pound Cake

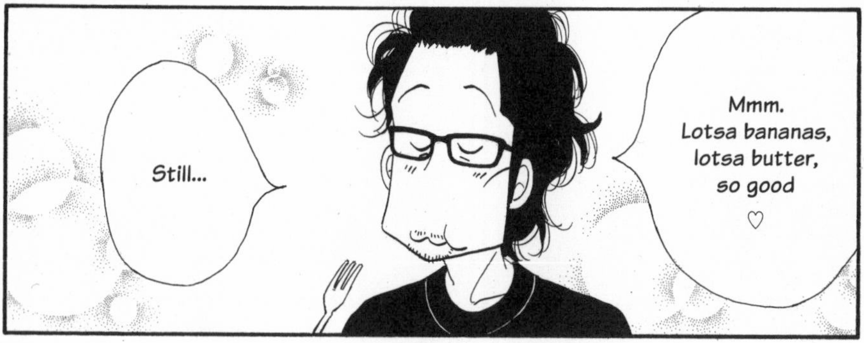
Mmm. Lotsa bananas, lotsa butter, so good ♡
Still...

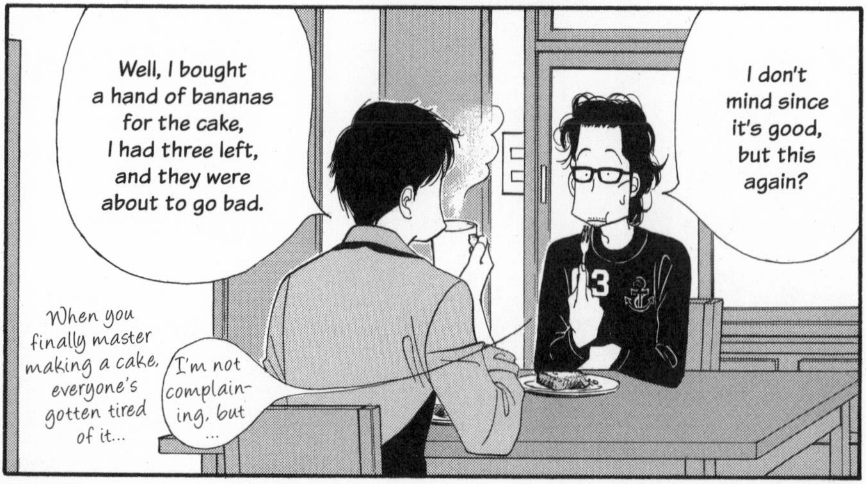
I don't mind since it's good, but this again?
Well, I bought a hand of bananas for the cake, I had three left, and they were about to go bad.
I'm not complaining, but ...
When you finally master making a cake, everyone's gotten tired of it...

#38 END

For a 7 oz bag of pancake mix,
use **5 1/4 oz butter, 3 7/8 oz sugar,**
three eggs, and four bananas,
and it will come out about the same.
(You could use the same mold used in the story,
it will fit. About the same cooking time too.)
There are real bananas in there,
so it won't last too long.
Try to avoid making it in the summer,
and finish within three days of cooking.

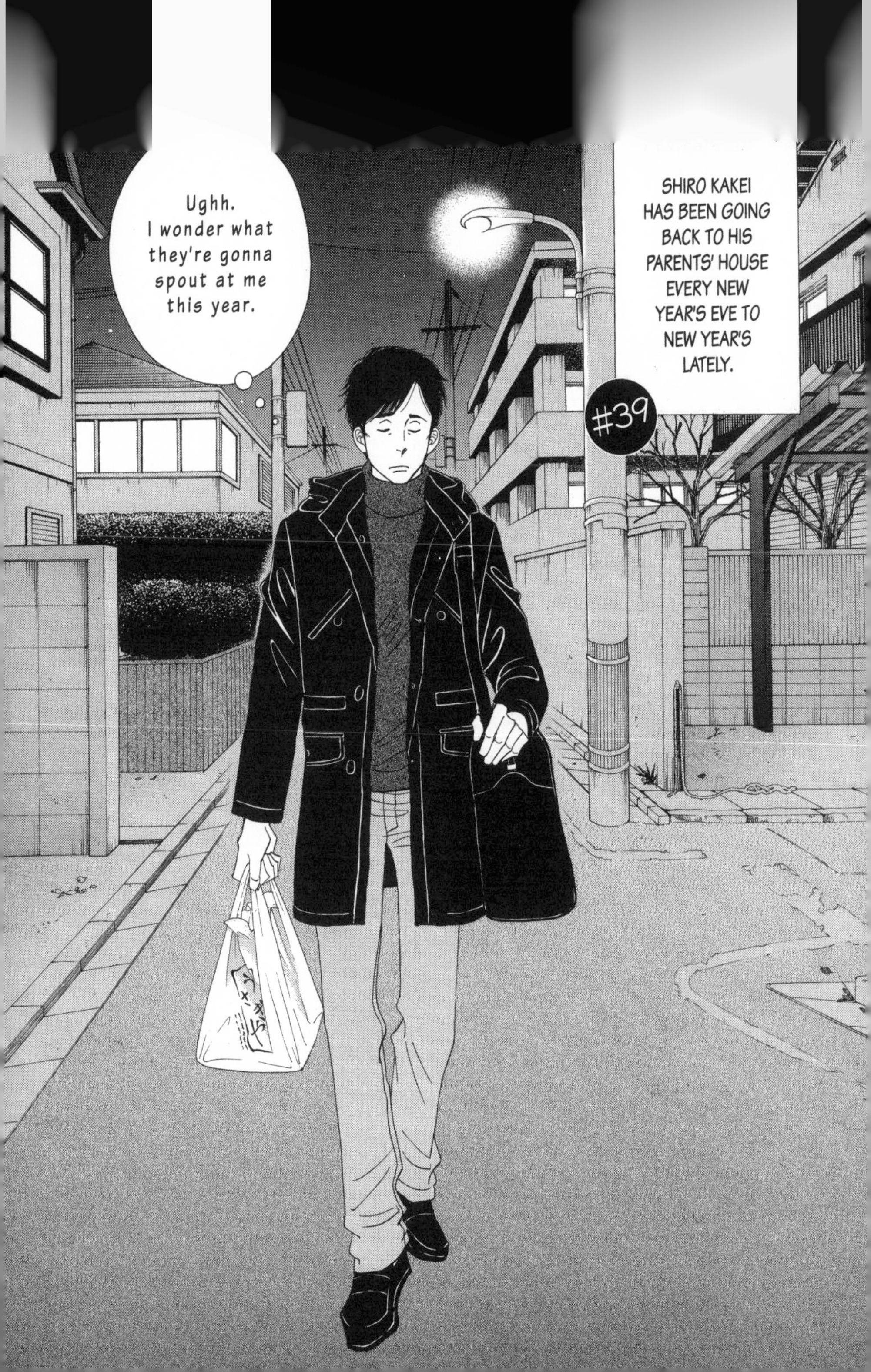
#39
SHIRO KAKEI HAS BEEN GOING BACK TO HIS PARENTS' HOUSE EVERY NEW YEAR'S EVE TO NEW YEAR'S LATELY.
Ughh. I wonder what they're gonna spout at me this year.

Shiro! Shiro!! The bar? On the screen of the computer. When that becomes vertical, how do you make it go back to horizontal?!

None of your business.

Shiro! Shiro, is everything going well with the man you're living with?! He hasn't ditched you, has he?!

DING DONG

Ugh. I'm dreading this...

Welcome home.

118

Ah, welcome home.

...

Dad, Shiro is here.

Why, thank you. I'll make you some tea now.

Oh yeah, this.

Yup. Very good.

Mm, this is good.

...

Dad, isn't this dorayaki good?

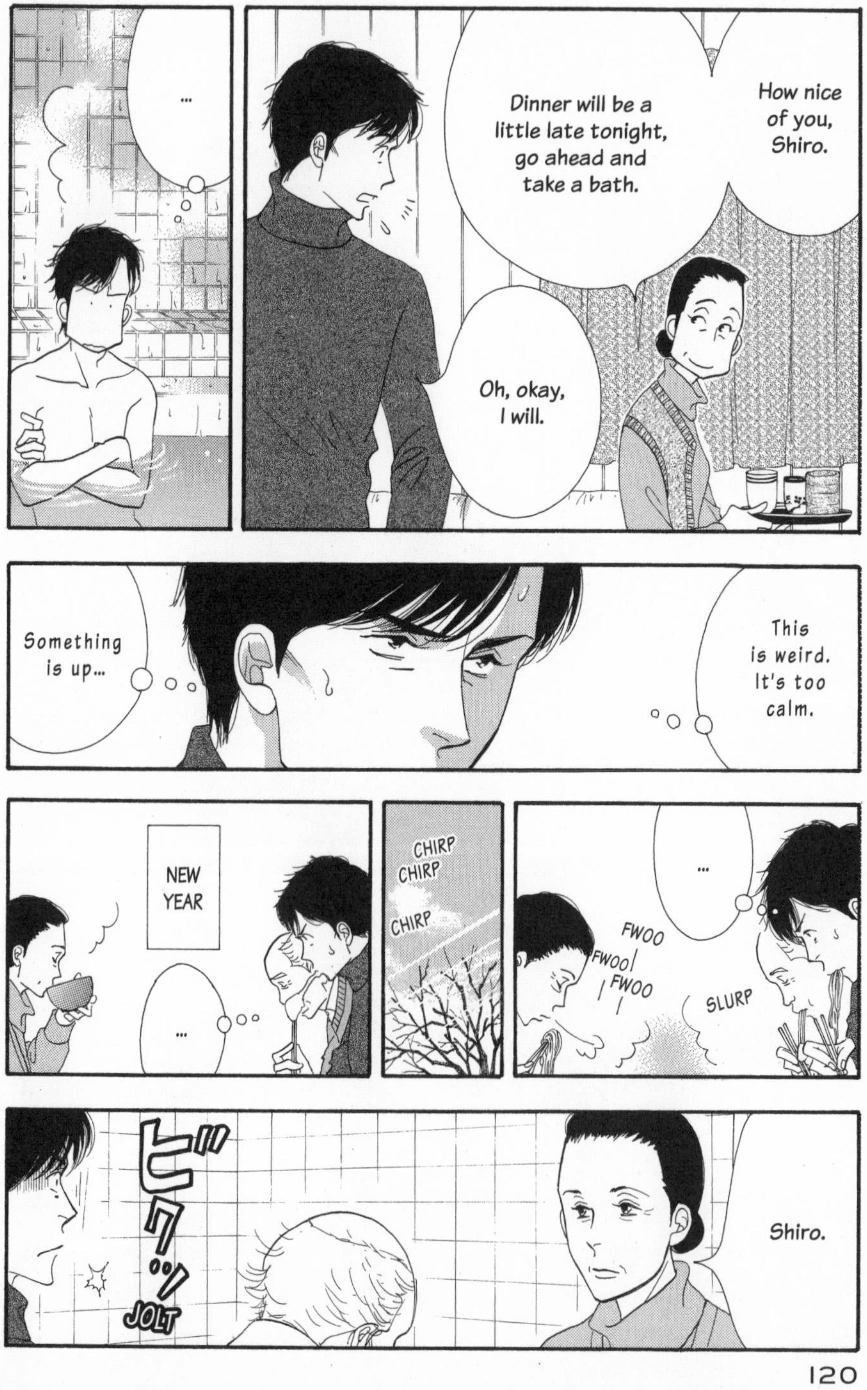
How nice of you, Shiro.
Dinner will be a little late tonight, go ahead and take a bath.
Oh, okay, I will.
...
This is weird. It's too calm.
Something is up...
...
FWOO
FWOO
FWOO
SLURP
CHIRP
CHIRP
CHIRP
NEW YEAR
...
Shiro.
ビク
JOLT

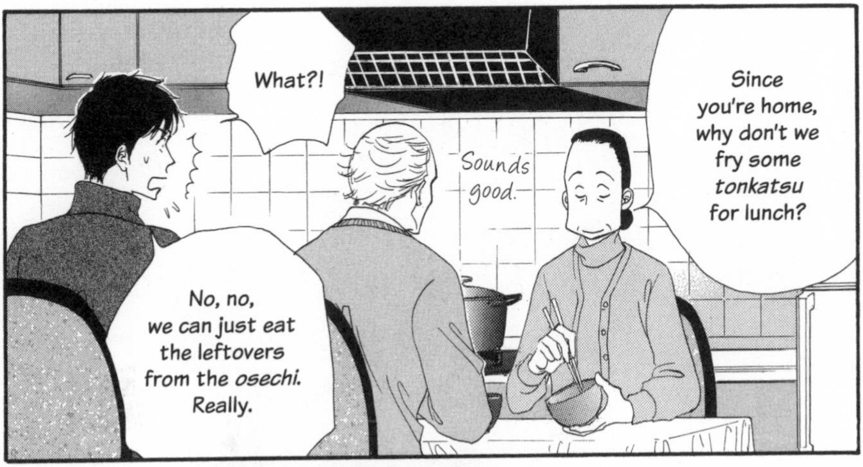
Since you're home, why don't we fry some *tonkatsu* for lunch?
Sounds good.
What?!
No, no, we can just eat the leftovers from the *osechi*. Really.

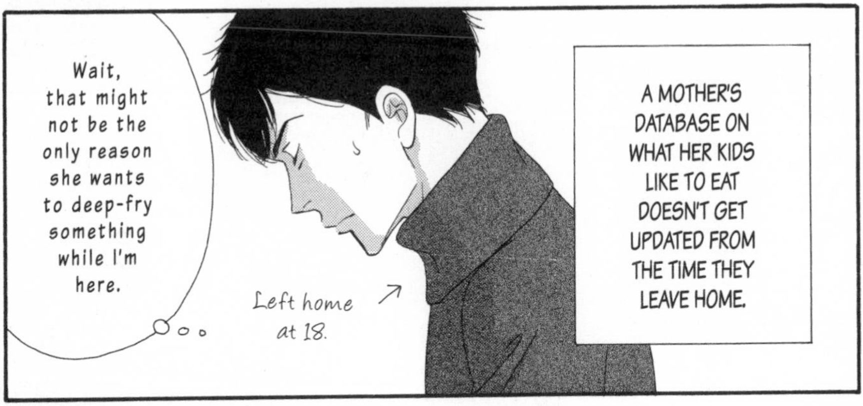
A MOTHER'S DATABASE ON WHAT HER KIDS LIKE TO EAT DOESN'T GET UPDATED FROM THE TIME THEY LEAVE HOME.
Left home at 18.
Wait, that might not be the only reason she wants to deep-fry something while I'm here.

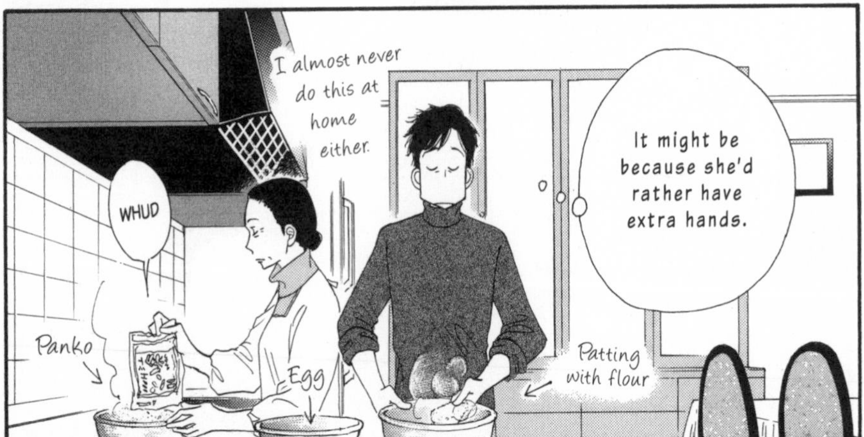
It might be because she'd rather have extra hands.
I almost never do this at home either.
Patting with flour
WHUD
Egg
Panko

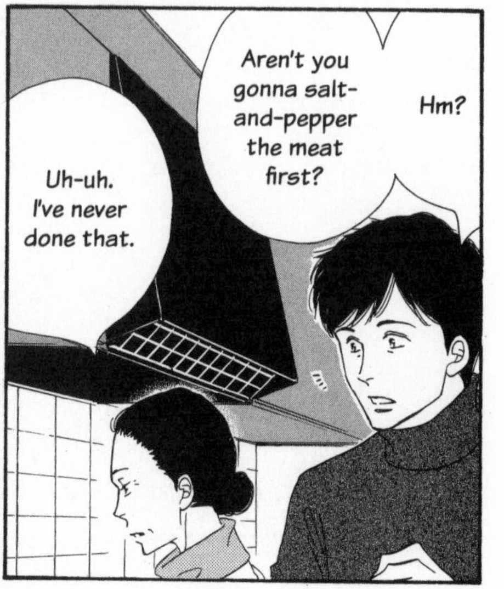
Hm?
Aren't you gonna salt-and-pepper the meat first?
Uh-uh. I've never done that.

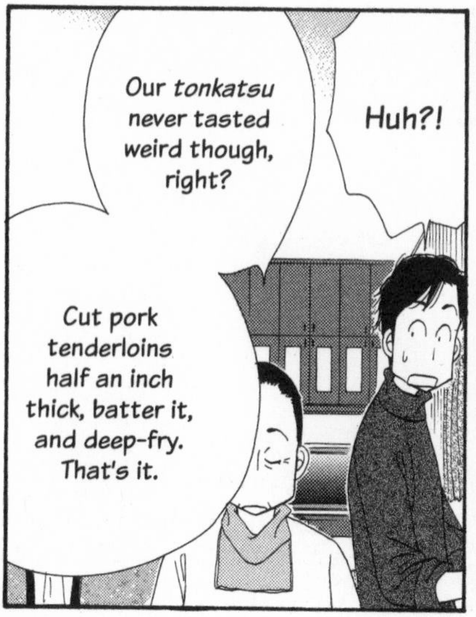
Huh?!
Our *tonkatsu* never tasted weird though, right?
Cut pork tenderloins half an inch thick, batter it, and deep-fry. That's it.

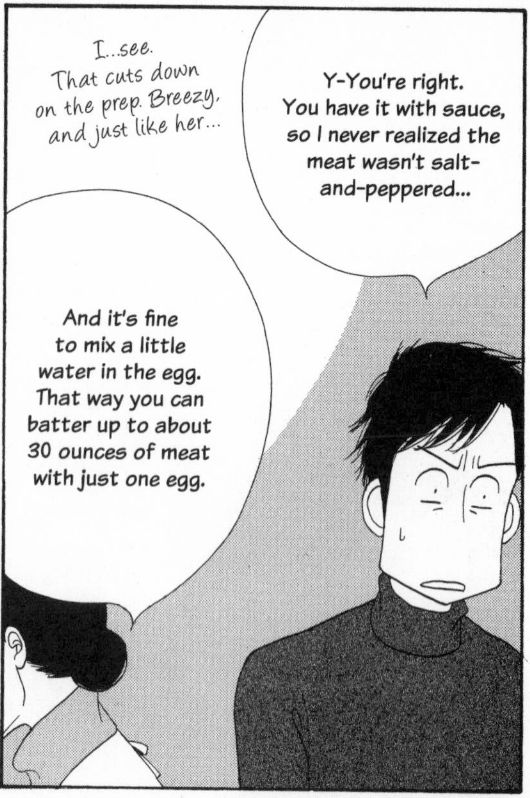
Y-You're right. You have it with sauce, so I never realized the meat wasn't salt-and-peppered...
I...see. That cuts down on the prep. Breezy, and just like her...
And it's fine to mix a little water in the egg. That way you can batter up to about 30 ounces of meat with just one egg.

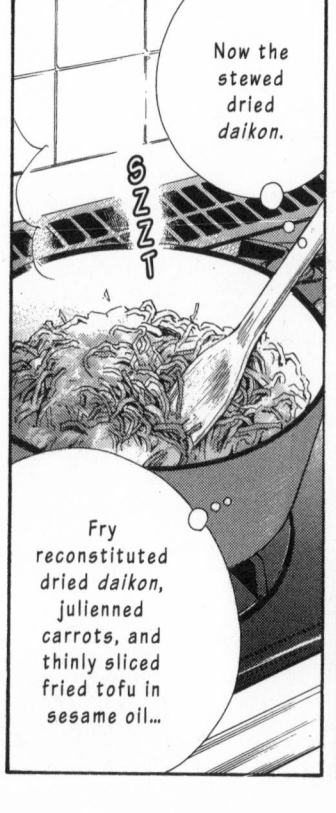

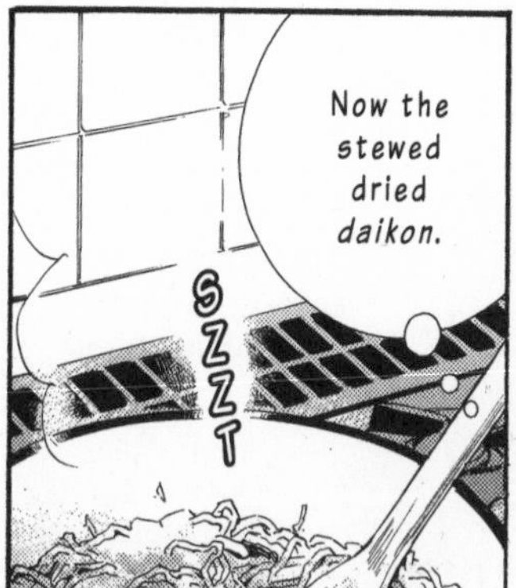
Now the stewed dried *daikon*.
SZZT
Fry reconstituted dried *daikon*, julienned carrots, and thinly sliced fried tofu in sesame oil...

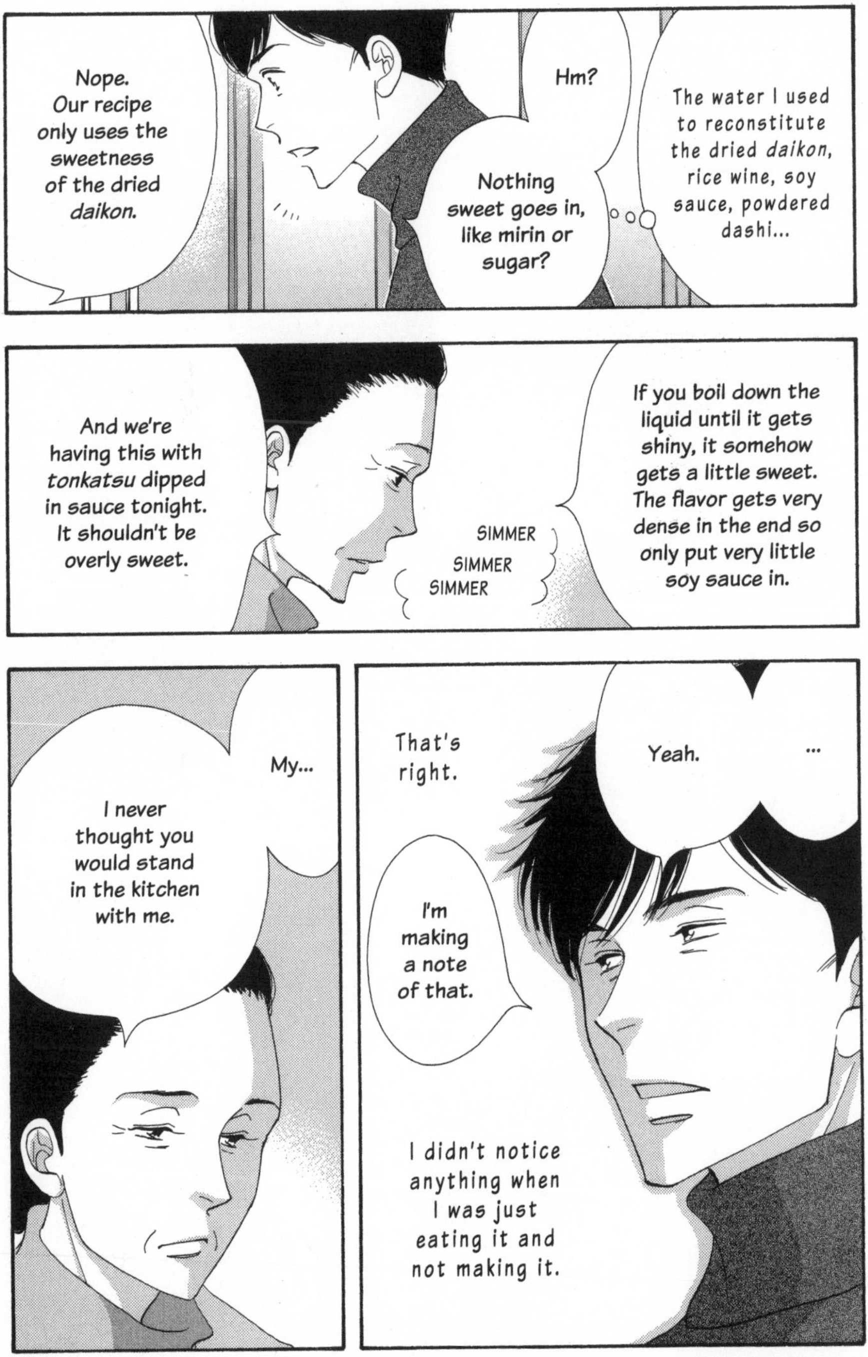
The water I used to reconstitute the dried *daikon*, rice wine, soy sauce, powdered dashi...
Hm?
Nothing sweet goes in, like mirin or sugar?
Nope. Our recipe only uses the sweetness of the dried *daikon*.
If you boil down the liquid until it gets shiny, it somehow gets a little sweet. The flavor gets very dense in the end so only put very little soy sauce in.
SIMMER
SIMMER
SIMMER
And we're having this with *tonkatsu* dipped in sauce tonight. It shouldn't be overly sweet.
...
Yeah.
That's right.
I'm making a note of that.
I didn't notice anything when I was just eating it and not making it.
My...
I never thought you would stand in the kitchen with me.

These are my
menu-building
roots...

Now,

we'll cook
a spaghetti
salad and call
it a night.

More
?!

Whaa
?!

*More
carbs
on top
of this
?!*

*7 oz
?!*

S-So the
salted, rinsed,
and dried thinly
sliced onion
and cucumber
technique was
for the spaghetti
salad...

Use that pot to
boil 7 oz spaghetti.
I'll make miso soup
while you do that.

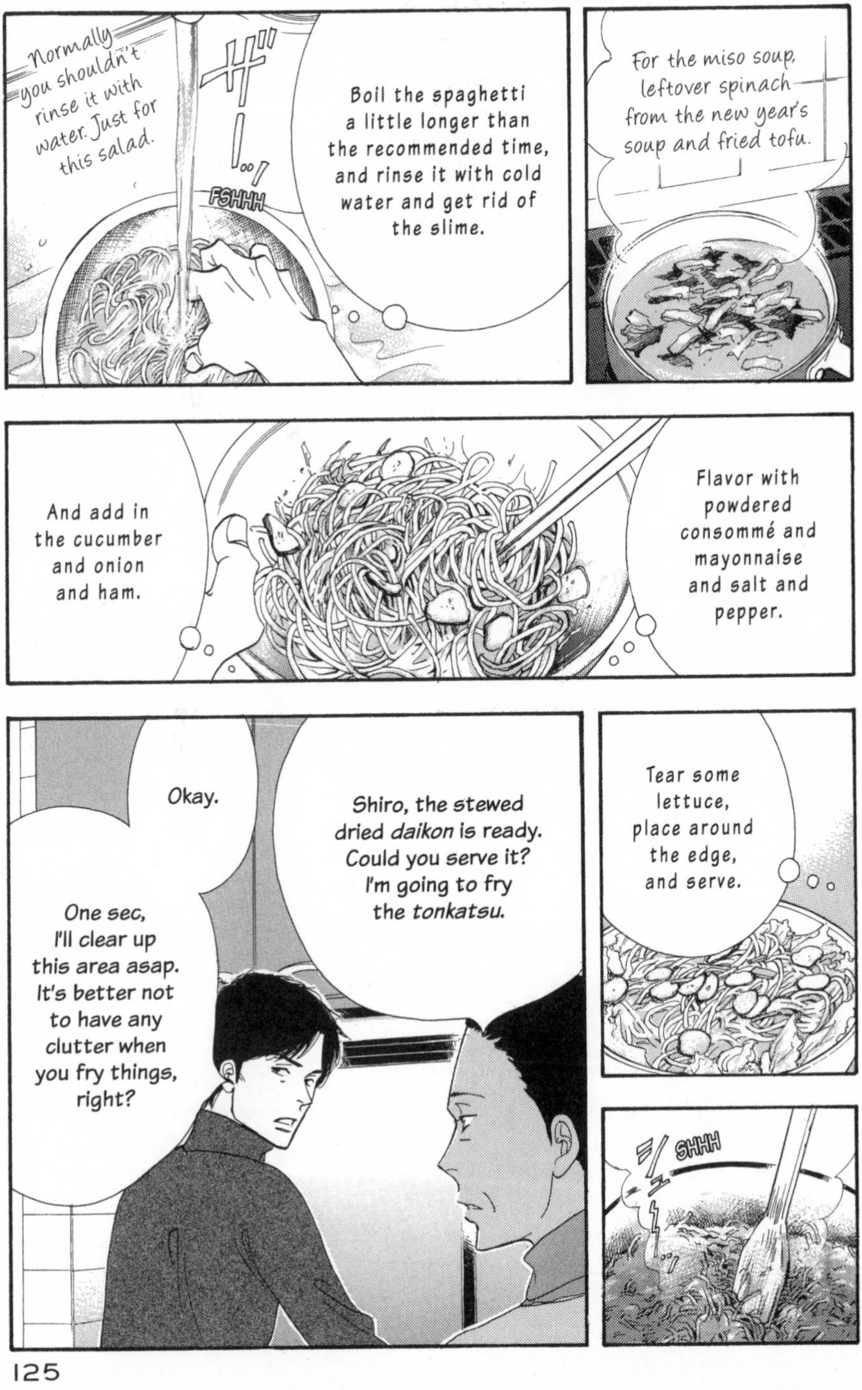
For the miso soup, leftover spinach from the new year's soup and fried tofu.
Boil the spaghetti a little longer than the recommended time, and rinse it with cold water and get rid of the slime.
FSHHH
Normally you shouldn't rinse it with water. Just for this salad.
Flavor with powdered consommé and mayonnaise and salt and pepper.
And add in the cucumber and onion and ham.
Tear some lettuce, place around the edge, and serve.
SHHH
Shiro, the stewed dried daikon is ready. Could you serve it? I'm going to fry the tonkatsu.
Okay.
One sec, I'll clear up this area asap. It's better not to have any clutter when you fry things, right?

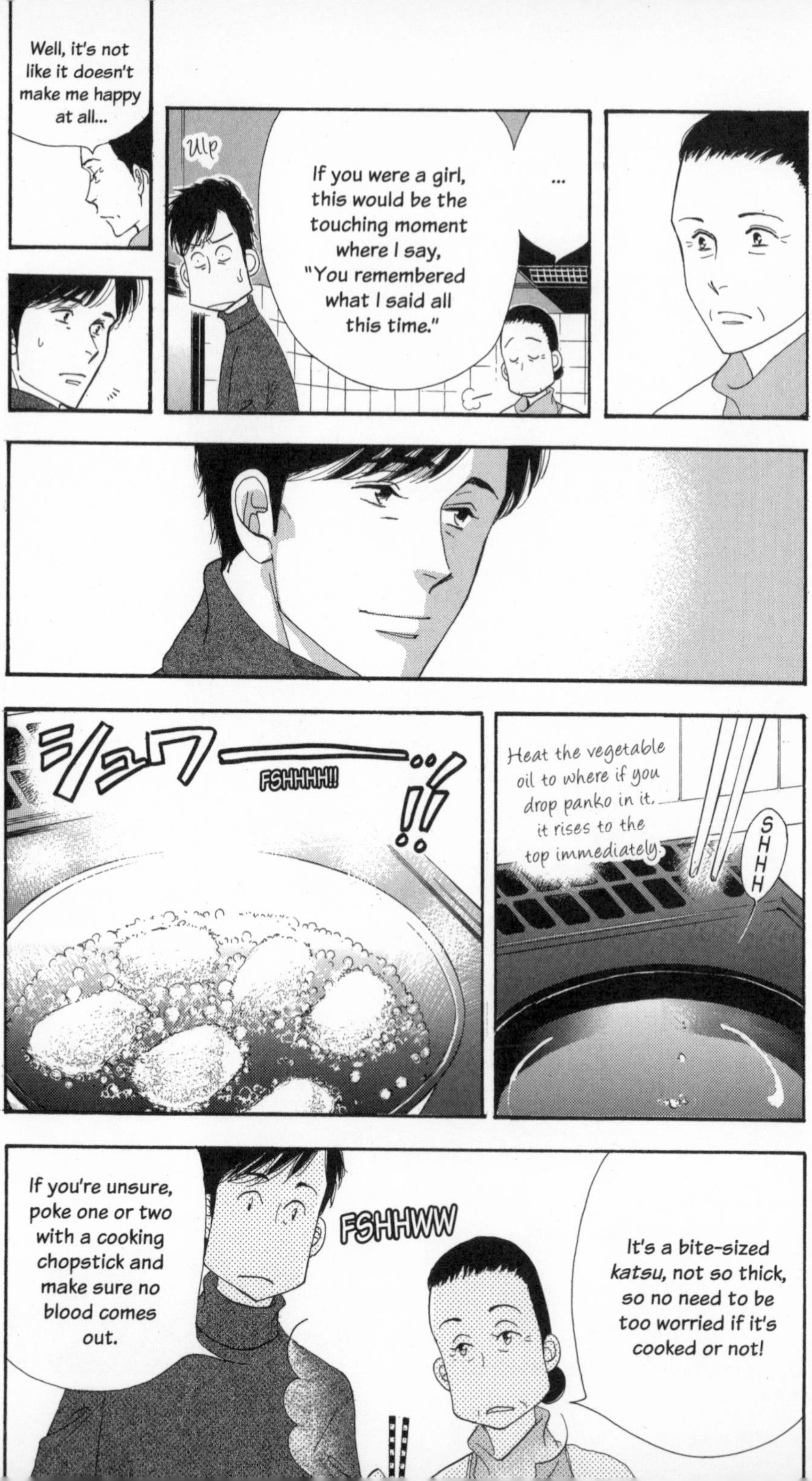
...
If you were a girl, this would be the touching moment where I say, "You remembered what I said all this time."
Ulp
Well, it's not like it doesn't make me happy at all...
Heat the vegetable oil to where if you drop panko in it, it rises to the top immediately.
SHHH
シュワー!!
FSHHHH!!
It's a bite-sized *katsu*, not so thick, so no need to be too worried if it's cooked or not!
FSHHWW
If you're unsure, poke one or two with a cooking chopstick and make sure no blood comes out.

SHH...

SWSH

SHH

FSHHWW

SWSH

A brown on the darker side.

Okaay.

Dad, it's dinner.

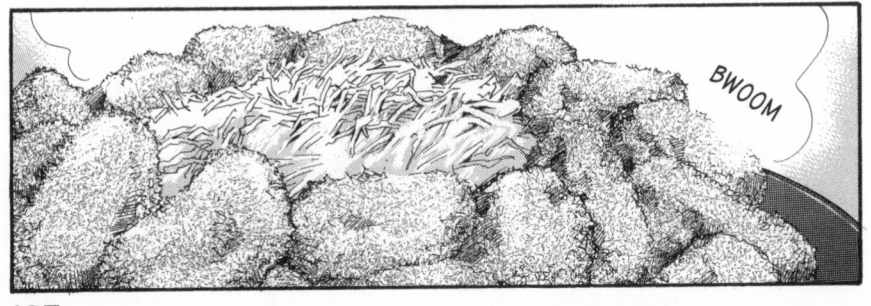

BWOOM

• *Tonkatsu*
  (deep-fried pork cutlet)
• *Stewed dried daikon*
• *Spaghetti salad*
• *Miso soup with spinach*
  and fried tofu

Thanks
for this
meal.

What is this...
The exact full-
stomach menu from
the 20th century
when I was in
high school...

Not a potato salad,
not a macaroni salad,
but a spaghetti salad.
So retro and last era.

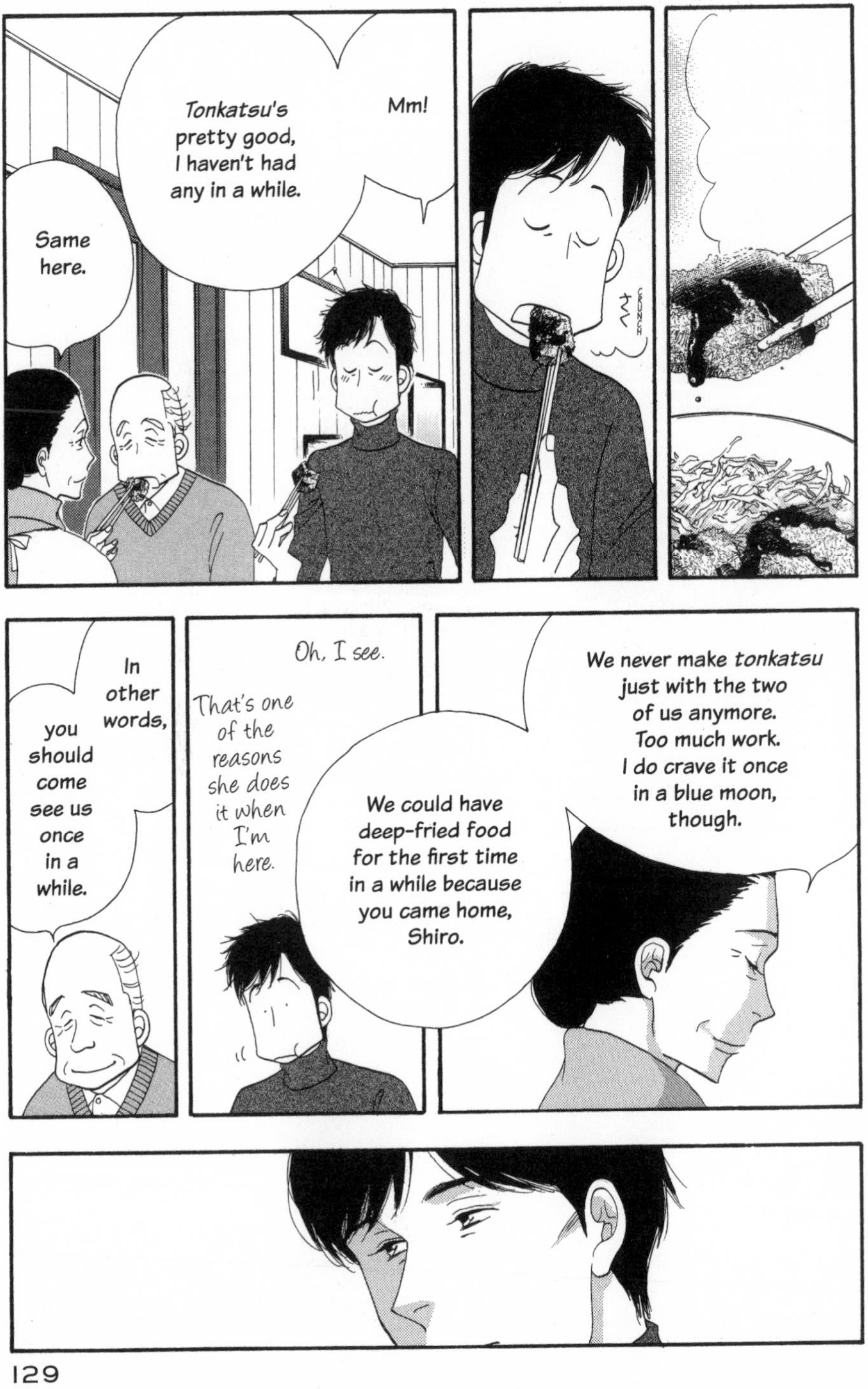
CRUNCH
Mm!
Tonkatsu's pretty good, I haven't had any in a while.
Same here.
We never make tonkatsu just with the two of us anymore. Too much work. I do crave it once in a blue moon, though.
We could have deep-fried food for the first time in a while because you came home, Shiro.
Oh, I see.
That's one of the reasons she does it when I'm here.
In other words,
you should come see us once in a while.

GFUFF

So much
left over...
↓

GFUFF

BUT THEY'RE
TWO ELDERLY
PEOPLE AND
A MIDDLE-
AGED GUY
AFTER ALL.

Oh...
Um, yeah,
thank you.

Bring it all home.
Finish it with him.
Your boyfriend is
home alone,
right?

Shiro.

SWSH   SWSH

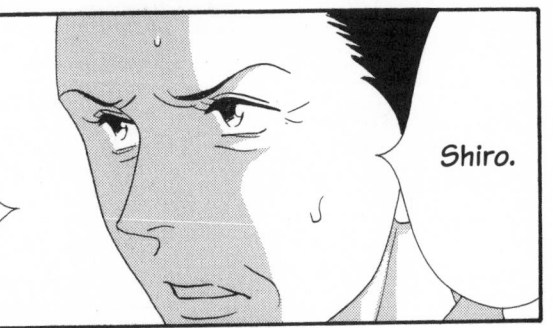

Next year, bring your boyfriend here with you. He has New Year's off too, doesn't he?!

Shiro.

A-A-A-Aren't you two pretty much married?! Isn't it common sense to introduce your spouse to your family?! Yes?!

This was it!! The quiet before the storm was for saying this!!

Th-

Well... But... It's not exactly like a guy-and-girl marriage... I mean, who knows, next year we might have broken up...

GLARE

Shiro!

A sweeter version of the **stewed dried** *daikon* comes up in volume two, #11.
Whichever one you prefer.

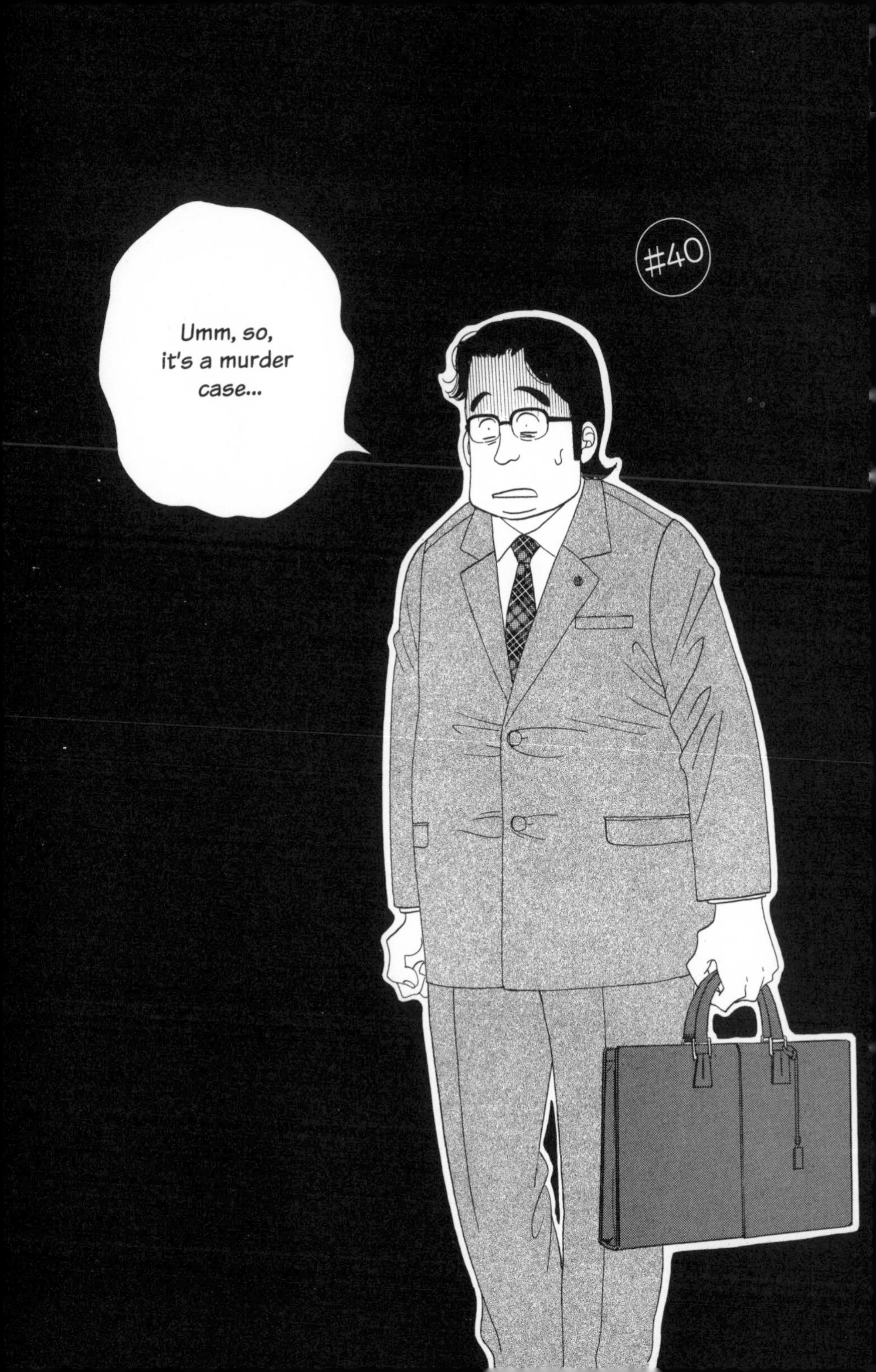
#40
Umm, so, it's a murder case...

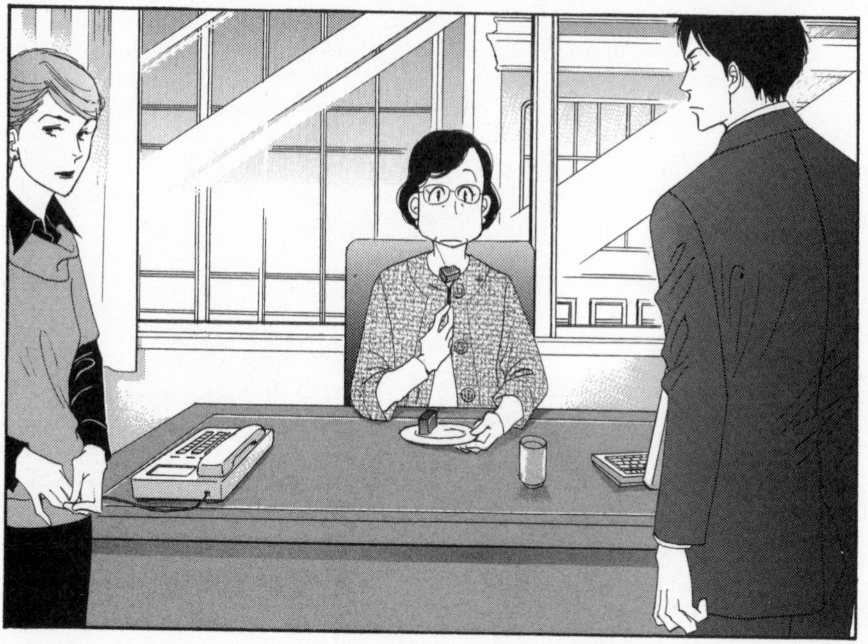
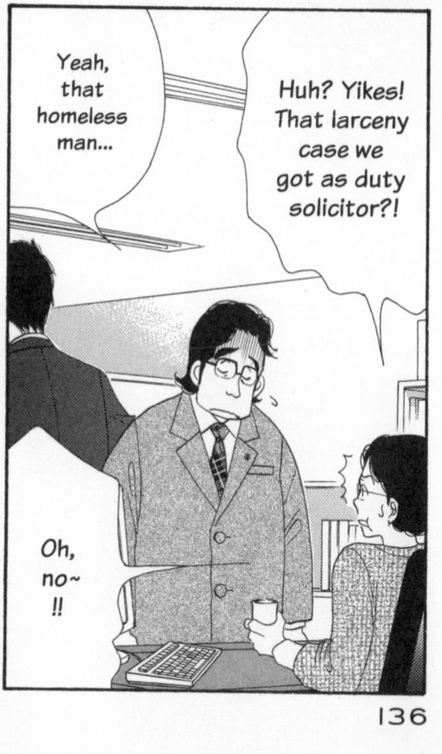
Huh? Yikes! That larceny case we got as duty solicitor?!
Yeah, that homeless man...
Oh, no~ !!
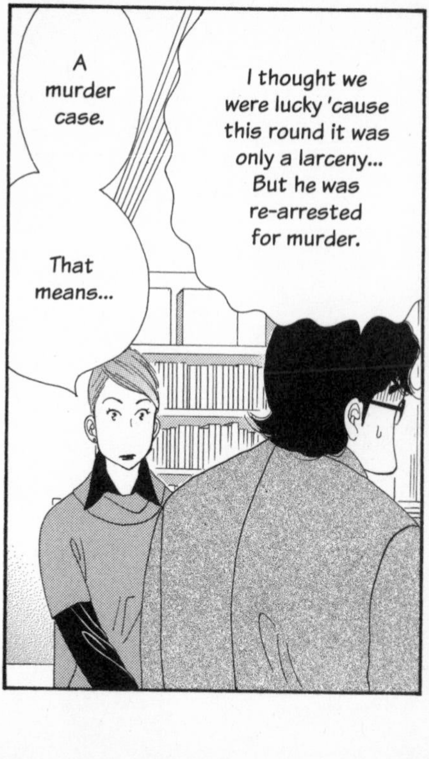
I thought we were lucky 'cause this round it was only a larceny... But he was re-arrested for murder.
A murder case.
That means...

a
jury
trial.

TIP-TOE

THE "B LIST" IS THE ROSTER OF LAWYERS WHO HAVEN'T UNDERGONE TRAINING FOR A TRIAL BY JURY, A RELATIVELY NEW SYSTEM IN JAPAN.

Waaah! What shall I do? I'm a B lister!

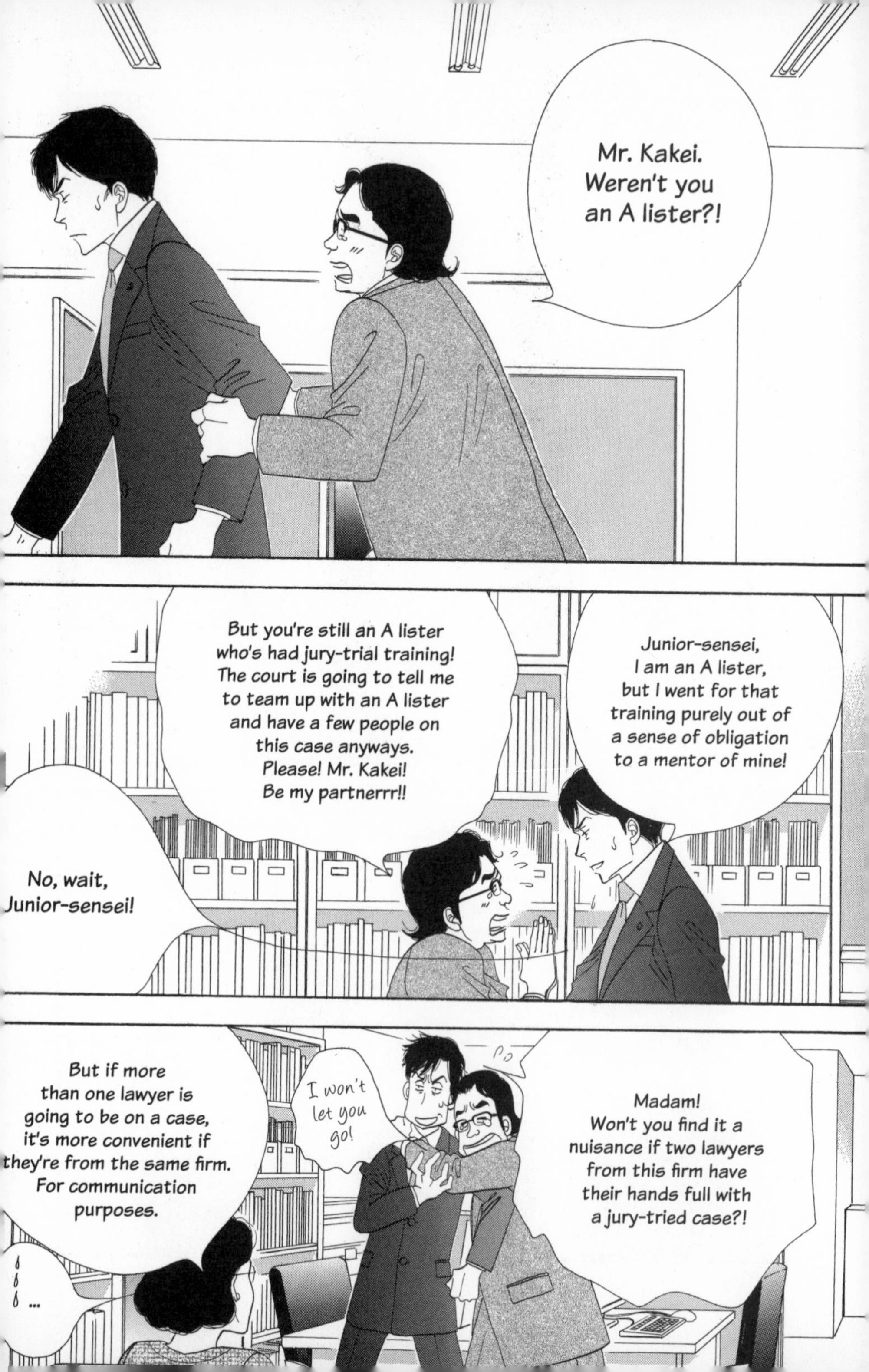
Mr. Kakei. Weren't you an A lister?!
Junior-sensei, I am an A lister, but I went for that training purely out of a sense of obligation to a mentor of mine!
But you're still an A lister who's had jury-trial training! The court is going to tell me to team up with an A lister and have a few people on this case anyways. Please! Mr. Kakei! Be my partnerrr!!
No, wait, Junior-sensei!
Madam! Won't you find it a nuisance if two lawyers from this firm have their hands full with a jury-tried case?!
I won't let you go!
But if more than one lawyer is going to be on a case, it's more convenient if they're from the same firm. For communication purposes.
...

But they don't look as good as you, Mr. Kakei...

I don't have enough experience in crim law to be relied on like this!

Junior-sensei, you have a friend from practical training who's much more experienced in crim law than I am, don't you? Why don't you ask someone like that?!

They've been preparing for trials by jury from years back, handpicking all the best-looking kids right out of practicals! The rumor is that they've built an army of pretty faces!!

Because, you know, the prosecutor's office doesn't play fair!

...

Only a rumor.

See, so I at least want someone who's easy on the eyes on our side as well! Looks really matter in jury trials, I'm not kidding!!

And they purposely have a young female prosecutor read the investigation record aloud so the jury will sympathize with the victim!

I'm chubby as you can see and have a high voice...

This is true. →

Then, the male suspect punched my face again even though I begged, "Please, don't hit me anymore!" Soon he started scrounging for items of value in my room...

I won't take part in this no matter what you say!

Ulp

That time you were the receiver for the jeweler's case...

...

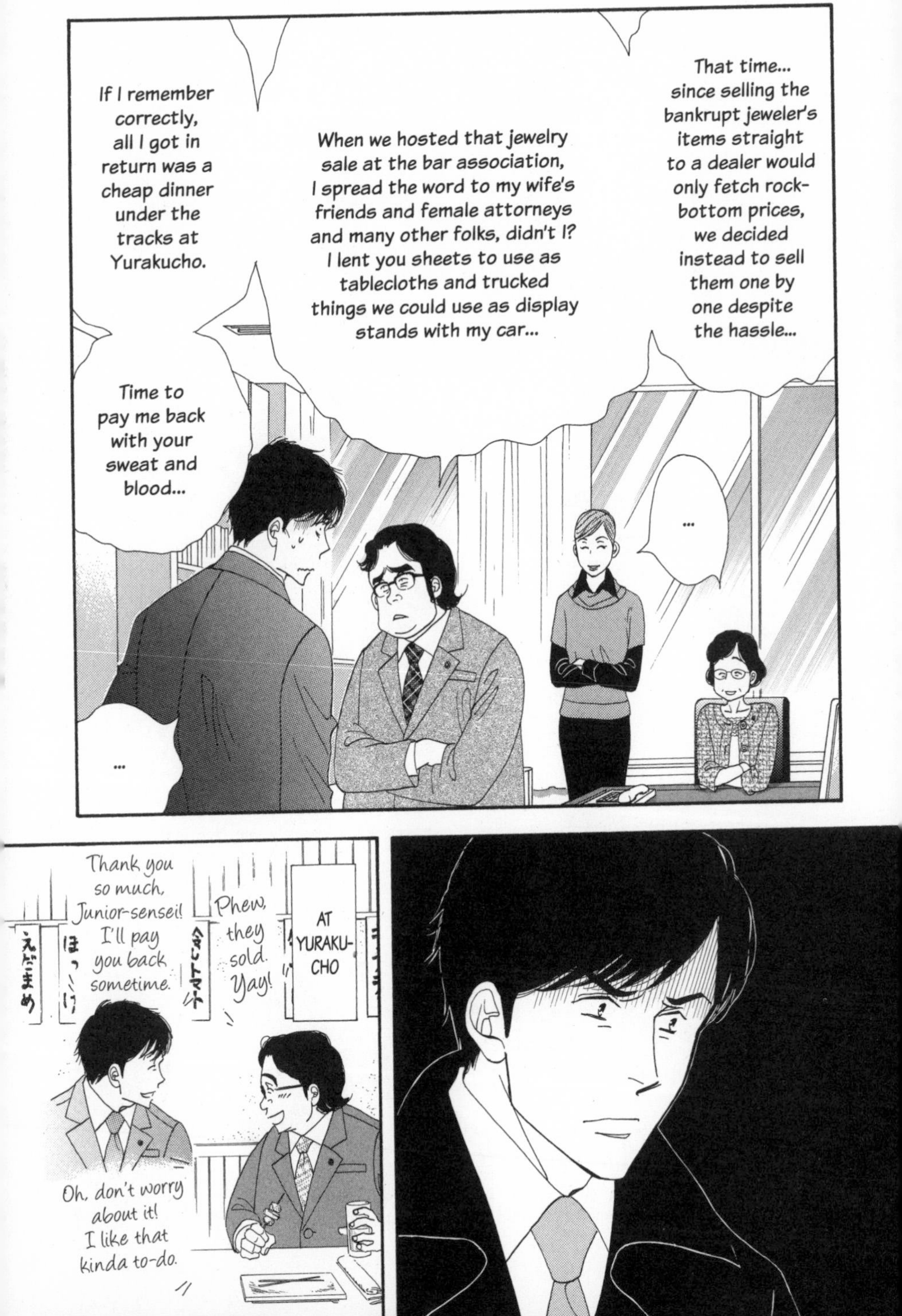
That time... since selling the bankrupt jeweler's items straight to a dealer would only fetch rock-bottom prices, we decided instead to sell them one by one despite the hassle...
When we hosted that jewelry sale at the bar association, I spread the word to my wife's friends and female attorneys and many other folks, didn't I? I lent you sheets to use as tablecloths and trucked things we could use as display stands with my car...
If I remember correctly, all I got in return was a cheap dinner under the tracks at Yurakucho.
Time to pay me back with your sweat and blood...
...
...
AT YURAKU-CHO
Phew, they sold. Yay!
Thank you so much, Junior-sensei! I'll pay you back sometime.
ほっけ
えだまめ
Oh, don't worry about it! I like that kinda to-do.

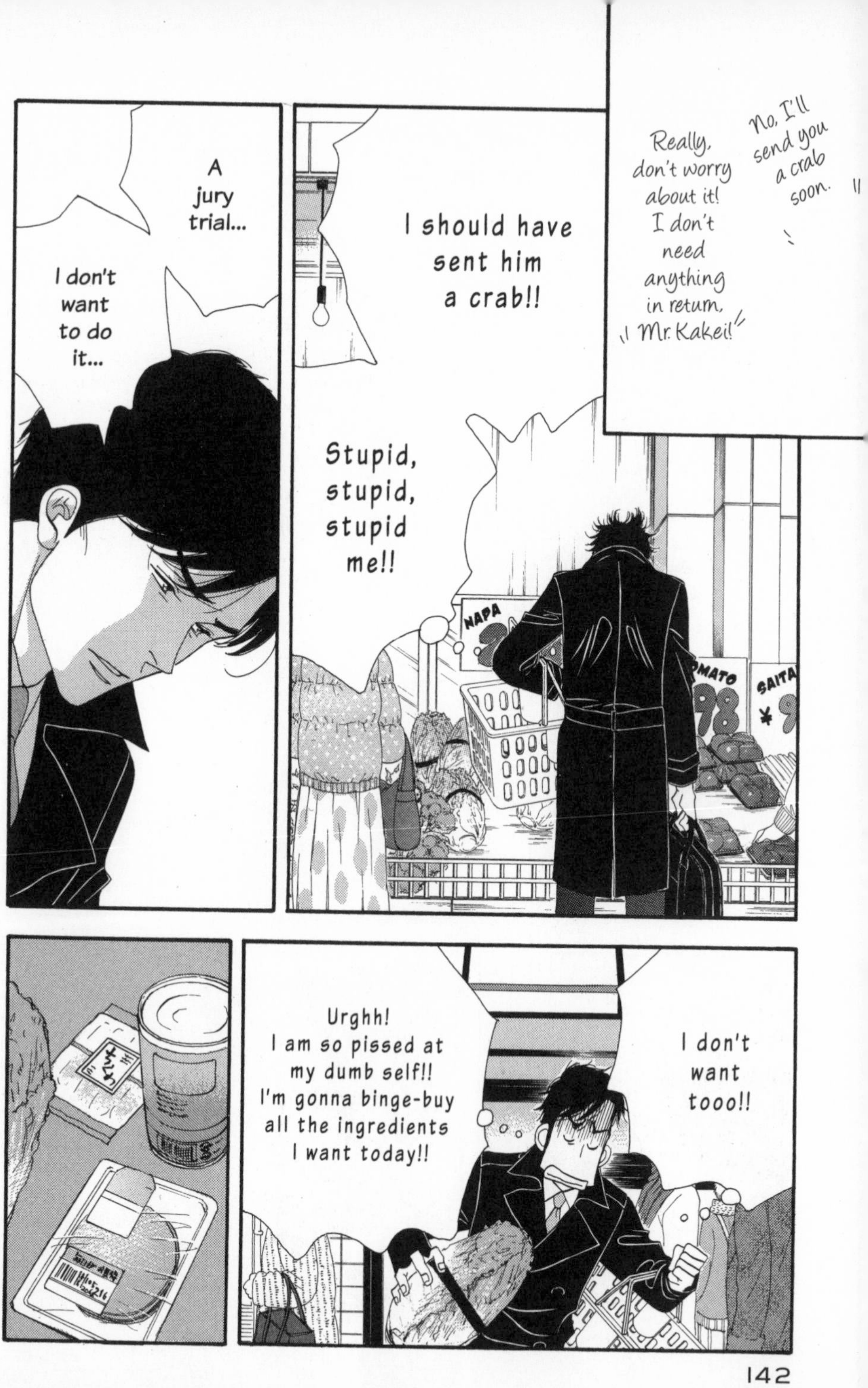
Really, don't worry about it! I don't need anything in return, Mr. Kakei!
No, I'll send you a crab soon.
I should have sent him a crab!!
Stupid, stupid, stupid me!!
NAPA
TOMATO
98
SAITA
A jury trial...
I don't want to do it...
I don't want tooo!!
Urghh! I am so pissed at my dumb self!! I'm gonna binge-buy all the ingredients I want today!!

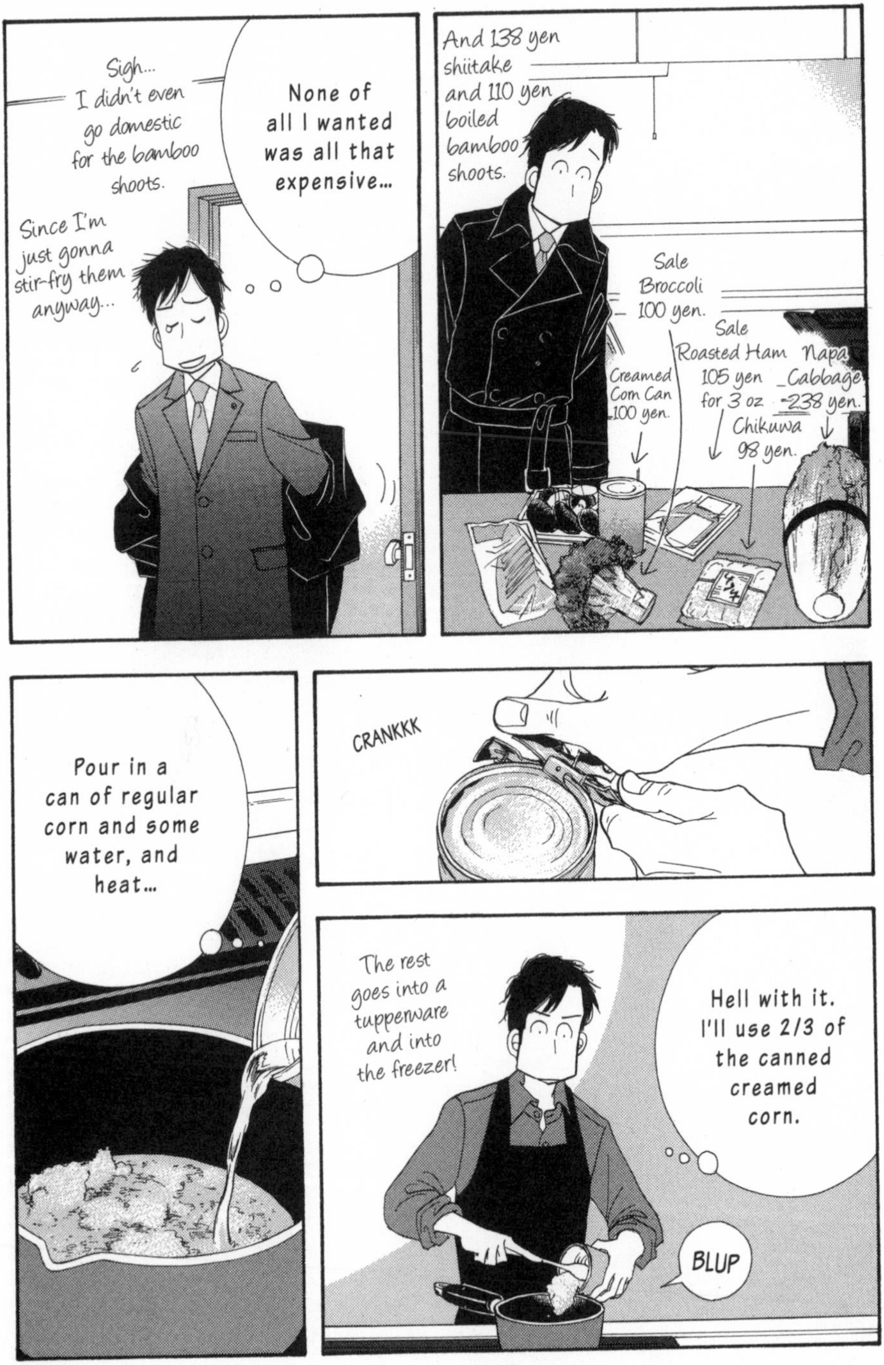
And 138 yen shiitake and 110 yen boiled bamboo shoots.
Sale Broccoli 100 yen.
Sale Roasted Ham 105 yen for 3 oz
Napa Cabbage 238 yen.
Creamed Corn Can 100 yen.
Chikuwa 98 yen.
None of all I wanted was all that expensive...
Sigh... I didn't even go domestic for the bamboo shoots.
Since I'm just gonna stir-fry them anyway...
CRANKKK
Hell with it. I'll use 2/3 of the canned creamed corn.
The rest goes into a tupperware and into the freezer!
BLUP
Pour in a can of regular corn and some water, and heat...

Stir it, and flavor with chicken broth and salt and pepper.
Once it starts to boil, pour one beaten egg into it...
KSH KSH KSH
and drizzle in sesame oil, and we have a Chinese soup with corn and egg.
BAM
BAM
Two 2" pieces of *daikon*, peeled and julienned.
TOK TOK TOK TOK TOK TOK TOK!
TOK
TOK TOK
Also julienne the white part of four 2" pieces of scallion.

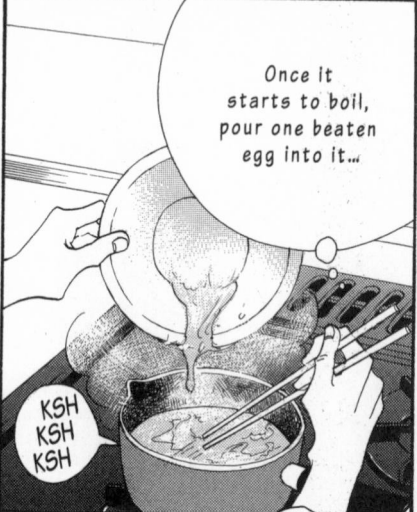

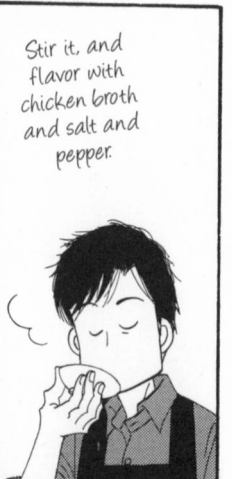

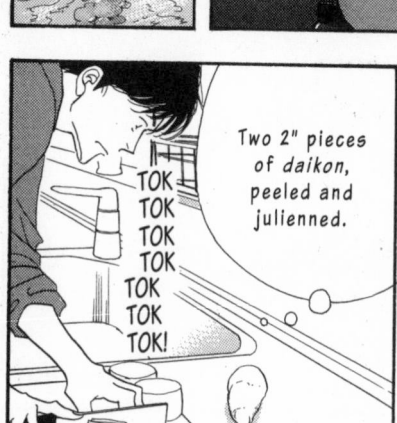

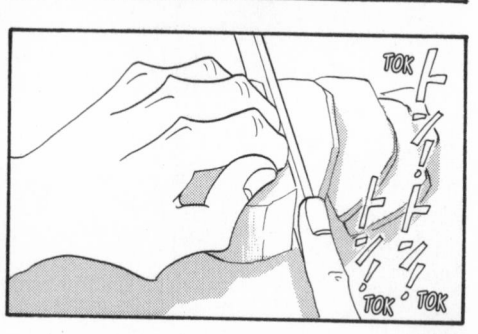

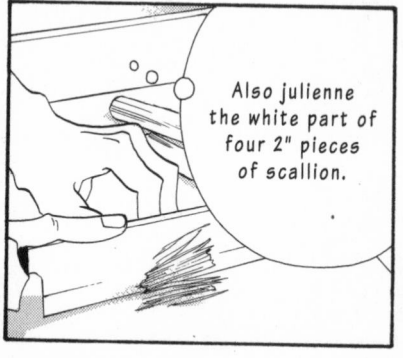

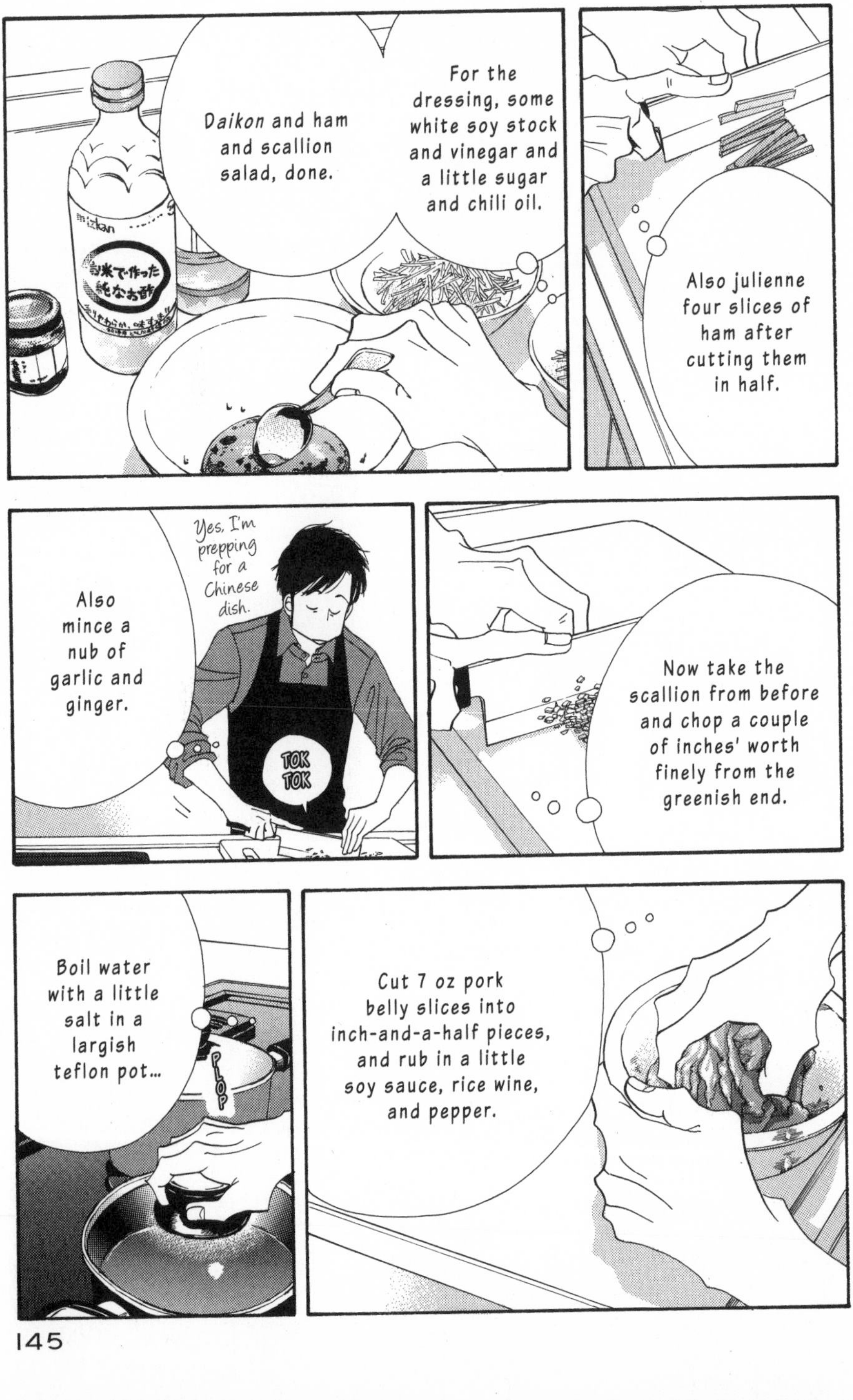
Also julienne four slices of ham after cutting them in half.
For the dressing, some white soy stock and vinegar and a little sugar and chili oil.
Daikon and ham and scallion salad, done.
mizkan
Now take the scallion from before and chop a couple of inches' worth finely from the greenish end.
Also mince a nub of garlic and ginger.
Yes, I'm prepping for a Chinese dish.
TOK TOK
Cut 7 oz pork belly slices into inch-and-a-half pieces, and rub in a little soy sauce, rice wine, and pepper.
Boil water with a little salt in a largish teflon pot...
PLOP

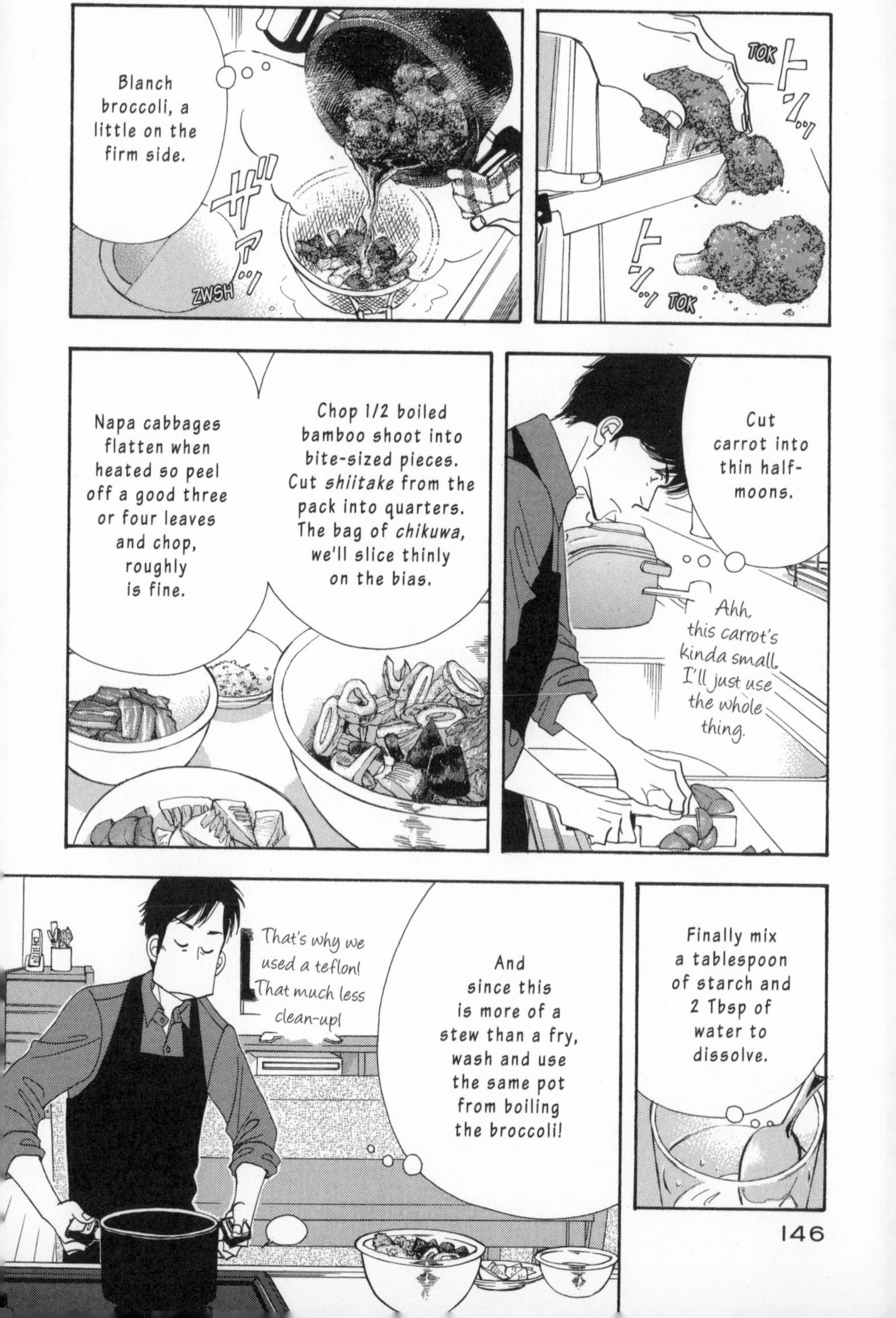
TOK
TOK
Blanch broccoli, a little on the firm side.
ZWSH
Cut carrot into thin half-moons.
Ahh, this carrot's kinda small. I'll just use the whole thing.
Chop 1/2 boiled bamboo shoot into bite-sized pieces. Cut *shiitake* from the pack into quarters. The bag of *chikuwa*, we'll slice thinly on the bias.
Napa cabbages flatten when heated so peel off a good three or four leaves and chop, roughly is fine.
Finally mix a tablespoon of starch and 2 Tbsp of water to dissolve.
And since this is more of a stew than a fry, wash and use the same pot from boiling the broccoli!
That's why we used a teflon! That much less clean-up!

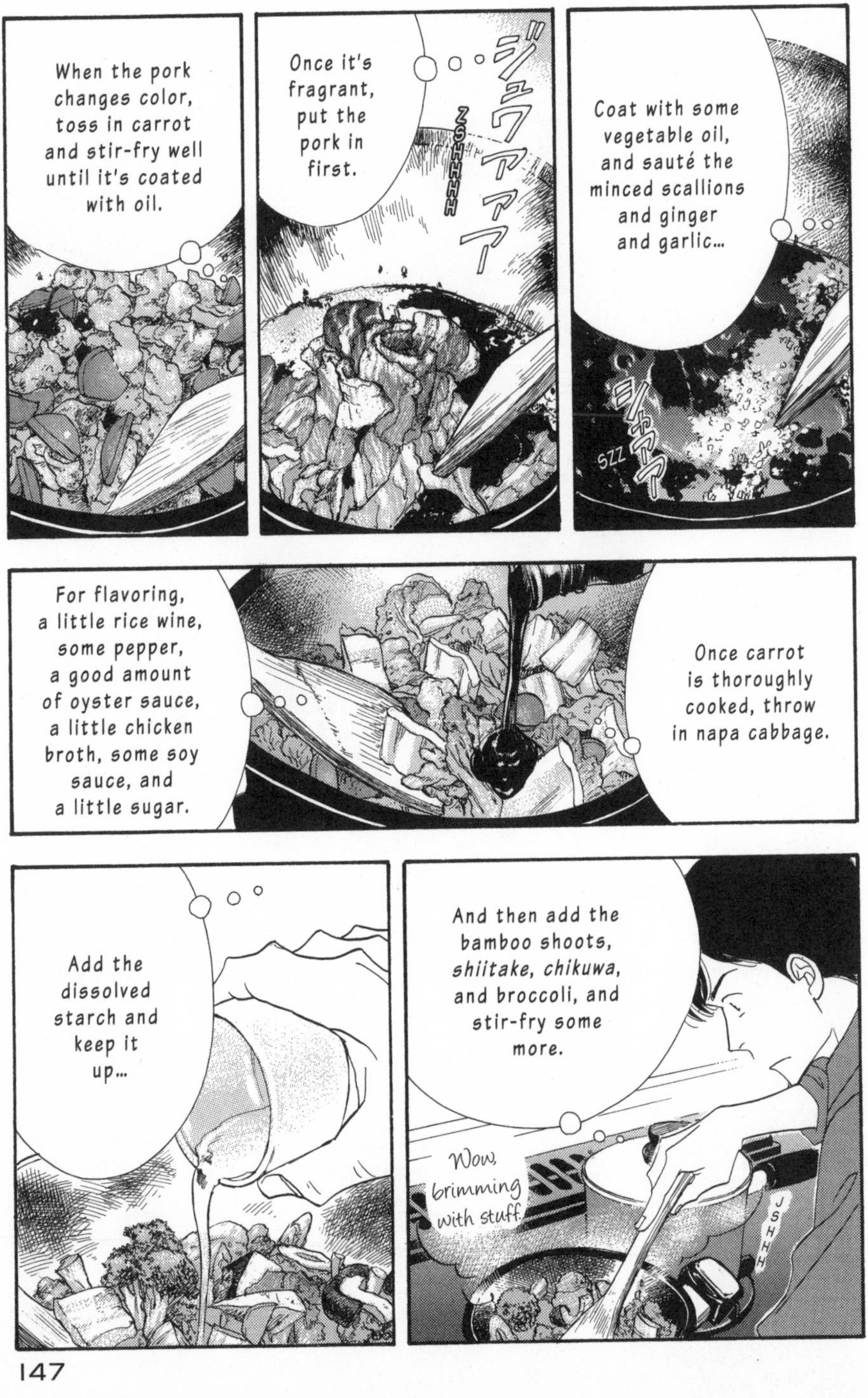
Coat with some vegetable oil, and sauté the minced scallions and ginger and garlic...
SZZ
Once it's fragrant, put the pork in first.
ZSHHHHH
When the pork changes color, toss in carrot and stir-fry well until it's coated with oil.
Once carrot is thoroughly cooked, throw in napa cabbage.
For flavoring, a little rice wine, some pepper, a good amount of oyster sauce, a little chicken broth, some soy sauce, and a little sugar.
And then add the bamboo shoots, *shiitake*, *chikuwa*, and broccoli, and stir-fry some more.
Wow, brimming with stuff.
JSHHH
Add the dissolved starch and keep it up...

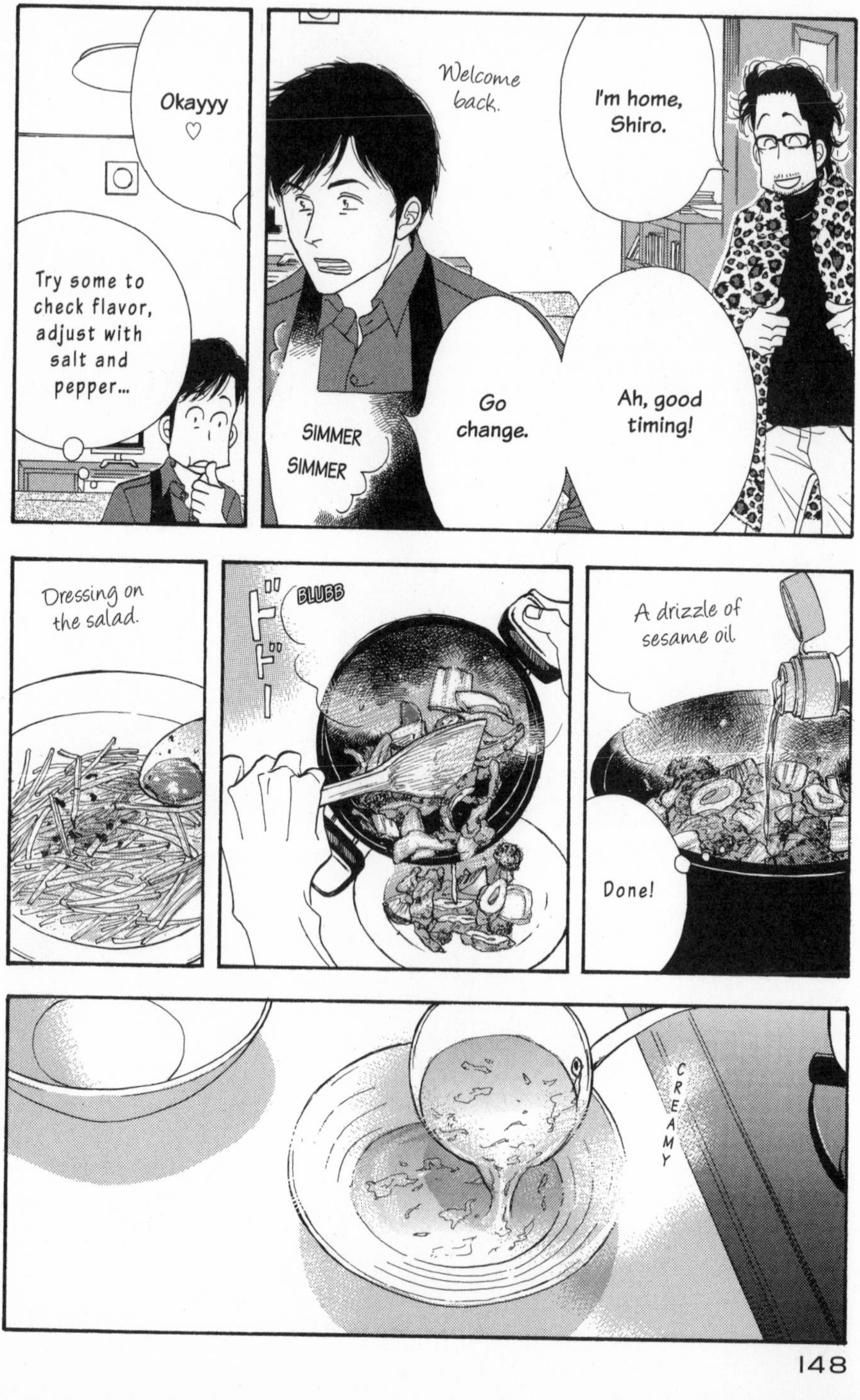
I'm home, Shiro.
Ah, good timing!
Welcome back.
Go change.
SIMMER SIMMER
Okayyy ♡
Try some to check flavor, adjust with salt and pepper...
A drizzle of sesame oil
Done!
BLUBB
Dressing on the salad.
CREAMY

Thank youuu!

Waah, this will warm me up ♡ A chop suey dinner!

- Pork and chikuwa chop suey
- Spicy daikon and ham and scallion salad
- Corn and egg soup

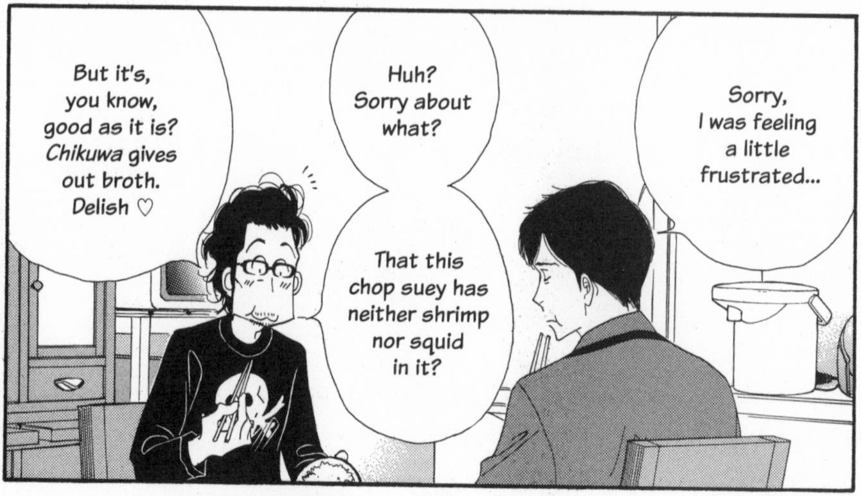
Sorry, I was feeling a little frustrated...
Huh? Sorry about what?
That this chop suey has neither shrimp nor squid in it?
But it's, you know, good as it is? *Chikuwa* gives out broth. Delish ♡

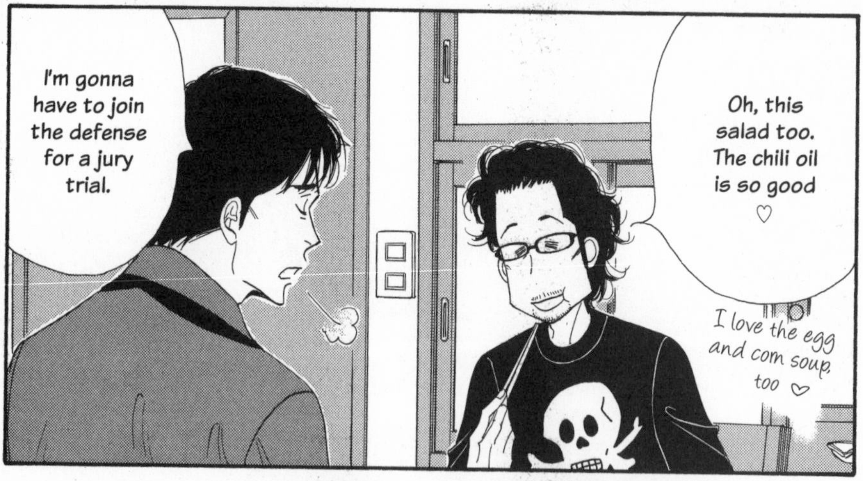
Oh, this salad too. The chili oil is so good ♡
I love the egg and corn soup, too ♡
I'm gonna have to join the defense for a jury trial.

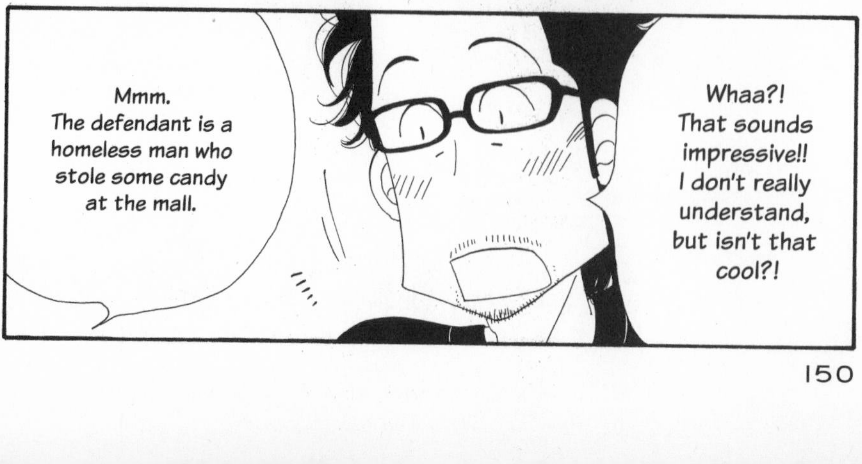
Whaa?! That sounds impressive!! I don't really understand, but isn't that cool?!
Mmm. The defendant is a homeless man who stole some candy at the mall.

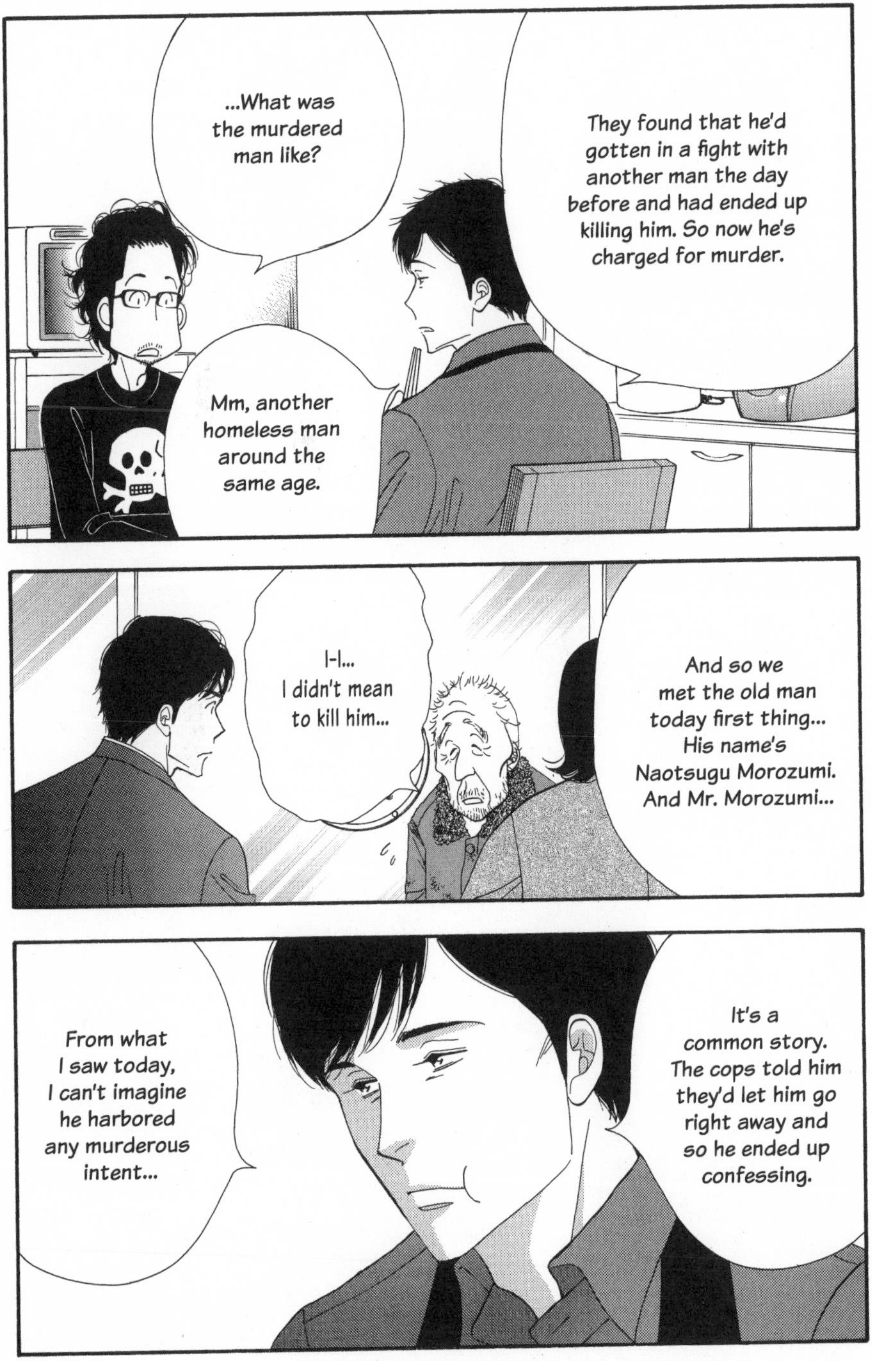
They found that he'd gotten in a fight with another man the day before and had ended up killing him. So now he's charged for murder.
...What was the murdered man like?
Mm, another homeless man around the same age.
And so we met the old man today first thing... His name's Naotsugu Morozumi. And Mr. Morozumi...
I-I... I didn't mean to kill him...
It's a common story. The cops told him they'd let him go right away and so he ended up confessing.
From what I saw today, I can't imagine he harbored any murderous intent...

Everything is compressed into a tight schedule, and that's really hard on lawyers who're dealing with multiple cases.

Ugh. It's not really cool like that... You can't keep the citizens there for long on these jury trials.

Whaaaa!! Oh my!! That's like one of those TV suspense shows!!

Ahhh. I wasn't really paying attention at my training. I gotta study all over again through the Japan Lawyers Association's e-learning...

SHIRO'S BURSTS OF FRUSTRATION: EXCEEDINGLY MODEST.

Uh huh... So frustrated I cooked two days' worth of everything.

Sorry.

So same menu tomorrow

...

And that's why you were frustrated?

You can freeze **chikuwas.**
Put the whole bag in the freezer when you buy it,
and take whatever you will use out of the freezer.
It will thaw in twenty to thirty minutes.

In the next
volume of

*what did you eat
yesterday?*

menu

steamed dumplings

Together, tomorrow too.

menu

sesame-dressed bok choy

menu

tofu with baby sardines, *natto* and *kimchi*

menu

bamboo shoot rice

menu

baby neck clam miso soup

menu

sashimi salad

menu

green asparagus dressed in white sauce

menu

etc, etc!

what did you eat yesterday?, volume 5

Translation: Yoshito Hinton
Production: Risa Cho
      Tomoe Tsutsumi

© 2014 Fumi Yoshinaga. All rights reserved.
First published in Japan in 2011 by Kodansha Ltd., Tokyo.
Publication rights for this English edition arranged
through Kodansha Ltd., Tokyo.
English language version produced by Vertical, Inc.

Translation provided by Vertical, Inc., 2014
Published by Vertical, Inc., New York

Originally published in Japanese as Kinou nani tabeta? 5 by Kodansha, Ltd.
Kinou nani tabeta? first serialized in Morning, Kodansha, Ltd., 2007-

This is a work of fiction.

ISBN: 978-1-939130-80-8

Manufactured in Canada

First Edition

Vertical, Inc.
451 Park Avenue South
7th Floor
New York, NY 10016
www.vertical-inc.com

Finally available in English: the award-winning comic about wine that has been a hit not just all over Asia but also in France! Learn about legendary bottles as well as affordable secrets while enjoying a page-turner that's not about superheroes but people with jobs to keep. When world-renowned wine critic Kanzaki passes away, his will reveals that his fortune of a wine collection isn't bequeathed as a matter of course to his only son, who in a snub went to work sales at a beer company. To come into the inheritance, Shizuku must identify— in competition with a stellar young critic— twelve heaven-sent wines whose impressions the will describes in flowing terms...

"Arguably the most influential
wine publication for the past 20 years."
—*Decanter Magazine*

Volumes 1-4 & New World available now!
approx. 400 pages and $14.95 each

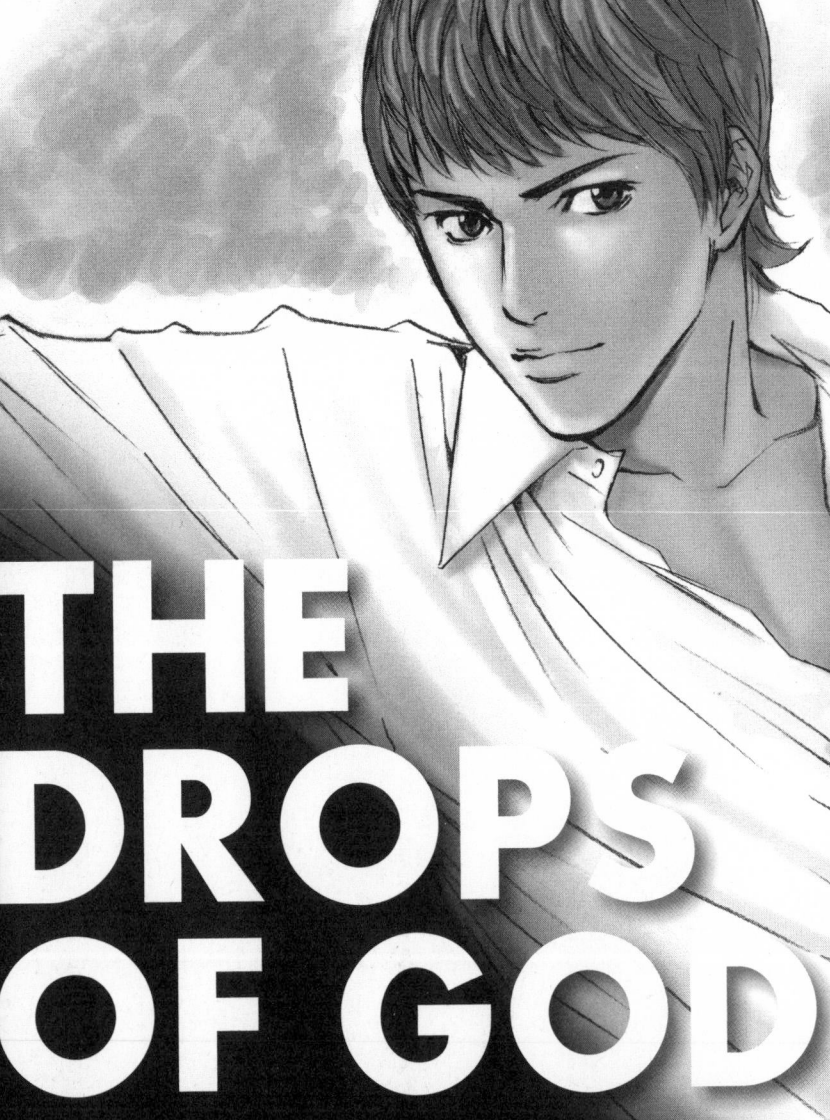

WINNER
GOURMAND COOKBOOK AWARDS
2009

THE
DROPS
OF GOD

WRONG WAY

Japanese books, including manga like this one,
are meant to be read from right to left.
so the front cover is actually the back cover, and vice versa.
To read this book, please flip it over
and start in the top right-hand corner.
Read the panels, and the bubbles in the panels,
from right to left,
then drop down to the next row and repeat.
It may make you dizzy at first, but forcing your brain
to do things backwards makes you smarter in the long run.
we swear.